'Anorexia nervosa is notoriously difficult to treat. Via a decade of systematic inquiry into why our treatments often fail individuals with this disorder, Dr. Tchanturia has documented an array of cognitive insufficiencies that may reflect core traits that underlie anorexia and impair patients' ability to engage in treatments that require cognitive flexibility. Richly referenced, Tchanturia and colleagues assist the reader with identifying and assessing neurocognitive profiles in individuals with anorexia and with applying interventions that aid patients in loosening their cognitive inflexibility in service of recovery. Scholarly and accessible, this volume is a must-have for clinicians and researchers working in the field of eating disorders.'
  – *Cynthia Bulik, PhD, FAED, Distinguished Professor of Eating Disorders, Director of the Center of Excellence for Eating Disorders, University of North Carolina, USA*

'The development of cognitive remediation therapy, which has been a landmark event in the treatment of eating disorders, has been pioneered by Dr. Tchanturia and colleagues. This approach seeks to find interventions that ameliorate traits that my constitute vulnerabilities that contribute to developing eating disorders. This excellent book now provides a state-of-the-art overview of progress in CRT. It is one-stop shopping for researchers interested in the concepts underlying this intervention, as well as studies assessing response to treatment, and for clinicians wanting to learn more about employing this theraphy.'
  – *Walter H. Kaye, MD, Professor of Psychiatry, Director of the Eating Disorders Program, University of California San Diego, USA*

'This compilation from the cutting-edge clinical research group brought together by the highly respected Dr. Kate Tchanturia explores the treatment approach of cognitive remediation therapy. It offers a unique opportunity to look at a highly innovative field of treatment for eating disorders.'
  – *Andreas Karwautz, Professor of Child and Adolescent Neuropsychiatry, Medical University of Vienna, Austria*

'Dr. Tchanturia's pioneering work on CRT for eating disorders represents a novel and promising addition to the clinician's armamentarium for the management of eating disorders and other complex mental disorders.'
  – *David Mataix-Cols, PhD, Professor, Karolinska Institutet, Sweden*

'Knowing how the brain's working affects an eating disorder helps patients and their families. They can feel less stigma when they understand more of the biological basis of the condition, and can find it easier to accept the treatment they need as a result. This book brings together leading research into this important novel area.'
  – *Susan Ringwood, Chief Executive, Beat, UK*

D1323454

COGNITIVE REMEDIATION THERAPY (CRT) FOR EATING AND WEIGHT DISORDERS

The effective treatment of anorexia nervosa remains a significant challenge. This has prompted new research into ways of engaging and keeping patients in treatment and ultimately achieving better outcomes, not only on a symptomatic level but also in broader aspects of life. In this book Kate Tchanturia brings together international experts from the field of eating disorders to discuss the effectiveness of cognitive remediation therapy for treating anorexia nervosa.

Cognitive remediation therapy (CRT) is a type of therapy that concentrates on improving neurocognitive abilities such as attention, working memory, cognitive flexibility and planning, and executive functioning – which leads to improved general functioning. Recent research has demonstrated the effectiveness of the approach for treating those with anorexia nervosa; cognitive improvements have been noted in patients, and the approach is associated with low drop-out rates from the treatment, and high levels of acceptability among both patients and therapists.

This book presents research focusing on:

- individual therapy with adults
- group format of CRT
- family-based therapy
- CRT with young people
- adapting interventions for people with comorbidities
- clinicians' experiences working with CRT.

Illustrated throughout with case studies, and integrating neuropsychological testing and brain imaging, this book discusses the latest research on this novel treatment approach. It will be key reading for researchers and academics in the eating disorders field wanting to trial the approach, as well as final year undergraduates and postgraduate clinical psychology students looking for a new perspective.

Dr. Kate Tchanturia is a Reader in the Psychology of Eating Disorders and a Consultant (Lead) Psychologist at King's College London, and at South London and Maudsley NHS Trust National Adult Eating Disorder Service, London, UK. Kate is a Fellow of the Academy of Eating Disorders and an Associate Fellow of the British Psychological Society.

COGNITIVE REMEDIATION THERAPY (CRT) FOR EATING AND WEIGHT DISORDERS

Edited by Kate Tchanturia

Routledge
Taylor & Francis Group

LONDON AND NEW YORK

First published 2015
by Routledge
27 Church Road, Hove, East Sussex, BN3 2FA

and by Routledge
711 Third Avenue, New York, NY 10017

Routledge is an imprint of the Taylor & Francis Group, an informa business

British Library Cataloguing in Publication Data
A catalogue record for this book is available from the British Library

Library of Congress Cataloging-in-Publication Data
A catalog record for this book has been requested

ISBN: 978-1-138-79402-3 (hbk)
ISBN: 978-1-138-79403-0 (pbk)
ISBN: 978-1-315-74926-6 (ebk)

Typeset in Bembo
by RefineCatch Limited, Bungay, Suffolk

Printed and bound in Great Britain by
TJ International Ltd, Padstow, Cornwall

CONTENTS

CONTRIBUTORS

Timo Brockmeyer, PhD, is a licensed clinical psychologist and research assistant at the Department of General Internal Medicine and Psychosomatics at the University Hospital Heidelberg, Germany. His research spans the clinical domains of eating disorders and depression, and he is most interested in topics of emotion regulation, cognitive-behavioral avoidance, cognitive flexibility, familial interaction patterns, and emotional processing in psychotherapy.

Unna Danner, PhD, is a senior researcher at Altrecht Eating Disorders Rintveld in the Netherlands. She completed her PhD at the department of social psychology at Utrecht University in the Netherlands. Her current work focuses on inefficiencies in neuropsychological functioning of individuals with eating disorders and the translation of more fundamental and experimental findings into clinical practice. Specifically, her interests lie with neuropsychological functioning in relation to compulsive and impulsive traits and emotion regulation. Her publications include peer-reviewed papers on both experimental and clinical studies in the field of cognitive remediation therapy, neuropsychological functioning and emotion regulation.

Helen Davies, PhD, is a trainee clinical psychologist at Exeter University, UK. She worked as a researcher in the Eating Disorders Unit, Institute of Psychiatry, King's College London, for eight years. She was involved in translational research, contributing to the development of the cognitive remediation programme. She completed her PhD on emotion expression in eating disorders and has authored peer-reviewed publications reporting on translational research and emotion processing in eating disorders.

Alexandra Dingemans, PhD, is a senior researcher at the Center for Eating Disorders Ursula in the Netherlands. The focus of her research is on investigating the effectiveness of treatments for eating disorders. She conducted several randomized controlled trials (RCTs). Her publications include evaluations of the effectiveness of cognitive remediation therapy in eating disorders and cognitive behavioral therapy in Binge Eating Disorder. Furthermore she is interested in the underlying mechanisms of binge eating. She has authored peer-reviewed articles reporting on experimental studies investigating the association between mood changes, depression, and binge eating.

Jonathan Espie is a Clinical Psychologist and part of the Senior Management Team in the Child and Adolescent Eating Disorder Service at the Maudsley Hospital, London. Jonathan is experienced in working with children and families across a broad range of behavioural, developmental and mental health difficulties. His publications include papers on cognitive biases in adolescents, parenting, and psycho-education for parents of children with autism spectrum conditions. Alongside his systemic approach to eating disorders, Jonathan offers specialist input as a CBT therapist.

Kathleen Kara Fitzpatrick, PhD, is an attending clinical psychologist in the Department of Psychiatry and Behavioral Sciences at Stanford University/ Lucile Packard Children's Hospital. Dr. Fitzpatrick's clinical work has focused on treatment of children and adolescents with eating disorders, particularly with family-based approaches and translational neuroscience protocols. Her research has focused on developmental neuroscience related to executive functioning and emotion regulation.

Caroline Fleming is a chartered counselling psychologist who has worked in the field of eating disorders for eight years. Since 2009 she has worked for the National Inpatient Eating Disorders Service at the Bethlem Royal Hospital, London, with Dr. Kate Tchanturia in the translation of research into good clinical practice, and is working to develop novel individual and group therapies within the inpatient setting. Prior to this she worked within the day and outpatient services for adults with eating disorders for Surrey and Borders NHS Foundation Trust.

Leon Fonville, MSc, worked with Dr. Kate Tchanturia as a MSc student and later as a research assistant on a brain imaging study on cognitive and emotional processing in eating disorders, investigating the neurocognitive profile of anorexia nervosa using magnetic resonance imaging. He is currently doing a PhD at the Institute of Psychiatry, Kings College London, in the field of Psychosis.

Hans-Christoph Friederich, Professor, MD, is a licensed psychotherapist, head of the eating disorders research group, and deputy head of the Department of General Internal Medicine and Psychosomatics at the University Hospital Heidelberg, Germany. His main research interests span neuroimaging, cognitive neuroscience, and emotion regulation in eating disorders as well as psychodynamic psychotherapy process research.

Eric van Furth, PhD, is Professor of Eating Disorders at the Department of Psychiatry of Leiden University Medical Center and Clinical Director at the Center for Eating Disorders Ursula in the Netherlands. After receiving his PhD in psychology from Utrecht University, Dr. van Furth went on to pen over fifty publications – primarily journals, chapters, educational videos, and conference papers on eating disorders. He has also published three books on the subject and is a member of the Editorial Advisory Board of the *International Journal of Eating Disorders* (IJED), *European Eating Disorders Review* (EEDR) and *Eating Behaviors.* He has been working clinically with patients with eating disorders for more than twenty-five years. He held a seat as the Chair of the Dutch Multidisciplinary Treatment Guideline Workgroup on Eating Disorders from 2004–06, and is currently a Fellow and Past-President of the Academy for Eating Disorders.

Amy Harrison, PhD, is a Chartered Clinical Psychologist with clinical and academic research interests in the field of eating disorders. She completed her PhD at the Institute of Psychiatry with Professor Janet Treasure and Dr. Kate Tchanturia, King's College London at the Department of Psychological Medicine. She has authored peer-reviewed articles reporting on the neuropsychological profile of people with eating disorders. She currently works with young people and their families at the Ellern Mede Ridgeway Service (private hospital) for eating disorders in London.

Phillipa Hay, MD, is Foundation Chair of Mental Health at the Centre for Health Research and School of Medicine, University of Western Sydney, Adjunct Professor of Psychiatry at the School of Medicine, James Cook University, and Co-Editor in Chief of *Journal of Eating Disorders.* Her research has encompassed community and primary care studies in the area of prevalence and burden from eating disorders, eating disorder mental health literacy, evidence-based eating disorder treatments, and has included controlled trials of psychological therapies. She is Deputy-Chair of the National Eating Disorders Collaboration and Chair of the Royal Australian and New Zealand College of Psychiatrists Working Group to develop national guidelines for treatment of eating disorders.

Suzanne Hutchison is a Systemic Family Therapist at Acorn Lodge Children's Unit, South London and Maudsley NHS Foundation Trust, London. She also works with families faced with eating disorders at The Child and Family Practice, London, and has prior experience of supporting adolescents with eating disorders and their families, in an inpatient setting in which she trained and began to use cognitive remediation therapy.

Katie Lang, MSc, is currently a PhD student investigating neurocognition and socio-emotional processing in children, adolescents and adults with anorexia nervosa. She has a strong interest in neuropsychology and neuroscience, and completed a master's qualification in Cognitive and Clinical Neuroscience. Before joining Dr. Tchanturia's research team, she worked as an Assistant Psychologist at the National and Specialist Obsessive Compulsive Disorder Clinic for Children and Young People, London.

Nick P. Lao-Kaim, MSc, is a neuroimaging researcher working with Dr. Tchanturia to identify the underlying neural patterns associated with the cognitive styles observed in people with anorexia nervosa, using functional MRI. Nick's main research interests involve executive brain processes, focusing primarily on improving our knowledge of the components of cognitive flexibility in order to construct more effective remedial therapy. He has co-authored peer-reviewed articles on brain function in anorexia nervosa.

Bryan Lask, MD, is an Emeritus Professor of Child and Adolescent Psychiatry at the University of London, Honorary Consultant at Great Ormond Street Hospital for Children and Medical Director for Mental Health Care UK. He has also been a Visiting Professor at the Universities of Oslo and British Columbia. He is a Past-President of the Eating Disorders Research Society and recipient of a Lifetime Achievement Award from the Academy for Eating Disorders (2011). His main area of clinical and research interest lies with early onset eating disorders. He has published twelve books, nearly two hundred peer-reviewed papers and numerous chapters in books edited by others. He has also been the Editor of *The Journal of Family Therapy* and *Clinical Child Psychology and Psychiatry*, and is Co-Editor of a new journal: *Advances in Eating Disorders – Theory, Research and Practice*.

Samantha Lloyd, MSc, is a current PhD student investigating perfectionism in adolescents and adults with anorexia nervosa, including potential associations between perfectionism and neurocognition. Before joining Dr. Tchanturia's team she completed an MSc in Mental Health Service and Population Research at the Institute of Psychiatry and has worked as a Research Assistant in both Chronic Fatigue and Eating Disorders services at the Institute of Psychiatry, London, UK.

James D. Lock, MD, PhD, is Professor of Child Psychiatry and Pediatrics in the Department of Psychiatry and Behavioral Sciences at Stanford University School of Medicine, USA, where he also serves as Director of the Eating Disorder Program for Children and Adolescents. Dr. Lock has published over two hundred articles, abstracts, books and book chapters. He is the past recipient of a National Institutes of Health (NIH) Career Development Award and a current recipient of a Mid-Career Award. He is active in research with four current NIH funded projects related to eating disorder treatment in children and adolescents and young adults, as well as participating in numerous national and international collaborations. His recent research focuses on integrating treatment research with neuroscience in eating disorders, including examining neurocognitive processes and their functional and neuroanatomical correlates. He has lectured widely in the US, Canada, Europe,

South America, Asia, Australia and New Zealand. Dr. Lock's current research focuses on interventions for anorexia nervosa and bulimia nervosa in younger patients and is funded by the NIH in the USA. He was awarded the Price Family Foundation Award for Research Excellence in 2010.

Naima Lounes, MSc, is a trainee clinical psychologist at Salomons, Canterbury Christ Church University, UK. Before joining Dr. Tchanturia's team, she was involved in research projects in emotional processing and in obsessive–compulsive disorder. She then worked as a psychology assistant in the Eating Disorders Unit, Institute of Psychiatry, King's College London, for two years. During this time and as part of her doctoral thesis, she was involved in various audit projects, including cognitive remediation therapy outcomes and therapists' experience of delivering the therapy. She is currently completing her clinical training.

Natalie Pretorius, DClin, is a clinical psychologist who has worked in the field of eating disorders for five years. She currently works in the Child and Adolescent Eating Disorders service at the Maudsley Hospital, London. Prior to this she has worked at the Institute of Psychiatry, King's College London carrying out research into eating disorders. Natalie's peer-reviewed publications include evaluations of cognitive behavioural therapy self-help interventions for adolescents with bulimia nervosa and of cognitive remediation therapy interventions for adults and adolescents with anorexia nervosa.

Jayanthi Raman is a clinical psychologist, with fifteen years of experience working with adults suffering from a broad range of mental health issues. She is a PhD candidate with Professor Phillipa Hay and Dr. Evelyn Smith, at the School of Medicine, University of Western Sydney, Australia, and holds the prestigious Training Fellowship in Psychiatric Research offered by the NSW Institute of Psychiatry. The focus of her doctoral research is on investigating the efficacy of cognitive remediation therapy in obesity. Furthermore she is interested in the underlying mechanisms involved in the maintenance aspects of obesity such as executive function, mood, emotion dysregulation, habitual cluster behaviours and health literacy.

Clare Reeder, PhD, DClin, is a chartered clinical psychologist and a Clinical Lecturer in the Department of Psychology at the Institute of Psychiatry, King's College London. She has been involved in a number of trials of cognitive remediation for schizophrenia and in developing a new computerised version of the therapy. She runs annual international cognitive remediation training courses at the Institute of Psychiatry. Her research interests are in understanding the links between cognitive and functioning change in schizophrenia, and particularly the role of metacognition. She is also currently adapting and investigating cognitive remediation for use with people with a borderline personality disorder diagnosis.

Alice Roberts is a Psychology undergraduate student currently studying at Cardiff University. She has a keen interest in clinical psychology and is particularly interested in child and adolescent clinical psychology and associated eating disorders. Learning about cognitive remediation therapy whilst working alongside Professor Bryan Lask on a placement year as part of her degree, Alice became convinced of its usefulness as a therapy for anorexia nervosa. Subsequently she has co-authored a paper concerning the benefits and feasibility of including the whole family unit in cognitive remediation therapy for anorexia nervosa.

Mima Simic, MD, MRCPsych, is a joint Head of the CAMHS National and Specialist Child and Adolescent Eating Disorder Service (CAEDS) and Consultant Child and Adolescent Psychiatrist for the adolescent DBT Service at the Maudsley Hospital, London. For more than twenty-five years, her clinical work has been focused on the treatment and development of new treatments for disorders in adolescence with a specialist interest in eating disorders and self-harm. Her main research interest has focused on testing the efficacy of the newly developed treatment modalities for eating disorders and self-harm, and results of the treatment trials she participated in continue to be published in peer-reviewed journals.

Emma Smith is a trainee clinical psychologist at the Institute of Psychiatry, Kings College London. Her pre-qualification roles included a number of posts in the field of neuropsychology before she joined Dr. Tchanturia's clinical team at the National Eating Disorder Service at the Maudsley Hospital. She has published a number of papers during these early stages of her career and hopes to continue with these academic interests once qualified.

Evelyn Smith, PhD, is a Research Fellow at the School of Psychiatry at the University of New South Wales and a consultant psychologist at St Vincent's Clinic, Sydney, Australia. She works primarily with adults and older adults with eating disorders and obesity and has published widely in this area. She is also an Honorary Associate at the University of Sydney where she is running a series of projects, including a randomised controlled trial on attention training therapy for bulimia nervosa. She is currently the Chief Investigator of a randomised controlled trial funded by the Diabetes Australia Research Trust to investigate the effectiveness of cognitive remediation therapy for obesity.

Kate Tchanturia, PhD, DClin, is a chartered clinical psychologist who has worked in the field of clinical and experimental psychology for thirty years. Over the last two decades, her clinical and academic work in the King's College London Department of Psychological Medicine and the South London and Maudsley NHS Eating Disorder Service has focused on translational research to promote good clinical practice. Dr. Tchanturia has published over one hundred peer-reviewed papers reporting experimental studies of cognitive processing and emotion in eating disorders, as well as their cultural presentations. In this book, she reviews the emerging evidence of cognitive remediation therapy for eating disorders with her international collaborators and colleagues, from the first case of CRT in anorexia, which she published in 2005, up until the present day. Currently, Dr. Tchanturia is the lead clinical psychologist for the National Eating Disorder Service at the Maudsley Hospital and a Reader in the Psychology of Eating Disorders at King's College London. She was honoured for her teaching excellence at King's College London in 2009 and is a recipient of Royal Society, Wellcome Trust, NHS Innovation, BRC and Swiss Anorexia Foundation awards. She has lectured internationally and trained clinicians and researchers in the UK, USA, Europe, South America, New Zealand and Australia in the neuropsychology of eating disorders and how to translate it into remedial approaches.

Heather Westwood studied undergraduate Psychology at Newcastle University and also gained a postgraduate Diploma in Mental Health Studies from the University of Southampton, UK. Heather has worked clinically in an outpatient service for eating disorders, facilitating group work within an intensive day treatment programme for anorexia nervosa and delivering CBT-based guided self-help for bulimia nervosa. Heather is doing a PhD with Dr. Kate Tchanturia at King's College London.

Til Wykes, PhD, DClin, is Professor of Clinical Psychology and Rehabilitation at the Institute of Psychiatry, King's College London. She has been involved in research on rehabilitation for many years both in the development of services and the evaluation of innovative psychological treatments. She is the director of the Centre for Recovery in Severe Psychosis (CRiSP) which has carried out a number of RCTs into the efficacy of cognitive remediation therapy, Group Cognitive Behaviour Therapy for voices, as well as motivational interviewing techniques in compliance and therapy to reduce the effects of stigmatization. She is also Co-Director in a collaborative venture, the Service User Research Enterprise (SURE), which employs expert researchers who also have experience of using mental health services. Til Wykes is the editor of the *Journal of Mental Health* and the director of the NIHR Mental Health Research Network which is a Department of Health funded research network responsible for providing the national NHS infrastructure for RCTs and other high quality research studies in mental health.

ACKNOWLEDGEMENTS

I would like to say a huge thank you to my supportive family: Simon, Alex, Sophie and Natia, you were so helpful. Many thanks to my son Alex Surguladze who designed the book cover, it means a lot to me. I would also like to thank Professors Janet Treasure, Ulrike Schmidt and Iain Campbell for their continuous support.

I would like to acknowledge my wonderful research collaborators. First of all my former PhD students who are now successfully continuing their journeys in different fields of Psychology all over the world: Helen Davies, Amy Harrison, Carolina Lopez, Marion Roberts; my wonderful clinical doctoral trainees, Dave Hambrook, Amanda Waldman, Naima Lounes and many others. Great researchers – voluntary therapists Natalie Pretorius, Emma Baldock, Abigail Eater, Hannah Curtis, Emma Smith, Eli Doris, Zoe Maiden, Becca Genders, Olivia Kyriacou, Jenna Whitney. Developing research and translating it in appropriate format for eating disorder population was very challenging, rewarding team work.

I am very grateful for my research and clinical colleagues: Lynn St Louis, Caroline Fleming, Amy Brown, Claire Baily and Robin Morris. Also a big thank you to my international colleagues for their time and contributions to this book. I have been supported financially by different funding resources throughout the research: Swiss anorexia nervosa Foundation, BIAL, the Psychiatry Research Trust, the NIHR Biomedical Research Centre for Mental Health at South London and Maudsley NHS Foundation Trust, the Institute of Psychiatry, King's College London, NHS Innovations, and Maudsley Charity Health in Mind.

I would like to thank all of our patients for taking part in the studies and for their helpful comments, permission to use anonymous cases, stories and examples.

INTRODUCTION

Why CRT for eating and weight disorders?

Kate Tchanturia

The purpose of this book is to present the current state of cognitive remediation therapy (CRT) for eating disorders. This book has descriptions of some CRT exercises but it is more of my attempt to bring current research evidence together. We decided to focus on anorexia in this monograph because this intervention is in the early stages of investigation in other diagnostic groups of eating disorders. Chapter 12 for example, describes the first application of CRT to the area of obesity.

It was relatively recently that we published the first case study of CRT in anorexia (Davies & Tchanturia, 2005). At this point, we were still piloting and adjusting the ideas from CRT work published in the literature. Professor Til Wykes and Dr Clare Reeder's work in the field of psychosis was particularly important and we are grateful for their training, comments and contributions during the development and introduction of CRT to the eating disorder research and clinical community.

This book now represents nine years of hard work from my research and clinical group, and work of the colleagues from the international community who took the time to research applications of CRT in eating disorders and to generate clinical and research evidence on this topic.

Cognitive remediation therapy quickly attracted the attention of clinicians, researchers, carers and patients themselves and we think there may be a number of reasons for this:

- There is a lack of strong evidence for the best choice treatment for anorexia.
- Experimental research into cognitive profiles in adult populations generated clear evidence that provided targets for the cognitive remedial work.
- A cognitive remediation intervention based on research evidence makes logical sense and furthermore is highly novel in the eating disorder treatment context.

- The motivational style of the intervention is well suited to the patients group.
- The focus on factors other than eating disorder symptoms, yet still targeting important maintaining factors in CRT has promise.

At this stage the acceptability, effectiveness and benefits of CRT were explored using various research designs (case studies, case series in both inpatient and outpatient settings, randomized treatment trials). CRT for anorexia has been studied in different clinical settings including the international labs – and of course in the UK (Institute of Psychiatry, King's College London) where it originates from – Stanford in the USA, Germany, the Netherlands and Norway. The largest randomized treatment trial is currently underway in Paris led by Doctors Sylvie Berthoz and Natalie Godart.

We made a great effort to invite colleagues who have already had training and experience with this intervention to share it with the readers.

At present, evidence from experimental studies shows that people with anorexia typically have problems with flexibility and 'bigger picture' thinking (for detailed discussion see Chapter 1). We also have a converging body of evidence from case studies (Chapters 2, 3), randomized treatment trials (Chapters 6, 7, 8), and evaluation from clinicians (Chapter 5), that CRT is an acceptable and effective form of treatment in the context of eating disorders in the one-to-one format. There are immediate improvements observed in treatment drop-out rates (Chapter 8), cognitive performance (Chapter 9), and quality of life (Chapter 7).

We made sure that we included in this book application of CRT in adolescent and adult patient groups (because originally CRT was developed and applied to adult population – Tchanturia *et al.*, 2007, 2008, 2010). We have also included in the book new applications of CRT in format- (Chapters 4, 9) and family-therapy contexts (Chapter 10), in obesity (Chapter 12), and have described early research in neuroscience of CRT in eating disorders (Chapters 7, 11). In sum, we have outlined the present state of art in terms of ongoing research and development of the cognitive remediation work in the field of eating disorders.

These research findings inspire confidence that exploring CRT further is a worthwhile venture. In particular, it will be important to investigate the following questions:

1   Who benefits from CRT most?
2   What are the active ingredients of the therapy?
3   What are the neurocorrelates of the cognitive styles and what are the changes produced on a neurocognitive level?
4   What is the right dosage of CRT in the treatment of anorexia?
5   How should CRT be modified for different age groups?
6   What is the minimal amount of training and supervision therapists can get?
7   Which are the best instruments to measure clinically meaningful benefits?

Some of these questions begin to be addressed in this book; however, further research and clinical exploration is needed. Hopefully this book will give an accurate picture of the current state of relevant research and clinical practice in order to promote interest from clinicians and academics alike and to encourage the formation of well-informed clinically meaningful hypotheses for the future.

I would like to thank all collaborators who contributed in this manuscript – from my research and clinical team, as well as international collaborators who joined me in this very exciting project – and generously gave time to inform all of you who will open this book and take interest in this fast developing area. I would like to say very special thanks to Helen Davies who helped enormously in developing a clinical manual of CRT and did lots of exciting work during her PhD studentship in our group. At this point Helen is doing her clinical psychology training and was not able to contribute her time to the book itself. I am very grateful to our publisher Jane Madeley who approached me at the British Association for Behavioural and Cognitive Psychotherapies London conference in 2013 and inspired me to put this project together.

I hope all our efforts will make a difference for the patients, families and professionals working in the field of eating disorders.

References

Davies, H. and Tchanturia, K. (2005). Cognitive remediation therapy as an intervention for acute anorexia nervosa: a case report. *European Review of Eating Disorders*, *13*, 311–316.

Tchanturia, K., Davies, H. and Campbell, I. (2007). Cognitive remediation for patients with anorexia nervosa: preliminary findings. *Annals of General Psychiatry*, *14*, 6–14.

Tchanturia, K., Davies, H., Lopez, C., Schmidt, U., Treasure, J. and Wykes, T. (2008). Neuropsychological task performance before and after cognitive remediation in anorexia nervosa: a pilot case series. *Psychological Medicine*, *38* (9), 1371–1373.

1

COGNITIVE PROFILES IN ADULTS AND CHILDREN WITH ANOREXIA NERVOSA AND HOW THEY HAVE INFORMED US IN DEVELOPING CRT FOR ANOREXIA NERVOSA

Kate Tchanturia and Katie Lang

Anorexia nervosa (AN) is a serious mental health disorder, with an enduring and chronic course, as well as high morbidity rates (Arcelus *et al.* 2011). In present times there is little in the way of effective treatments, and the National Institute of Clinical Excellence (NICE 2004) currently does not have a first line (best) recommended treatment for adult anorexia nervosa patients. It is therefore important for us to focus our attention on underlying cognitive traits that may be present in individuals with anorexia, and which may make engaging in conventional psychological therapies difficult.

To be beneficial, many talking therapies such as Cognitive Behaviour Therapy (CBT) and Cognitive Analytical Therapy (CAT) require the individual to engage in complex cognitive processes. CBT, for example, is based on the principle of making behavioural changes, and learning more adaptive behaviours in order to affect cognitive processes. If, however, someone's cognitive style makes it difficult for them to think flexibly and biases them to focus on detail rather than in a gistful way, they are likely to find this process incredibly difficult. Therefore, whether or not an individual will find psychological treatments such as CBT helpful will largely depend on factors such as IQ and neurocognitive style. We use CBT here as an example, but it largely applies to any kind of therapy, because psychological (talking) therapies are based on the premise that patients can learn to replace maladaptive behaviours with more adaptive ones.

Recent research has highlighted a particular neuropsychological profile in AN, in which certain inefficiencies in cognitive processing have been observed. In particular, such inefficiencies have been identified in the areas of set-shifting and central coherence (e.g. for more details our published work, Tchanturia *et al.* 2011, 2012; Lang *et al.* 2014a; Roberts *et al.* 2007; Lopez *et al.* 2008a,b). *Set-shifting* refers to the ability to move *flexibly* from one behaviour or mental set to another and adapting to a changing and unpredictable environment (Lezak 2008). In everyday behaviour, set-shifting is expressed in flexibility of thinking. Another important cognitive feature in the literature associated with anorexia is extreme attention to detail versus bigger picture thinking; many researchers refer to this as central coherence. *Central coherence* is the ability to contextualize information and integrate it into the 'bigger picture' (Frith 1991). With an extremely focused rigid and detailed processing style, it is understandable why individuals with anorexia might find conventional psychological treatments difficult. The idea of such cognitive traits acting as maintaining mechanisms was proposed by Schmidt and Treasure (2006), who suggested that these cognitive styles might be one of the four main factors maintaining anorexia.

This chapter shall therefore focus on set-shifting and central coherence and review the evidence for the cognitive profile of adults and children with anorexia.

Set-shifting

Outside of the eating disorders field, flexibility has been implicated as a strong predictor of response to psychological treatment in a range of mental health disorders, as well as being beneficial for general health and wellbeing (Kashdan and Rottenburg 2010).

Within the sphere of anorexia, many patients report anecdotally that they find problem-solving challenging, due to their inflexible or rigid thinking style. This is coupled with our clinical observations that a majority of patients with anorexia find it difficult to accept the idea of recovery (particularly when very underweight and nutritionally compromised), or to change their behaviours not only around eating but also everyday routines.

Such observations have sparked an interest into mental flexibility, and about a decade ago our attention became focused on research into flexibility of thinking in the adult population in people with anorexia (e.g. Tchanturia *et al.* 2001, 2002, 2004a,b, 2011, 2012).

Neuropsychological tasks assessing mental flexibility have been used to examine set-shifting and test our clinical observations. Table 1.1 lists the most common of these tasks.

The findings from our early experimental studies (e.g. Tchanturia *et al.* 2004a,b) matched our clinical observations, and confirmed that due to their more inflexible thinking styles, people with anorexia found cognitive flexibility tasks particularly challenging compared to those without eating disorders. We have continued this line of research for more than a decade now, and as experts within the field, we are convinced that this inflexible thinking pattern is present not only in patients currently ill with anorexia but also in individuals who have recovered from the disorder, in comparison to non-eating-disorder groups. It is still not clear whether this is the case for patients with bulimia and other eating disorders (Tchanturia *et al.* 2012, 2011; Roberts *et al.* 2013, 2007; Harrison *et al.* 2012; Van den Eynde *et al.* 2011).

The best and most robust way of examining the experimental evidence is through study replication and critical appraisal of the literature. Two decades ago

TABLE 1.1 Description of popular experimental set-shifting tasks

Name of task	Description
Wisconsin Card Sorting Task (WCST, Heaton et al. 1993)	Originally this test was developed using cards, but it is now computerised to minimise experimenter bias/error and to save time. Participants are presented with a stimulus card and required to match it to one of four category cards (1 red triangle, 2 green stars, 3 yellow crosses or 4 blue circles). The correct way to sort the cards is unknown and the participant must use feedback on whether they have sorted correctly, to guide their next move. The sorting rule changes unpredictably and the participants must adapt to the rule change. The number of perseverative errors is used as a measure of set-shifting. The largest dataset on WCST in eating disorders is published in an open access journal (Tchanturia et al. 2012) and can be found at www.ncbi.nlm.nih.gov/pmc/articles/PMC3257222/
Trail Making Task (TMT, Delis et al. 2001)	Originally developed as pen and paper task, there are now computerised versions available (it is sub-test of D-KEFS test battery). TMT consists of two parts: In Part A, participants are required to connect twenty-five numbered dots in numerical fashion as quickly and accurately as possible. In Part B, participants are asked to connect the dots, but this time alternating between numbers and letters (e.g. 1-A-2-B etc.). A measure of set-shifting ability is taken from the amount of time taken to complete Part B.
The Brixton (Burgess and Shallice 1997)	A blue dot is displayed either on pages, or in the computerised version on a screen, and moves around in a sequence. Participants are asked to predict the next position where it will appear. The sequence changes unpredictably and participants need to adapt to the new sequence in order to guess its next position correctly. The largest dataset published to the data in eating disorders can be found in an open access journal (Tchanturia et al. 2011) at www.ncbi.nlm.nih.gov/pmc/articles/PMC3115939/

it was impossible to understand neurocognitive profiles in eating disorders for two main reasons: Firstly, the number of studies was extremely limited. Our first attempt in 1999 to critically appraise the eating disorders literature in neuropsychology was unsuccessful, due to the twelve existing studies' variability in methodology, leading to unclear findings. Such studies concluded that neuropsychological functioning was 'intact', even in the starved phase of anorexia. Secondly, studies were looking at general executive functions and not using a hypothesis-driven approach to guide their investigations. This meant that these studies were not focusing on the most clinically relevant aspects of cognition, namely set-shifting and central coherence.

Hypothesis-driven research started in 2000 and now there are many adult population-based studies from different parts of the world confirming our original experimental findings, that cognitive flexibility is problematic for people who are in the actively ill state of anorexia. Studies are available from various groups from Italy

(Tenconi *et al.* 2010; Abbate Daga *et al.* 2012); Germany (Fredrick *et al.* 2011, 2013); USA (Steinglass *et al.* 2006) and the Netherlands (Danner *et al.* 2012) to name but a few.

Data analysis

The best way to visually show the results of a meta-analysis (combining results from multiple studies) is by using forest plots, whereby all of the evidence is put together in one graph. Effect sizes (a standardised way – usually Cohens d – of measuring the difference between two groups) are displayed on the *x* axis with each individual study plotted on the *y* axis. In regard to measurements, 0.30 and under is seen to be a small effect size, 0.30–0.50 a medium effect size and 0.50 or more is a large effect size. The effect size for each individual study can be seen, with an overall sum of effect sizes displayed on the bottom.

Figure 1.1 displays a forest plot of the available anorexia nervosa (AN) WCST studies. The top half of the forest plot depicts adult AN WCST studies. The graph shows that across the various studies, adults with anorexia made more perseverative

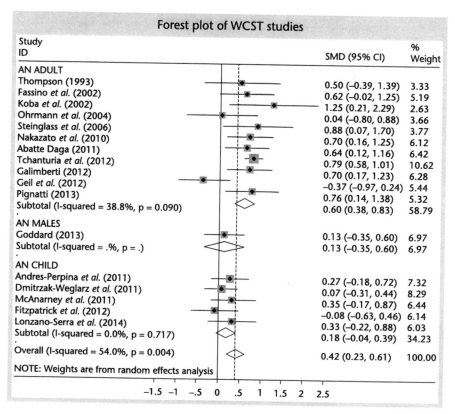

FIGURE 1.1 Forest plot of WCST studies: adults with AN (top half) and children with AN (bottom half)

errors (as the studies sit to the right of the line), with an overall effect size of 0.60 (large effect size). This means that they found it difficult to switch to new rules – dropping redundant rules and strategies and adapting to the changing environment – when the conditions of the task changed. Instead they tended to continue to follow the old rule, thus exhibiting perseverative errors. It should also be highlighted here that Goddard et al. (2013) has been separated from the other adult studies as this study only contained male AN patients.

The evidence based on the research in the adult population with anorexia clearly shows (with the exception of one study, Geil et al. 2012) that patient groups are performing less efficiently than controls on set-shifting tasks.

More recently the attention of the field has turned to examine the neuropsychological profile of children and adolescents with anorexia. This interest has been spurred on by the hypothesis that inefficient set-shifting may be an endophenotype for the disorder. An endophenotype is a measurable biological, behavioural or cognitive marker which is present more often in individuals with a disorder than in the general population (Gottesman and Gould 2003).

Endophenotypes must fulfil four criteria:

1   They must be associated with a certain population (e.g. anorexia)
2   They must be present regardless of whether or not the illness is in the acute phase or recovered stage (i.e. not state-dependant)
3   They must be heritable, and
4   Must also be present to a higher degree in non-affected family members, such as siblings or parents (Gottesman and Gould 2003).

As well as evidence of inefficient set-shifting in individuals currently ill with anorexia, the trait has also been observed following recovery and also in unaffected sisters of those with anorexia (Roberts et al. 2010), providing support for the endophenotype hypothesis. However, a recent meta-analysis of the child and adolescent set-shifting data in anorexia did not reveal a clear difference in performance on set-shifting tasks between children with and without anorexia (Lang et al. 2013). A forest plot displaying studies using the WCST with children with AN can be also be found in Figure 1.1 (bottom half).

As can be seen from this graph, the overall sum of effect sizes from the child studies is much smaller (0.15) than that of the adults (0.60). We should however, keep in mind that in comparison to the adult studies, the data from children is still very preliminary, as there are currently only five studies with 179 adolescent patients, compared with 14 studies totalling 540 patients in the adult literature. The review by Lang (2013) suggested that the interpretation of the data was clouded by methodological constraints within the current literature and that this was an area of research requiring more attention.

To summarise, the evidence for the existence of set-shifting inefficiencies in the adult anorexia population is strongly supported by the literature; however, the profile of children and adolescents is unclear and in need of further investigation.

Central coherence

Another cognitive characteristic stimulating the development of cognitive remediation therapy was extreme attention to detail and weak central coherence (WCC). This cognitive style refers to the tendency to focus on small details at the 'expense of bigger picture/gestalts' of the information. Similarly to set-shifting, this area of research was driven by the clinical observations that patients with anorexia tended to become very preoccupied with tiny details at the expense of the context of the information. Table 1.2 displays popular neuropsychological tests that are used to examine central coherence.

The most popular test of central coherence that has been used in the anorexia nervosa population is called the Rey-Osterrieth Complex Figures test (ROCFT). The way in which an individual chooses to go about drawing this figure can offer insights into whether they are employing a global or a fragmented strategy to process the figure. If the larger or more global structures of the shape are drawn first (e.g. the large rectangle) it suggests that the individual is seeing the context of the picture. However, if smaller more detailed features are drawn first it suggests that the individual has a preference for detail. In some cases an individual can be so detail-focused that the outcome of the drawing is highly fragmented and incoherent and

TABLE 1.2 Popular neuropsychological tests of central coherence

Name of test	Description of test
Rey Osterrieth Complex Figures Test (Osterrieth 1944)	A pen and paper task, in which participants are required to copy a complex figure as accurately as they can. The drawing style adopted by the individual can reveal central coherence abilities. The CCI is obtained from calculating the style index and the order index as defined by Happé's group (see Lopez *et al.* 2008b and Booth 2006 for references). A higher CCI score indicates a more global processing strategy. Detailed instructions and protocol can be found in: http://media.wix.com/ugd/2e1018_e10dcd4e42414639a83c5d70db55977f.pdf
Group/Embedded Figures Test (GEFT/EFT; Witkin 1971, 2002)	Participants are required to locate a simple shape within a much more detailed and complex shape. The time taken to find the embedded shape is recorded. Shorter times are indicative of detail-focused processing.
Object Assembly (OA; Wechsler 1974, 1981)	Participants are required to complete five jigsaw puzzles depicting familiar objects. The main outcome measure is the time taken to complete each puzzle. Time scores are then scaled, whereby higher scores indicate better global integration.

does not represent the shape they were asked to copy. The main outcome of the ROCFT is the central coherence index (CCI), with a lower CCI being more indicative of a detail-focused style. (A detailed description of how to conduct and interpret the data can be found on our website, www.katetchanturia.com under the section clinical protocols: http://media.wix.com/ugd/2e1018_e10dcd4e424146 39a83c5d70db55977f.pdf.)

A meta-analysis performed by Lopez *et al.* (2008b) demonstrated that individuals with anorexia struggled with tasks that required a global processing style. The authors could not, however, conclude that those with anorexia had superior detail-focused processing and therefore were unable to conclude that they had weak central coherence. Having said that, there have been numerous studies since this 2008 review, employing detail-focused tasks which have demonstrated superior detail-focused processing in adults with anorexia nervosa (for updated meta-analysis see Lang *et al.* 2014a).

Figure 1.2 displays a forest plot of studies using the ROCFT in patients with anorexia and shows that patients in adult populations use more fragmented, detailed approaches to draw the figure as they fall to the left of the line, demonstrating a lower CCI score – unlike the non-eating-disorder controls who had higher CCIs. This profile of superior detail-focused processing and weak global integration does not appear to be specific to AN, and can also be seen across the spectrum of eating disorders, for example in patients with Bulimia Nervosa (Lang *et al.* 2014).

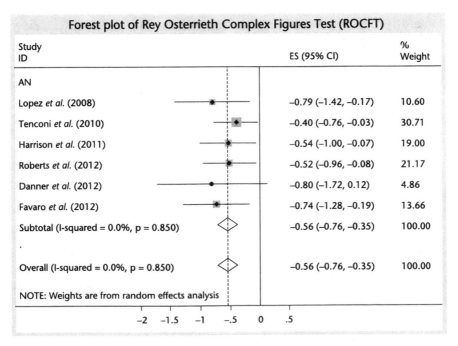

FIGURE 1.2   Central coherence studies: forest plot for adults with AN

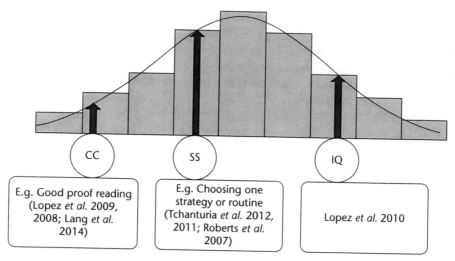

FIGURE 1.3 Graph of cognitive styles in anorexia nervosa (CC – central coherence; SS – set-shifting)

Currently, evidence of weak central coherence in children is lacking and inconclusive. A review of the literature found only four studies investigating central coherence in children with anorexia. Many of these studies reported different outcomes, making a synthesis of the data impossible (Lang and Tchanturia, 2014b).

Intelligence Quotient (IQ)

A further cognitive characteristic worth mentioning is the higher than average IQ reported in patients with anorexia. A few years ago we conducted a careful analysis of the literature looking at good quality studies which reported a formal assessment of the general intelligence of people with anorexia and found that most of the studies reported higher than average IQ of 110–115, compared to the general population norm of 100 (Lopez et al. 2010).

How has the neurocognitive profile of AN helped to develop treatments?

The discovery of the distinct neuropsychological profile of adults with anorexia has led to the adaptation and development of cognitive remediation therapy for anorexia. cognitive remediation therapy has a long and successful history in the field of brain lesion and psychosis and is now emerging in the field of other disorders (Ben-Yishay and Diller 1993; Wykes et al. 2011).

The experimental finding of inefficient set-shifting and weak central coherence in anorexia have given the field specific targets to aim CRT at, and we are now beginning to tailor CRT to address such cognitive features, and to use the high IQ of those with AN to discover and reflect on their own cognitive style, think about alternative ways of thinking and doing, and to apply this learning to their everyday life. This approach of remedial therapy in the adult population is showing some promise, as will be demonstrated in Chapters 2, 3, 4, 6, 7 and 8.

Regarding children and adolescents, there have been encouraging findings which are outlined in Chapters 8 and 9. The pilot studies of CRT have shown feasibility and efficacy; however, larger studies are needed to help us to understand the cognitive profile of children and adolescents, and whether CRT can produce any beneficial changes in cognition.

Research into the cognitive profiles of individuals with eating disorders has helped us to tailor cognitive remediation programmes specifically for the adult anorexia population. The work within the psychosis field has broadly addressed not only cognitive flexibility but major components of CRT, focused on working memory and planning (Wykes and Reeder 2005).

As previously described in this chapter, the areas showing the most inefficient processing in anorexia are flexibility and central coherence. Therefore, we have adapted CRT for anorexia by including a flexibility module as well as 'bigger picture' exercises. These areas were the main adaptation in terms of content of the manual and conceptual framework for the application of CRT for anorexia. It is worth mentioning that recent appraisal of the literature and experimental data has not supported inefficiencies in working memory, even in the acute anorexia population (for details of the study see Chapter 11, and Lao-Kaim et al. 2013) There is also little research support for planning inefficiencies in adult patients with anorexia, therefore not many exercises focusing on these areas of cognition were included in the CRT manuals for anorexia (Tchanturia et al. 2006 and Tchanturia et al. 2010 revised version: www.katetchanturia.com).

Delivery of CRT

Another important aspect that we would like to highlight is the way in which CRT can be delivered. Our work was informed and stimulated by the work in psychosis, but adapting and tailoring the principles of CRT for anorexia needed careful consideration as well as a good understanding of the clinical picture and the research findings in the anorexia field.

With these factors in mind we modified many of the instructions and made sure that emphasis of the tasks were coherent with the clinical picture and patients' needs in eating disorders. For example, in the psychosis manual (Delahunty et al. 2002), patients are encouraged to improve their performance and complete the tasks and exercises more quickly and accurately as time goes on, and initially we followed the same framework. However, after a significant amount of clinical work and supervision, we realised that aiming to complete tasks faster and more efficiently was feeding competitiveness and was giving patients the impression that it was about their performance, when our actual aim was reflection, whereby patients perform simple cognitive tasks, observe their thinking style and reflect on how it may apply to real life. They then go on to apply this knowledge to new behavioural experiments and new behaviours.

We also aimed to change the perfectionistic approach many anorexia patients had towards the tasks, and to help them become satisfied with being 'good enough'. A good example to demonstrate what we mean by this is the line bisection task – described in Chapters 2 and 3 and present on the cover page of the manual.

In the task, the patient is asked to estimate a middle point in every line. Many patients with psychosis find this task challenging and a majority of individuals with the condition perform it inaccurately. The therapist then encourages them to use strategies to complete the task as well as they can. However, in anorexia we observed that the patients spent a long time making sure that the dot was as accurate as possible, as the 'estimation' element of this task made patients uncomfortable and anxious. This exercise helps therapists to explore reasons why it is so difficult for people with anorexia to estimate, guess or make little mistakes. The therapist can then explore if this is similar in other behaviours and everyday activities that the patient performs. It also opens up a discussion to set up behavioural experiments and try to do things differently. As a result of this exercise, one of the patients we worked with tried to be more relaxed about the rules. (More specific examples are described in two cases in Chapters 2 and 3 – Tchanturia and Hambrook 2009 and Lopez *et al.* 2012 respectively.)

To try and address central coherence inefficiencies, we developed tasks facilitating 'global' thinking, for example, asking patients to describe pictures of busy street scenes. Most patients give excessive amounts of detail in their descriptions, whereas therapists use concise descriptions. When the therapist and patient compare the description, it facilitates interesting discussions about pros and cons of detailed- and bigger-picture cognitive styles (more details of CRT in the following chapters), and what we can learn from how we approach the tasks and how this applies to real life.

Current practice

The initial CRT framework for anorexia (Davies and Tchanturia 2005) has continued to evolve over time with clinical work and supervision. Our annual CRT workshops in the Institute of Psychiatry, King's College London have stimulated research and clinical work in the Eating Disorder field; for example, Chapters 5, 6, 7, 8, 9, 10 and 12 are a result of this training. Updated manual can be found in the following webpage: www.national.slam.nhs.uk/wp-content/uploads/2014/04/Cognitive-remediation-therapy-for-Anorexia-Nervosa-Kate-Tchanturia.pdf.

It is very encouraging to continue to see developments and growing evidence for CRT in anorexia, but at the same time we need to be mindful that there may be subtle differences in the way in which CRT is being delivered throughout the world. Although all authors involved in the book were trained on our CRT course, there are still subtle differences in each group's protocol. For example, our German colleagues only focus on flexibility and have removed the central coherence component (Chapter 7); colleagues from the USA (Chapter 8) have adopted the very first version of our CRT manual and continue to use it in its original format; and the Norwegian version has been adapted to include additional exercises, along with their own neuropsychological assessment battery, the Ravelo profile (Chapter 10), as well as child group protocol (Chapter 9). Therefore, as can be seen, each group has tailored the protocol slightly from the original training, to suit the needs of their patient groups.

In summary, CRT for eating disorders has developed a lot over the last nine years. Most of the work presented in this book and in ongoing trials (in France and Japan) follow the principals and clinical manual that we developed, but inevitably as the field is growing it will be a challenge to have identical protocols across groups due to difficulties with clinical resources, setting, and research agenda.

As a final note in this chapter, we would like to express our excitement for how the work we started nine years ago has evolved, and we are looking forward with enthusiasm and curiosity as to how it will continue to develop, and further evidence be gathered in the field of eating disorders in the future.

References

Abbate-Daga, G., Buzzichelli, S., Amianto, F., Rocca, G., Marzola, E., McClintock, S. and Fassino, S. (2012). Cognitive flexibility in verbal and nonverbal domains and decision making in anorexia nervosa patients: a pilot study. *BMC Psychiatry*, *11* (1), 162.

Arcelus, J., Mitchell, A. J., Wales, J. and Nielsen, S. (2011). Mortality rates in patients with anorexia nervosa and other eating disorders: a meta-analysis of 36 studies. *Archives of General Psychiatry*, *68* (7), 724.

Ben-Yishay, Y. and Diller, L. (1993). Cognitive remediation in traumatic brain injury: update and issues. *Archives of Physical Medicine and Rehabilitation*, *74* (2), 204–213.

Booth, R. (2006). *Local-global processing and cognitive style in autism spectrum disorders and typical development*. London: Institute of Psychiatry, King's College London.

Burgess, P. W. and Shallice T. (1997). *The Hayling and Brixton Tests*. UK: Thames Valley Test Company Ltd.

Danner, U. N., Sanders, N., Smeets, P. A., van Meer, F., Adan, R. A., Hoek, H. W. and van Elburg, A. A. (2012). Neuropsychological weaknesses in anorexia nervosa: Set-shifting, central coherence, and decision making in currently ill and recovered women. *International Journal of Eating Disorders*, *45* (5), 685–694.

Davies, H. and Tchanturia, K. (2005). Cognitive remediation therapy as an intervention for acute anorexia nervosa: a case report. *European Review of Eating Disorders*, *13*, 311–316.

Delahunty, A., Reeder, C., Wykes, T., Morice, R. and Newton, E. (2002). *Cognitive Remediation Therapy: Manual*. London: Institute of Psychiatry.

Delis, D., Kaplan, E. and Kramer, J. (2001). *The Delis-Kaplan executive function system*. San Antonio, TX: The Psychological Corporation.

Dmitrzak-Weglarz, M., Słopien, A., Tyszkiewicz, M., Rybakowski, F., Rajewski, A. and Hauser, J. (2011). Polymorphisms of the SNAP-25 gene and performance on the Wisconsin Card Sorting Test in anorexia nervosa and in healthy adolescent participants. *Archives of Psychiatry and Psychotherapy*, *13* (1), 43–51.

Frith, U. (1991). *Autism: explaining the enigma*. 16–26. Oxford: Blackwell Scientific Publications.

Gottesman, I. I. and Gould, T. D. (2003). The endophenotype concept in psychiatry: etymology and strategic intentions. *American Journal of Psychiatry*, *160* (4), 636–645.

Harrison, A., Tchanturia, K. and Treasure, J. (2011). Measuring state trait properties of detail processing and global integration ability in eating disorders. *The World Journal of Biological Psychiatry, 12* (6), 462–472.

Harrison, A., Tchanturia, K., Naumann, U. and Treasure, J. (2012). Social emotional functioning and cognitive styles in eating disorders. *British Journal of Clinical Psychology, 51* (3), 261–279.

Heaton, R. K., Chelune, G. J., Talley, J. L., Kay, G. G. and Curtiss, G. (1993). *Wisconsin Card Sorting Test Manual: Revised and expanded.* Odessa, FL: Psychological Assessment Resources.

Kashdan, T. B. and Rottenberg, J. (2010). Psychological flexibility as a fundamental aspect of health. *Clinical Psychology Review, 30* (7), 865–878.

Lang, K., Stahl, D., Espie, J., Treasure, J. and Tchanturia, K. (2013). Set shifting in children and adolescents with anorexia nervosa: an exploratory systematic review and meta-analysis. *International Journal of Eating Disorders*, DOI: 10.1002/eat.22235.

Lang, K., Lopez, C., Stahl, D., Tchanturia, K. and Treasure, J. (2014). Central coherence in eating disorders: an updated systematic review and meta-analysis. *World Journal of Biological Psychiatry*, DOI: 10.3109/15622975.2014.909606.

Lang., K. and Tchanturia, K. (2014). A systematic review of central coherence in young people with anorexia nervosa. *Journal of Child and Adolescent Behavior.* DOI: 10.4172/jcalb.1000140.

Lao-Kaim, N., Giampietro, V., Williams S. C. R., Simmons A. and Tchanturia, K. (2013). Functional MRI investigation of verbal working memory in adults with anorexia nervosa. *European Psychiatry*, DOI: 10.1016/j.eurpsy.2013.05.2003.

Lezak, M. (2007). *Neuropsychological Assessment.* Oxford: Oxford University Press.

Lopez, C., Davies, H. and Tchanturia, K. (2012). 'Neuropsychological Models and eating Disorders', in J. Fox and K. Goss (Eds.), *Eating and It's Disorders*, pp. 185-199. Oxford: Wiley-Blackwell.

Lopez, C., Tchanturia, K., Stahl, D., Booth, R., Holliday, J. and Treasure, J. (2008a). An examination of the concept of central coherence in women with anorexia nervosa. *International Journal of Eating Disorders, 42* (2), 143–152.

Lopez, C., Tchanturia, K., Stahl, D. and Treasure, J. (2008b). Central coherence in eating disorders: a systematic review. *Psychological Medicine, 38* (10), 1393–1404.

Lopez, C., Stahl, D. and Tchanturia, K. (2010). Estimated IQ in anorexia: a systematic review of the literature. *Annals of General Psychiatry, 23* (9), 40.

Lozano-Serra, E., Andrés-Perpiña, S., Lázaro-García, L. and Castro-Fornieles, J. (2014). Adolescent anorexia nervosa: cognitive performance after weight recovery. *Journal of Psychosomatic Research, 76* (1), 6–11.

McAnarney, E., Zarcone, J., Singh P., Michels, J., Welsh, S., Litteer, T., Hongyue, W. and Klein, J. D. (2011). Restrictive anorexia nervosa and set-shifting in adolescents: a biobehavioral interface. *Journal of Adolescent Health, 49*, 99–101.

Merwin, R., Timko, C. A., Moscowich, A., Konrad Ingle, K., Bulik, C. and Zucker, N. (2011). Psychological inflexibility and symptom expression. *Anorexia Nervosa Eating Disorders, 19*, 62–82.

NICE. 'Eating disorders – core interventions in the treatment and management of anorexia nervosa, bulimia nervosa and related eating disorders.' NICE Clinical Guideline no. 9. London: NICE, 2004: www.nice.org.uk.

Osterrieth, P-A. (1944). The test of copying a complex figure: a contribution to the study of perception and memory. *Archives of Psychology, 30*, 206–356.

Roberts, M. E., Tchanturia, K., Stahl, D., Southgate, L. and Treasure, J. (2007). A systematic review and meta-analysis of set-shifting ability in eating disorders. *Psychological Medicine, 37*, 1075–1084.

Roberts, M. E., Tchanturia, K. and Treasure, J. (2010). Exploring the neurocognitive signature of poor set-shifting in anorexia and bulimia nervosa. *Journal of Psychiatric Research, 44* (14), 964–970.

Roberts M. E., Tchanturia, K. and Treasure, J. (2013). Is attention to detail a similarly strong candidate endophenotype for anorexia and bulimia nervosa? *World Journal of Biological Psychiatry, 14* (6), 452–463.

Schmidt, U. and Treasure, J. (2006). Anorexia nervosa: valued and visible. A cognitive-interpersonal model and its implications for research and practice. *British Journal of Clinical Psychology, 45*, 343–366.

Steinglass, J. E., Walsh, B. T. and Stern, Y. (2006). Set shifting deficit in anorexia nervosa. *Journal of the International Neuropsychological Society, 12* (03), 431–435.

Tchanturia, K., Morris, R., Brecelj, M., Nikolau, V. and Treasure, J. (2004a). Set Shifting in anorexia nervosa: An examination before and after weight gain, in full recovery and the relationship to childhood and adult OCDP traits. *Journal of Psychiatric Research, 38,* 545–552.

Tchanturia, K., Brecelj, M., Sanchez, P., Morris, R., Rabe-Hesketh, S. and Treasure, J. (2004b). An examination of cognitive flexibility in eating disorders. *Journal of the International Neuropsychological Society, 10*, 513–520.

Tchanturia, K., Campbell, I. C., Morris, R. and Treasure, J. (2005). Neuropsychological Studies in anorexia nervosa. *International Journal of Eating Disorders, 37*, 572–576.

Tchanturia, K. and Hambrook, D. (2009). 'Cognitive Remediation', in C. Grilo and J. Mitchell (Eds.), *The Treatment of Eating Disorders; Clinical Handbook*, pp. 130–150. New York: Guilford Press.

Tchanturia, K., Davies, H., Reeder, C. and Wykes, T. (2010). www.national.slam.nhs.uk/wp-content/uploads/2014/04/Cognitive-remediation-therapy-for-Anorexia-Nervosa-Kate-Tchanturia.pdf.

Tchanturia, K., Harrison, A., Davies, H., Roberts, M., Oldershaw, A., Nakazato, M., *et al.* (2011). Cognitive flexibility and clinical severity in Eating Disorders. *PLoS ONE, 6* (6), e20462.

Tchanturia, K., Davies, H., Harrison, A., Roberts, M., Nakazato, M., Schmidt, U., *et al.* (2012). Poor cognitive flexibility in Eating Disorders: Examining the evidence using the Wisconsin Card Sorting Task. *PLoS ONE, 7* (1), e28331.

Tchanturia, K., Lloyd, S. and Lang, K. (2013). Cognitive Remediation in eating disorders. *International Journal of Eating Disorders, 46* (5), 492–496.

Tenconi, E., Santonastaso, P., Degortes, D., Bosello, R., Titton, F., Mapelli, D. and Favaro, A. (2010). Set-Shifting abilities, central coherence, and handedness in anorexia nervosa patients, their unaffected siblings and healthy controls: exploring putative endophenotypes. *World Journal of Biological Psychiatry, 11*, 813–823.

Van den Eynde F., Guillaume S., Broadbent H., Broadbent H., Campbell I., Schmidt U. and Tchanturia, K. (2011). Neurocognition in bulimic eating disorders: a systematic review. *Acta Psychiatrica Scandinavica*, 1242, 120–140.

Wechsler, D. (1974). *Manual for the Wechsler intelligence scale for children.* California: Psychological Corporation.

Wechsler, D. (1981). *WAIS-R manual: Wechsler adult intelligence scale-revised.* California: Psychological Corporation.

Witkin, H. A. (1971). *A manual for the embedded figures tests.* California: Consulting Psychologists Press.

Witkin, H. A. (2002). *Group embedded figures test.* Mind Garden.

Wykes, T. and Reeder, C. (2005). *Cognitive remediation therapy for schizophrenia.* Abingdon: Routledge.

Wykes, T., Huddy, V., Cellard, C., McGurk, S. R. and Czobor, P. (2011). A meta-analysis of cognitive remediation for schizophrenia: methodology and effect sizes. *American Journal of Psychiatry, 168* (5), 472–485.

Zastrow, A., Kaiser, S., Stippich, C., Walther, S., Herzog, W., Tchanturia, K., Belger, A., Weisbrod, M., Treasure, J. and Friederich H. (2009). Neural correlates of impaired cognitive-behavioral flexibility in anorexia nervosa. *American Journal of Psychiatry, 166,* 608–616.

PART I

Individual format of CRT: complex cases

2

A CASE STUDY OF CRT WITH AN INPATIENT WITH ANOREXIA NERVOSA

Caroline Fleming and Kate Tchanturia

Individual psychological work with underweight and nutritionally compromised patients who are newly admitted to the inpatient ward is a highly challenging process. The patients are often ambivalent, not believing that they require treatment in hospital; rather, they believe that they are able to maintain their health outside of the ward. Within this context, over the past nine years we have been developing individual cognitive remediation therapy (CRT) for inpatients with anorexia nervosa.

As we discussed in Chapter 1, our main focus was to highlight to the patients the research findings about cognitive styles in eating disorders; to tailor and adjust specific exercises from CRT developed in other areas of psychiatry in order to help them to 'observe' their cognitive style, and for us to facilitate the process of reflection on cognitive styles during the therapy sessions. During later sessions, our aim was to help them to set up behavioural experiments, practice outside of the sessions and generalise their newly acquired knowledge and skills to their lives outside of the inpatient ward environment.

Increasingly, we started to notice how powerful the motivational engaging component of this intervention was. In this case we present a complex patient with whom the therapist (CF) used CRT as a component of treatment. In supervision sessions (CF, KT), we routinely reflected on the dynamic of the therapeutic relationship. In this and other cases (based on the analysis of videotapes and supervision notes), it is clearly demonstrated that the CRT style (whether it is in individual or in group format) is light-hearted and playful. As patients become more confident in their reflective capacity and curious about, rather than critical of, their thinking styles, the therapy process becomes more relaxed, which appears to contribute to patients' ability to experiment with behavioural change. Both authors of this chapter have experience of delivering various and varied individual and group interventions in the inpatient ward. From the facilitators' perspective, CRT is the most structured, helpful and, to a certain degree playful intervention which allows a gradual building up of relationships and movement towards a more complex psychological intervention once this stage has been completed. Interestingly, this observation is supported with research on clinicians' views on CRT (for details see Chapter 5).

Introducing Julie's case (patient name is anonymised and permission was obtained; the pseudonym was chosen by the patient herself) will help us to outline the clinical reality of delivering CRT, and demonstrate some specifics of how to deliver exercises and the means by which this can complement the rest of the individual work with patients.

Case introduction

Julie was a 29-year-old female who was referred to the inpatient ward due to severe anorexia nervosa binge/purge subtype. Prior to her admission, she had managed to continue functioning sufficiently well to work full time within a busy company. However, her eating disorder had become increasingly out of control to the point that, at admission, she was bingeing and purging between 15 and 20 times per day. She was extremely fearful of the associated physical health implications and described being terrified that she may die, but had not been able to break this cycle in any meaningful way as an outpatient. As a result, her community team referred her to our national ED inpatient ward.

Presenting complaints

Julie found it very difficult to manage the dynamics on the inpatient ward and felt herself to be very different from other inpatients as she was so appreciative of the opportunity to work towards recovery and was motivated to do so. She was also highly sensitive to others' emotional states and would often find herself in the 'caring' position for others – which she recognised – but this also led to her feeling overwhelmed at times and that her needs were not being met. At the time of her admission there were also quite significant disruptions pertaining to outbursts from other patients which triggered her own fear response in relation to traumatic experiences from early childhood.

History

Family

Julie is the elder of two siblings, with a younger sister two years her junior. She was brought up by both parents but described an unpredictable and invalidating early environment. She described a closer relationship to her father than her mother, although he did shift-work so was not often available; additionally, she described him as holding exceptionally high standards and expectations of Julie which she worked hard to live up to, but she never felt herself to be good enough. Julie described a volatile and difficult relationship with her mother, explaining that she was intensely critical and physically punished her for any misdemeanours when she was a child. Additionally, she described her mother as being overly concerned with weight and shape but she did not offer healthy meals for the family and they never ate together, so Julie described never having developed a sufficient understanding of healthy eating.

Education/career

Julie did not enjoy school; she was shy and intelligent which she perceived as contributing to her being bullied throughout school. She achieved well academically and completed her degree in law after which, as mentioned, she worked full time in a busy company. Prior to this, she had been working towards a career as a professional dancer and had been successful within this, gaining parts in shows at the ages of 13 and 14 – which also contributed to bullying from others, who she perceived as envious of her success. However, when she became too tall to continue with this trajectory, she took the advice of her father and teachers and turned her academic abilities towards a professional career.

Social

Julie did not enjoy an active social life. She described living within a small community and was socially isolated as many of those she could have socialised with she had known from school, so she did not experience close connections with anyone. Additionally, owing to the extent of her eating disorder symptoms and behaviours, she did not have any available time to embark on any pleasurable or enjoyable activities that would have provided her with the opportunity to meet new people.

Medical and mental health

Julie had not experienced any major illness. There was no family history of diagnosed medical, psychiatric or eating disorder. The onset of her eating disorder difficulties started at age 15 and seemed to develop in the context of her stopping her dancing career. She began to comfort eat and put on weight for which she received a lot of criticism from her mother in particular. At 18 years of age, she moved to England to go to university and, in the first term, decided to go on a healthy eating diet to lose weight. She lost a stone in three months and received positive comments from her family as a result. She continued to restrict her nutritional intake and became unwell, being diagnosed with anorexia at the age of 20. She had to return home and continued her studies by distance learning. Julie had continued with an unremitting anorexia since this time and gradually the pattern of bingeing and purging developed and worsened.

Case conceptualisation

It seems that Julie experienced an adverse and invalidating early environment in which her needs were not met and needed to be suppressed. The only means by which she could experience a sense of validation was through her achievements, but this was never deemed by her to be good enough. She did not develop secure attachments outside the family, experiencing bullying throughout her schooling, which appeared to leave her continually hypervigilant to threat or criticism and she tried to be 'invisible'. Additionally, in relation to weight and shape concerns, it seems that her mother was overly concerned about her and her daughters' weight and shape, which contributed to her sensitivity to her body size.

It appears that, within this context, she developed the core beliefs of vulnerability to harm, emotional deprivation, a sense of unworthiness and overall experience of defectiveness, perceiving herself as a failure despite evidence to the contrary. It seems that to prevent activation of this belief system, Julie developed unrelenting perfectionistic standards for herself, and held a tendency to people-please. It seems that her eating disorder also held a function of managing her emotional experience as she described any negative emotion as fundamentally 'bad'.

Course of treatment and assessment of progress

Format

As a result of the assessment process, Julie and her therapist (CF) agreed that CRT would prove a potentially very helpful intervention in exploring and working towards managing Julie's perfectionism, as well as exploring her 'all or nothing' thinking and her tendency towards a negative bias. Additionally, due to Julie's difficulties with forming trusting relationships – fearing others criticism of her, thereby contributing to a reticence to permit herself to be fully open with others – it was felt that CRT would be relatively safe and supportive in relation to this, enabling her to fully engage with a more in-depth therapy through forming a good therapeutic relationship.

With regard to exploring the work of CRT with Julie, this case study will take a more helicopter perspective ('bigger picture' view), exploring some of the exercises that were carried out within sessions but focusing in greater detail on the reflective process and behavioural experiments that were conducted between sessions. In addition, there will be consideration given to how the learning of CRT was taken forward to inform further therapeutic intervention.

Commencement

During the first two sessions, Julie and Caroline (CF, therapist) explored the nature and purpose of CRT (this involves an outline of the research evidence in a friendly fashion, the gist of which is described in the Chapter 1) through a variety of

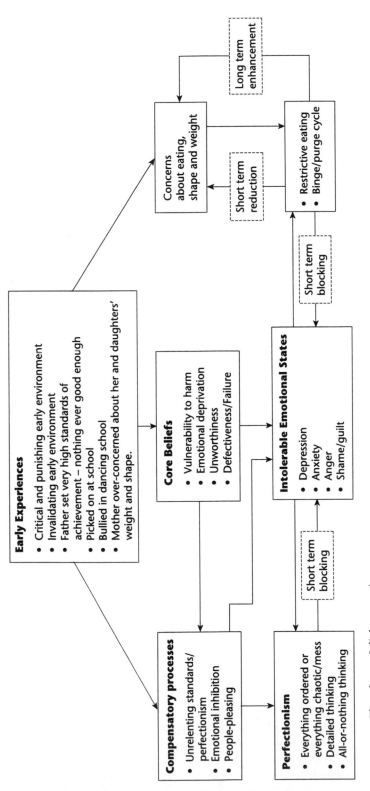

FIGURE 2.1 Flowchart – Julie's presenting state

exercises, which highlighted her detail-focused and perfectionist thinking styles: for example, exercises asking the patient to come up with a catchy title for 'busy' text, describing a busy picture, summing up three positive things you did during your admission.

In the first session, Julie engaged with the line bisection task as mentioned previously, where patients are asked to estimate the midpoint of a number of horizontal lines. She took a long time to complete the task, clearly aiming for accuracy as to where she should place her mark on each of the lines – highlighting the elevated levels of perfectionism discussed in Chapter 1. Reflecting on her discomfort in relation to the task, Julie was able to relate how difficult she found estimation or a 'good enough' position in day to day life.

At school, her need for accuracy led to her never being permitted a mistake, that she was not allowed to cross things out and she would re-write pages of texts rather than make an error. At university, she recalled almost being late handing in work as she never felt she had done enough research to ensure her arguments were accurate. This had continued into her working life: she described her manager as highly critical, so worked exceptionally long hours to ensure all documents were one hundred percent accurate rather than facing the possibility of criticism for a mistake, which would have felt unbearable. Julie remarked how surprised she was that the bisection task, even though so simple, could elicit so much information.

Additionally, we explored Julie's reflective abilities through a variety of exercises with regard to her capacity to relate the exercises to everyday life, and also explored any barriers to fully engaging in the therapy. As a result of the assessment process we appreciated Julie's tendency to people-please and agreed that it would be useful to remain vigilant to this potential, through the therapeutic process.

Through this approach, we were able to identify Julie's cognitive strengths and difficulties. With regard to the former, Julie conveyed a genuine motivation and willingness to engage in CRT. She exhibited an interest in the exercises and worked hard to engage with each, despite her anxiety that she would make mistakes, get things wrong and that the therapist would necessarily judge and criticise her for this. Julie was highly articulate and insightful in relating the learning to everyday life. Additionally, she was clearly invested in the therapeutic process, attending regularly and seeking additional support when conducting behavioural experiments between sessions if she was struggling with these. In terms of difficulties, perfectionism, an all or nothing thinking style, a negative bias and low self-esteem seemed to contribute to a slowness to complete exercises despite her willingness to do so.

Progress

As a result, it seemed important in early sessions to pay attention to exploring her inner critic as this seemed to be impacting negatively on the therapeutic process. Through this process we appreciated that she was fearful of 'getting things wrong' which would lead to criticism, judgement and possible rejection. We explored together her internal self-talk prior to starting a CRT exercise and she was able to share highly punitive thoughts such as: 'you can't do this', 'see, you're hopeless, pathetic, you'll show yourself up', 'you're wrong, you'll make the wrong decision'. We worked with this unhelpful thinking process throughout the intervention and developed towards a stance of 'curiosity and interest' rather than 'harsh judgment' – which she was able to take on board – and this appeared effective in shifting the dynamic of the therapeutic relationship to a more collaborative stance.

Challenges: looking inside the box

The goals for the remaining seven sessions were concerned with focusing on exercises that challenged Julie's inflexible thinking as well as exploring different perspectives (work concentrating on the set-shifting inefficiencies discussed in Chapter 1). Additionally, we worked towards challenging her perfectionism through moving from a detail-focused perspective to a focus on the bigger picture. This was achieved through reflecting on and managing her inner critic when she was clearly struggling to engage with tasks, focusing on exercises that involved switching between different stimuli, and working towards improved decision making between sessions.

An example of one of these exercises was the 'maps' task, in which Julie was asked to describe various routes and directions across a map (shifting from one perspective to another). Initially she found the task impossible and became distressed and tearful as she felt bombarded and overloaded with information. However, she continued despite her discomfort, which enabled us to explore how to develop a more helicopter perspective and to think towards the bigger picture both in specific tasks as well as in everyday life.

Through this process, Julie was able to move from a position of 'I can't' to 'I can do it'. She learned to take a deep breath to calm her anxiety, took a step back from the task and made a plan of action. She incorporated new self-talk such as: 'I'm not a failure, I am capable', and permitted herself to experience a sense of achievement and pride in small but significant accomplishments.

Decision-making

As we mentioned, another significant area of difficulty Julie identified through the exercises and reflecting on these, was in decision making. Again, through moving towards an 'I can' stance, we explored this further within a prioritising task: 'how to plant a sunflower'. In this task Julie was asked to describe the process of planting a sunflower, providing instructions in a succinct way. To highlight Julie's detail-focused thinking style, she started by providing an immensely detailed explanation of the process. She described the route from the ward to the garden centre, including where and how it would be safe to cross various roads. She described the layout of the garden centre, all the different types of soil that could be purchased, various sized pots and suggesting one that would potentially work well. However, as she had been learning in previous sessions, she stopped herself, started again and provided a more gistful explanation, surprising herself that she had the capacity to change perspective. Reflecting on this task in relation to everyday life, Julie described the process of being overwhelmed with choice, fearing making a mistake or the wrong decision and this being criticised negatively by others.

For instance, she described how painful a process decision making was for her by explaining the struggles she had had in attempting to purchase a diary – something that she had been desperately wanting to do for five years. She explained the process. Firstly she would have to go to every stationary shop on the high street and look at all of the possible options. She would return to each shop five times to ensure she had all of the potential information and nothing had been missed. She would then return home and continue to research further options on the internet. By the end of this process she was so overloaded with information that she would essentially give up. As a result, we developed a behavioural experiment based on the prioritising Julie had been able to achieve in CRT. Her choices were limited by only being permitted to enter three shops and her options were further limited relating to her preferences for size, price, colour, and any added features. This enabled her to purchase her diary, and she could feel genuinely proud of her achievement.

Food

Although not a direct aim of this therapeutic intervention, Julie was able to disclose the anxiety she was experiencing in choosing her menu for the week. She explained how she would spend hours ruminating over the menu, ask all other patients what they were choosing, and then painstakingly going through each option weighing up the pros and cons before making a choice. Ultimately, when eating her meal, she ruminated over making the wrong decision, which served to reinforce her sense of confusion and frustration with herself. To support this, we utilised the learning of CRT with regard to prioritising and her new found stance of curiosity. As a result, rather than her default position of 'I've got it wrong', she took a step back, distanced herself from others, and became curious about whether this was a meal that would be manageable. She found this freed her up considerably to fill out menus in good time, and prevented her from continually ruminating over the menu choices, in between meals. We also identified that, as food was such a rarity in life prior to admission, when she did eat she wanted the plate of food to look and taste perfect. Now that she was eating on a regular basis, 'good enough' was a more appropriate stance, and so she could relax more in the dining room.

Identifying and addressing traits

Considering Julie's perfectionist and all-or-nothing thinking further in relation to day to day life, it was possible to identify how she had to ensure everything was neat and in order, that one task had to be completed prior to another being started, that no mistakes were permitted and, if it was not exactly as she had expected or anticipated, she had to start again. However, if she could not meet the standards she had set, she would give up completely and do nothing – which activated her defectiveness/failure belief system.

To take this forward, Julie conducted a number of behavioural challenges towards developing a less demanding standard of herself, so that leisure activities could be just that, rather than another chore to be endured. For instance, she allowed herself to start a second project in Occupational Therapy prior to completing the first; she left a book unfinished that she was not enjoying and tried another; and went on a 'random' and mindful walk around the grounds of the hospital. Additionally, she found it quite liberating to use a dice game to purchase an item for fun and entertainment. In this we identified six potential items and then rolled a dice to make the choice. She used this approach again when on home leave, deciding what she and her sister could do together on an afternoon out.

By completion of the ten sessions of CRT, Julie had begun to feel more confident, particularly in relation to decision making. Additionally, she was able to engage in more pleasurable activities, both on the ward and when on home leave. In our final session we drew out the cycle of perfectionism and the inner critic that we had been working with throughout the therapy. Within this, we appreciated that her initial reaction to being faced with any task was 'I can't do it', leading to feelings of anxiety, fear and panic – culminating in the thought that 'I'm a failure' – and either avoiding the task completely or ensuring it was completed perfectly without any mistakes. We acknowledged that neither of these positions was tenable, as the former reinforced the belief, and the latter culminated in her feeling stressed, distressed and exhausted much of the time.

We considered means by which Julie could move out of this cycle sufficiently to be able to engage with exercises and the changes she had made between sessions. She reflected for herself on her newly developing strategy of 'taking a step back' and positive self-talk such as 'give it a go, I might possibly be able to do it', removing the performance pressure and taking a more curious stance.

Complicating factors

Due to the dominance of Julie's inner critic, it was important to continually reinforce the stance of curiosity and interest, as she would quickly return to a judgemental stance towards herself. Additionally, as we mentioned, Julie was inclined to 'people please' and thus we needed to remain aware of her wanting to be the 'perfect patient'. However, she did appear to be authentically engaged with the materials, and honest about the experiences she was discussing.

Follow up

It seemed that Julie found it hard to hold onto the positive changes she had made as a result of CRT. It appeared that, within her all or nothing thinking style, it was exceptionally difficult for her to appreciate and acknowledge small but significant changes and this required external reinforcement, as she held a tendency to ignore or minimise these. It also seemed feasible that, in managing her eating disorder symptoms more effectively, it meant that she was no longer inhibiting her emotional experience, and this seemed to be contributing to an exacerbation of depressive symptoms in particular. Ongoing therapeutic work therefore focused more specifically on her depression in the context of perfectionism and Julie started a course of anti-depressant medication to support this, something that she had been somewhat reticent about before.

Julie and her therapist (CF) continued to work together but, unfortunately, her funding ran out and she was discharged before she felt she had a sufficient foundation in place to manage her eating disorder completely at home. She maintained her determination, particularly as she was feeling physically much healthier through managing her eating disorder on the ward, but fearful that the changes would not be sustainable. Unfortunately, there was not a local specialist service available to her and so she did not have access to specialist follow-up post-discharge.

As such, our last sessions together targeted the progress she had made, to attempt to support her in developing her confidence in her ability to change through reflecting on the significant changes she had made. We also focused our attention to continuum thinking in the process of recovery, as black and white thinking appeared to be impeding her progress. In Table 2.1 we have presented some of the outcome measures we were able to obtain before and after the CRT with Julie.

Clinical outcomes show a small improvement in Body Mass Index (BMI) and little improvement in cognitive performance as measured by the Brixton Spatial Anticipation Test and Rey Osterrieth Complex Figure task for central coherence

TABLE 2.1 Summary of outcome measures before and after ten sessions of CRT

	Time 1	Time 2	Direction
Clinical			
BMI	15.3	15.8	+
EDE-Q (global score)	2.33	4.06	−
HADS anxiety	18	21	−
HADS depression	16	21	−
Neuropsychological			
Brixton (errors)	7	5	+
Rey	0.19	0.34	+
Other			
CFS	39	39	=
WSAS	38	39	−
MR: Importance	10	10	=
MR: Ability	0	0	=

Key: Time 1 – outcome before sessions; *Time 2* – outcome after sessions; *Direction:* +, −, = indicate changes over time – improvement, deterioration, or no change respectively.

assessment. We presented the Eating Disorder Examination questionnaire (EDE-Q), Hospital Anxiety and Depression scale (HADS), the Cognitive Flexibility Scale (CFS), the Work and Social Adjustment Scale (WSAS) and the motivational ruler measures.

For more details of this outcome-related research, please visit the following website: www.katetchanturia.com

The therapist's final thoughts from a therapist perspective

This case was chosen for presentation for a number of reasons.

Firstly, despite her motivation and determination, Julie's eating disorder was extremely entrenched and, as she had not been able to shift her relationship with her illness in any meaningful way, she was feeling hopeless, helpless and despairing that any therapeutic intervention would be supportive of change. CRT was helpful in shifting perspective as it enabled her to experience positive change, developing her confidence in the possibility she could be effective in this to some degree.

Secondly, Julie expressed a deep sense of shame in relation to her eating disorder symptoms, so, engaging with a therapy that did not directly focus on the illness seemed effective in enabling the development of a secure, non-judgmental therapeutic relationship that appeared to support her in speaking more openly about her illness.

Thirdly, Julie's dominant defectiveness schema meant that she found it very difficult to hold onto any positives and, through enabling opportunities for achievement in general day to day functioning, she was able to explore and appreciate positive steps with regard to managing her eating disorder. For instance, on home leave she binged and purged on one occasion and, rather than discounting the whole leave as a failure, she could appreciate the significant improvement compared with life prior to admission.

Finally, for a therapist working with complex cases, CRT can prove an exceptionally useful tool in developing a secure therapeutic relationship based on curiosity and interest, which can be further developed within a more in-depth psychotherapy.

Supervisor's thoughts, and putting it in the context

We learned from Julie's case that some patients will benefit from extended sessions of CRT. Additionally, involving the multi-disciplinary team is helpful - for example, occupational therapist to help practice with everyday behaviours, skills and consolidate reflections obtained in the sessions. The idea of implementing elements of CRT within family therapy is also helpful from our point of view, to facilitate the maintenance of progress from CRT within the real life context (Chapter 10 outlines more details of CRT in family setting).

3

ADAPTING CRT TO INCREASE AWARENESS OF THINKING STYLES IN PEOPLE WITH SEVERE ANOREXIA AND COMORBID DISORDERS

Amy Harrison and Kate Tchanturia

Overview

This chapter aims to explore how cognitive remediation therapy (CRT) might be adapted for working with people with severe and enduring Eating Disorders (EDs) who also have severe comorbid illnesses, such as anxiety problems. Firstly, a brief review regarding the use of CRT in illnesses commonly comorbid with EDs will be presented. Ideas about how CRT can be adapted for working with these individuals will then be illustrated through a case example – 'Sarah' (pseudonym), an adult with severe anorexia nervosa and obsessive compulsive disorder (OCD).

An outline of the CRT provided will be given, alongside quantitative and qualitative outcomes. The chapter will include discussions about how CRT was integrated into the formulation developed by the wider treatment team. It will also explore how CRT was introduced to the patient, the practical adaptations offered to enable the patient to access treatment, how the CRT exercises and the material brought to the session by the patient were used to expand awareness of thinking styles in everyday life. Finally, we will also explore how small behavioural experiments were designed and used to increase flexibility and bigger-picture thinking, with the overall aim of increasing the individual's ability to function more independently.

Use of cognitive remediation therapy in conditions commonly comorbid with eating disorders

The use of CRT in schizophrenia is well documented elsewhere (see, for example, the review by Wykes and Spaulding, 2011). This section will focus on providing a brief review of how CRT has been used in conditions commonly comorbid with EDs, including depression and anxiety problems like OCD, from which Sarah was also suffering alongside her anorexia.

There is overwhelming research and clinical evidence that people with EDs have a variety of comorbid conditions, such as depression (Lewinsohn, Striegel-Moore, and Seeley, 2000; Santos, Richards, and Bleckley, 2007; Zaider and Cockell, 2002). For example, one study found forty-six percent of female inpatients also met DSM-IV criteria for a coexisting major depressive disorder (Blinder, Cumella, and Sanathara, 2006). As in anorexia, the cognitive problems observed in people with depression are perhaps best described as cognitive inefficiencies (as discussed in Chapter 1), rather than deficits, and for both illnesses, the cognitive problems are less marked than in schizophrenia (Porter, Bowie, Jordan, and Malhi, 2013). Cognitive inefficiencies have been clearly established as a core feature of major depressive disorders (Porter *et al.*, 2013) and, as in anorexia (Tchanturia *et al.*, 2011, 2012; Harrison, Tchanturia, and Treasure, 2011), the data indicate that some of these problems might remain despite symptom improvement (Douglas, Porter, Knight, and Maruff, 2011).

Porter *et al.* (2013) reviewed the published literature on cognitive remediation for the cognitive functioning problems observed in depression and found ten studies had been published which reported on the development and evaluation of cognitive remediation treatment packages for people with depression. In general, these studies reported improvements in cognitive functioning following treatment. For example, Elgamal *et al.* (2007) found that cognitive remediation, added to treatment as usual, was associated with significantly larger improvements in attention, verbal learning and memory, psychomotor speed and executive function, than was observed in those who received treatment as usual only. This positive outcome for cognitive remediation in depression is supported by another study which used a computerised form of treatment, and significantly, improvements in visual and verbal memory, with medium to large effect sizes compared to waiting list controls were reported (Naismith *et al.*, 2011). Whilst there were improvements in cognitive functioning, these studies did not find that cognitive remediation improved symptoms of depression. This is a finding which echoes systematic reviews published on cognitive remediation in schizophrenia, where CRT contributes to clear cognitive and general functioning benefits with medium effect sizes, but minimal symptom reduction (e.g. McGurk *et al.*, 2007).

However, one, albeit small, pilot study, which deviates from this pattern of results used Adrian Wells' attention training technique (Wells, 2011) to improve patients' cognitive control, and found that nineteen patients who received six, thirty-five minute cognitive training sessions reported lower depression symptomatology than a control group of seven patients who received treatment as usual (Siegle *et al.*, 2007). In patients with severe and enduring forms of depression, Bowie *et al.* (2013) reported that their treatment group of seventeen patients showed significant improvements in verbal memory, attention and processing speed after cognitive remediation, compared to the waiting list control group (n = 16). Another case series which looked at the impact of cognitive remediation in eight people with severe and enduring depression who were receiving electro-convulsive therapy, reported small-sized changes in memory functioning after cognitive remediation

(Choi *et al.*, 2011). Thus, the available evidence indicates that cognitive remediation can help to improve cognitive functioning in both moderate and severe forms of depression. The next section explores the use of CRT in people with OCD.

CRT and OCD

Like depression, anxiety disorders commonly co-occur alongside EDs. A large study of 762 participants with EDs found that 64% had at least one comorbid anxiety disorder. These disorders included social phobia (20%), generalised anxiety disorder (10%) and specific phobia (15%). However, by far the most common anxiety problem was OCD, affecting 41% of ED patients (Kaye *et al.*, 2004). Like depression, for many years it has been suggested that OCD is also underpinned by neuro-psychological inefficiencies (Menzies *et al.*, 2007). Due to the inflexible behaviour associated with the drive to perform rituals, set-shifting or cognitive flexibility was proposed to be one form of cognitive inefficiency associated with OCD.

An earlier review of the literature reported inconsistencies, such that although a wealth of studies provided support for this hypothesis, others did not find that set-shifting is affected in people with OCD (Kuelz, Hohagen, and Voderholzer, 2004). It has been suggested that the discrepancies in findings may be due to the fact that the vast majority of studies had small sample sizes of between fifteen and thirty participants, the use of different measurements, and a range of illness severity (Kashyap, Kumar, Kandavel, and Reddy, 2013). In order to address these issues, Kashyap *et al.* (2013) investigated the neuropsychological profile of 150 participants with OCD compared to 205 healthy controls.

They found that, after controlling for age, gender and education, patients with OCD demonstrated significant inefficiencies in scanning, planning time, concept formation, decision-making and encoding of non-verbal memory relative to healthy controls – a profile that they argue, suggests the presence of executive functioning problems, with patients experiencing particular challenges when they needed to develop strategies, organise stimuli and use their cognitive resources to their maximum efficiency. This study was published after the most recent available review for neuropsychological performance in OCD, which included 88 studies and found that people with OCD demonstrate specific inefficiencies (with small to medium effect sizes observed) in visuo-spatial memory, executive function and verbal fluency (Shin, Lee, Kim, and Kwon, 2013).

Further findings

There are few published reports of CRT being used to support cognitive functioning in OCD. It is possible that this might be explained by the aforementioned debate regarding the presence or absence of cognitive inefficiencies in these patients. However, one theme emerging from the literature is that psychological therapies do have the ability to functionally affect the brain, because in their review, Barsaglini *et al.* (2013) found that around half of the available published studies pointed to changes in activation in the caudate nucleus in patients with OCD after treatment. To our knowledge, there are currently two studies which have used a form of cognitive training to support cognitive functioning in OCD, although these studies looked at the treatment effect on neuropsychological outcomes rather than brain activity itself. One group designed a cognitive training package with the aim of improving difficulties in organising information.

Their thirty-five OCD patients were randomly assigned either to a training, or no training condition. In the brief training, they were taught adaptive and meaningful ways of organising complex visuo-spatial information using the Rey-Osterrieth Complex Figure Test (Osterrieth, 1944). Those who received the cognitive training showed greater organisational and memory strategies when completing a copy and recall trial of the figure at a later time than those who did not receive the training (Buhlmann et al., 2006). Another group led by Dr Stefan Moritz in Germany (clinical trials reference NCT01035242) are currently investigating the impact of adding cognitive remediation – delivered using a programme called CogPack – to cognitive behavioural therapy on both OCD symptoms and cognitive functioning. A previous study by Kuelz et al. (2006) reported that cognitive behaviour therapy in itself may help patients to be able to think and behave in more flexible ways, which contributes to the development of more effective cognitive strategies. They conducted neuropsychological assessments on thirty OCD patients before and after cognitive behaviour therapy for OCD, and the data suggest that patients who responded to treatment also improved their scores on measures of set-shifting and global processing.

In summary, the available evidence points to the presence of cognitive inefficiencies in people with OCD, in particular in the domain of executive functioning and there is interest in using CRT to support cognitive functioning in these patients.

Thus far, the Chapter has explored the presence of co-occurring depression and OCD in people with EDs, and a brief review of the literature on neuropsychological functioning in these illnesses; the use of CRT as a tool to ameliorate cognitive inefficiencies has also been explored. In the next section, a case study of an individual with anorexia who also had co-occurring depression and OCD will be presented, to highlight some of the additional challenges these comorbid conditions can place on treatment, and the way in which CRT for anorexia could be adapted to best support improvements in cognitive functioning which may help to account for this complex presentation. Despite the high co-occurrence of EDs and OCD, there is little research available which suggests how to treat these complex cases (Simpson et al., 2013). Therefore, this case study is published with the aim of exploring whether CRT might be a useful and effective treatment in this context.

Case description

'Sarah' was a 44-year-old female patient of mixed ethnicity. She had experienced problems with anxiety throughout her life but despite this, she had successfully completed school and obtained a job working in an office. When she was 24 years old, she left work after experiencing bullying from a male colleague which occurred over a period of two years. She explained that she developed OCD at this time and also had an episode of depression. Sarah had been unable to work since and at the time of admission she was living with her mother. Her father had passed away fifteen years prior to the admission due to cirrhosis of the liver. She had been admitted informally for treatment as an inpatient.

On admission, Sarah had a body mass index (BMI) of 13.8 (37.5 kg) and she was suffering with the physical symptoms of starvation including amenorrhoea, lanugo hair, cold and blue extremities, fatigue, difficulties with concentration and attention, and hair loss. She had comorbid diagnoses of depression, for which she was taking anti-depressant medication, and she also had severe OCD. The obsessions were related to beliefs that all foods were contaminated with sugar which was dangerous for the body, particularly the teeth, and that the environment was dirty. These intrusive thoughts were often unwanted but at times were egosyntonic, as Sarah had a strong personal interest in maintaining a 'pure' body. The obsessions were present for the majority of her waking hours. Sarah's compulsions included severe avoidance of any foods that contained sugar, shopping only from organic baby food stores on the internet, eating only 'pure' organic baby foods that she had checked several times with the producer had not been processed with sugar, using cutlery that had been sealed inside protective cellophane, excessive interest in dental hygiene and excessive hand washing, bathing rituals and teeth cleaning, as well as an intense interest in looking at 'pure' pictures and reading about purity in body and mind.

The compulsions took up a significant proportion of Sarah's day. For example, taking a bath could take around 3 hours and making a cup of coffee at home could take up to 2 hours. As a consequence of the severe food avoidance, Sarah's BMI was dangerously low and her physical health was severely compromised. Because of the time taken by the rituals and the extreme need to perform them to a perfect standard, she was unable to adequately attend to her personal hygiene and this had a strong impact on her personal presentation. Sarah had been receiving cognitive behavioural therapy (CBT) for OCD, involving exposure and response prevention (ERP) from a clinical psychologist, supported by her key worker and other nurses in the ward. This had had some impact on her physical and mental health, as she had been able to increase the range of foods she was willing to consider eating.

An initial formulation (shown below) was developed to understand the current factors maintaining Sarah's low weight, poor physical health and difficulties functioning independently.

- *Current symptoms*: Severely low weight, excessive washing of hands and cutlery, excessive avoidance of sugar in foods, extreme focus on dental hygiene, depression.
- *Precipitating factors*: Experience of bullying at work aged 20–24.
- *Predisposing factors*: Episode of depression aged 22; father had depression and alcohol dependency.

- *Maintaining factors:* Severe avoidance, focus on detail, inflexible cognitive style, a desire to hold onto OCD because it provides safety and purity, a belief that tasks must be completed in a particular way at all times, otherwise it is no use completing them at all.
- *Protective factors:* Close relationship with mother; good social skills.

Based on the initial formulation, after discussions with the psychology team and the broader multidisciplinary team, CRT was offered as a treatment with the aim of:

1 Helping Sarah to become more aware of her thinking styles when she approached tasks during the day to improve general functioning;
2 Helping Sarah to practice flexible thinking and being more flexible in her behaviour to support the ERP she was doing in her CBT sessions;
3 Helping Sarah to develop bigger picture thinking skills to help her move away from becoming stuck in excessive detail with the objective of her increasing her independent functioning.

The rationale for offering CRT was also based on a review of the literature on cognitive functioning in depression and OCD summarised above, and the consideration that 'on-going cognitive impairment may hamper the process of psychological therapy, give rise to significant psychosocial impairment, remain after the main syndrome is treated and be a risk factor for relapse' (Porter *et al.*, 2013, pp. 1172–1173).

Thus, the specific treatment goals were established, and are shown in Figure 3.1.

Description of treatment

Ten hour-long weekly, individual sessions were attended by the patient. The treatment was delivered by a Trainee Clinical Psychologist (AH) who was in the final year of her clinical training and was supervised by a Consultant Clinical Psychologist (KT). The sessions took place over a period of four months.

Support improvement in BMI by helping Sarah to develop more flexible, bigger picture thinking skills	Increase cognitive flexibility and global processing skills measured using neuropsychological tasks
Increase options available when approaching tasks – improve functioning	Doing something different with thinking to attempt to break maintenance cycles

FIGURE 3.1 Treatment goals

Explaining cognitive remediation therapy to the patient

Initially, Sarah was very reluctant to consent to participate in the sessions, as she was terrified that CRT might reduce her OCD symptoms which, as previously highlighted, she was keen to hold on to. After more information was given by both authors regarding the nature of the CRT and the fact that we had no strong evidence that it would eliminate OCD but were interested to see if it might help to improve functioning, Sarah agreed to the sessions. She said that she would try something new if it might be able to make her life a bit easier and might help her to gain some skills to help her to live independently out of the hospital. Sarah was curious, but at the same time she was also anxious.

The sessions themselves were conducted in a small living room on the inpatient ward, because Sarah did not feel comfortable accessing the treatment rooms as they might be dirty or contaminated. Giving her more time to think about whether she wished to access the treatment, and changing the usual location of the therapy were two important adaptations that were required at the start to help Sarah to engage in CRT. Being flexible in this way also provided for Sarah a concrete example of some of the thinking styles explored in CRT.

Beginning

In the initial session, the therapist and patient worked together to explore what Sarah understood about thinking styles and her goals for therapy. This was conducted in a collaborative, curiosity-based way to facilitate the development of an environment where there were no right or wrong ways of approaching tasks. This was particularly important given Sarah's strongly held belief that she must complete tasks in a specific way and if unable to maintain this standard, then she may as well not complete the task at all. Sarah began to talk about her previous employment and this topic was then used in an exercise which explored the range of thinking styles required for different professions. An example of this exercise is shown in Figure 3.2.

This conversation generated several strong themes related to thinking styles. The first was that Sarah had an excellent eye for detail and this was particularly evident in the way she discussed memories. She included an extremely large amount of detail and it took her a long time to convey a simple story. The second was that Sarah was inflexible in her thinking and behaviour. She found it extremely difficult to switch from thinking about one thing to thinking about something else and this was particularly evident in the fact that she would become highly distressed several times during the day, in part because she became fixed on one image or piece of information and was unable to switch her attention to something else.

She had also become very stuck doing rituals, particularly around bathing, and she was unable to multitask when completing these activities, which meant they were taking up a significant part of her day to complete. She explained that could not estimate each component of a task, as everything had to be conducted in a

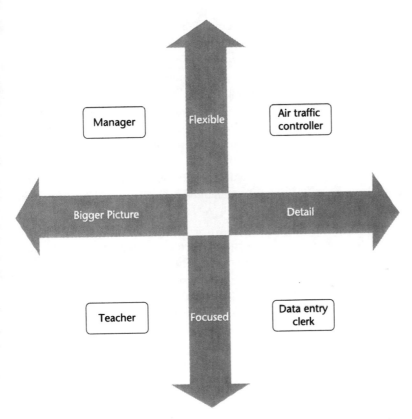

FIGURE 3.2   Identifying thinking styles associated with different professions

particular way. For example, Sarah explained that she needed to spend exactly two minutes cutting and filing each nail and she timed this with a stop watch. The therapist helped her to explore some of the advantages and disadvantages of this approach. This initial discussion helped to frame the focus of the exercises during the remaining sessions.

In the following section, the cognitive skills that were practised during the CRT sessions are reviewed, and an exploration of how functioning in these areas were targeted is provided.

Bigger picture thinking

To increase awareness of global thinking skills, we used the geometric figures exercise. In this exercise, Sarah described a shape for the therapist and the therapist had to draw it without having seen it. This helped to identify that Sarah often got stuck on small details, such as the size of a component of the shape, compared to the other components. This meant that it took her quite a long time to complete the task and the information was very overwhelming. Sarah linked this to everyday life and explained that this was evident in the way she organised her possessions in her room. She placed a great deal of emphasis on how her things should be stored and this related to very minute details, such that cutlery had to be stored wrapped in cellophane in a cardboard box inside a bag. This linked with her OCD obsessions about cleanliness.

We reflected on the bigger picture of hygiene generally on the ward and Sarah found that by getting out of the detail, she could actually now notice that cleaners were circulating regularly and that stepping back and widening her awareness, she saw that the hygiene standards were actually higher than she had previously realised. Although this did not translate to a reduction in her rituals around the cutlery, it did enable her to take a bath on the ward which she had not been able to do for a week because of fears about cleanliness.

Another exercise used to practice bigger picture thinking was summarising letters and generating headlines. This involved Sarah summarising in three bullet points – or a text or twitter message – the content of a one page letter. At first Sarah found this extremely hard and she was overwhelmed with the amount of information available. However, with practice, it became easier and she developed some useful strategies to cope with her propensity to go into extreme detail.

The ideas behind these strategies came from another CRT exercise about prioritising. Sarah was asked to prioritise the different tasks required to set up a birthday party. She used the strategy she learnt from this task to summarise the letter effectively by listing the top three most important points. These cognitive skills related to an important aspect of her everyday functioning, which was talking about difficult experiences she had had when she was bullied at work. She noticed that she tended to go into extreme details about the experience, but now practiced stepping back and generating a headline of what happened. For example 'cruel office worker bullied colleague.' This provided her with some distance from the negative experience and allowed her to put the memory into the context of the overall picture of how people generally had treated her in her life, for example, 'most people are kind and loving towards me.'

Flexibility

We used the ski lift and ladders tasks – where Sarah had to switch direction when following information on a page – and the Stroop material, where Sarah had to switch between saying the colour that the item was printed in, to saying what the item was itself, to explore flexible thinking skills. Sarah linked these exercises to real life and gave lots of examples of how her thinking and behaviour were inflexible. For example, she was not able to switch to eating a range of foods and felt certain that she wanted to continue to eat a narrow range of baby food. This was explored in a curious and motivational style, looking at the pros and cons of sticking with the same foods and the pros and cons of switching to including other foods, and culminated in Sarah completing an experiment where she tried to be more flexible with her cutlery. Rather than leaving the cutlery in a sealed package in her room, she experimented with having the spoon out on the table in the dining room for ten minutes before she ate. This was linked to the ERP focused on tolerating the anxiety she experienced around cutlery being contaminated with sugar. Using a different thinking style, being flexible rather than inflexible, was one rationale behind trying to expose herself to the anxiety rather than sticking with old ways of doing things. Sarah also changed the time of a beauty appointment to better suit her schedule, whereas before, she would have kept the original appointment even though it was very inconvenient and meant she had to wake up very early in the morning to make sure she was on time.

Sarah also practised being more flexible around taking other people's perspectives. For example, she struggled daily with the idea that she had been an inpatient for several months and she felt that she did not need to be on the ward and it was very distressing for her to be there at times. Sarah and the therapist practised taking other people's perspectives to understand different viewpoints about Sarah's admission. This was a useful way of linking the flexibility skills developed around the CRT exercises, to Sarah's real-life situation and functioning.

Estimation

To explore estimation skills, we completed the line bisection task, shown in Figure 3.3. This required Sarah to bisect the lines at different places. For example, to indicate where 50% or 80% were. Sarah took a very exact approach to the task and she observed that this made her slow and caused a lot of unnecessary anxiety.

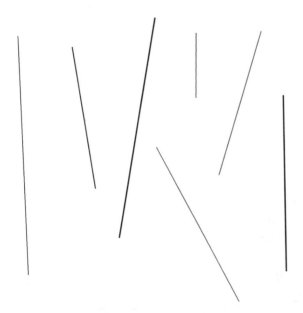

FIGURE 3.3 Line bisection task

Reflecting on this approach, she was supported to explore this, linked to her everyday functioning. She explained that she had to carry out rituals in a very exact and precise way. For example, she had to check everything in her room very precisely before she could leave. From this, Sarah generated some experiments to practice doing things 'just right.' For example, she practised checking only nine out of ten of the items that she usually checked in her room. Again, this very much linked with the ERP she was doing for her OCD, and allowed her to leave her room more quickly and so, she was less likely to be as late for appointments as she had been previously.

Multitasking

We used the Stroop material and time zones exercises to explore multitasking. When practising the Stroop task, switching between saying the name of the picture and saying the colour of the ink, Sarah noted that it was difficult to have to do several things at once: to block out irrelevant information, at the same time as labelling something and also trying to ignore the intrusive thoughts generated by the OCD obsessions. On the time zones task, Sarah had to hold one piece of information in mind (for example 'what time it is now?') and then manipulate other pieces of information in her mind (for example, the time zone of another country and what time it would be there). Sarah explored some strategies that helped, such as taking her time, focusing her attention and remaining calm. She linked these exercises to everyday life, and noticed that when she multitasked, she could do several things at once and complete a task more quickly than previously, when for example, conducting her bathing routines, she tended to do only one thing at a time, in part, due to exacting standards. The therapist and Sarah had a discussion about how she might try to do things differently to speed up a task. This change was extremely difficult for Sarah to contemplate but she reflected that having successfully completed the Stroop task and the time zones task, she felt that she did have the capacity to multitask.

Results

Weight as an outcome variable

During the admission, Sarah's weight increased. With the support of the re-feeding programme on the ward, before CRT was started, her weight increased, which can be seen in Figure 3.4. During the CRT sessions, her weight continued to increase and she maintained her weight gain at one month follow up, after self-discharge from the ward. This gain was not maintained three months post discharge.

Neuropsychological outcome variables

Before and after the ten sessions of CRT treatment, a brief battery of neuropsychological measures was administered, which included the Brixton Task (Burgess and

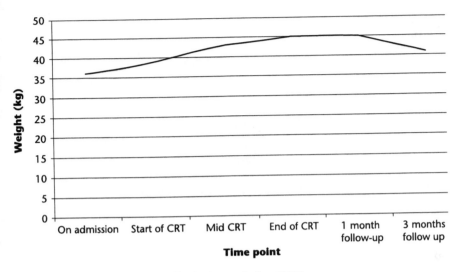

FIGURE 3.4 Sarah's weight profile during and after CRT

Shallice, 1997), used to measure set-shifting, and the Rey-Osterrieth Complex Figure (Osterrieth, 1944) which was used to explore the degree to which information was processed in a global cognitive style. This brief battery was selected with the aim of minimising patient burden and was also based on the use of the Brixton Test as a sensitive measure of set-shifting – as published in the largest database of eating disorder and healthy controls using this measure (Tchanturia et al., 2011).

As shown in Figure 3.5, Sarah made fewer errors on a parallel form of the Brixton task after, as compared to before CRT, indicating that she was able to demonstrate greater cognitive flexibility after CRT. Note that a lower number of errors indicate greater cognitive flexibility. Based on a dataset which accumulated our research group's published studies using this measure in people with eating disorders, the mean number of perseverative errors demonstrated by people with anorexia (n = 215) on this measure is 12.8 (SD = 6.2; see Tchanturia et al., 2011). Sarah's baseline score indicated she demonstrated a greater number of perseverative errors than others with AN (22 vs. 12.8) and she also showed poorer set-shifting skills than the large sample of healthy controls (n = 216) in Tchanturia et al.'s (2011) study, who made on average 9.8 (SD = 4.2) perseverative errors on this measure. After CRT, Sarah made fewer perseverative errors on the task (16 vs. 22), indicating improved set-shifting skills. Whilst the scores were moving in the right direction, her performance continued to be less efficient than healthy controls.

Figure 3.6 shows the change in Sarah's cognitive style with regard to global versus detailed processing of information. Note that a higher central coherence index on the Rey-Osterrieth Complex Figure relates to a more global information processing style. Previous studies have found that people with anorexia (n = 50) have a mean central coherence index on this measure of 1.35 (SD = 0.42), compared to a healthy control mean (n = 89) of 1.56 (SD = 0.33) (Harrison et al., 2011).

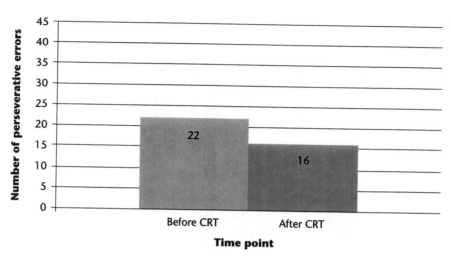

FIGURE 3.5   Sarah's perseverative errors, before and after CRT

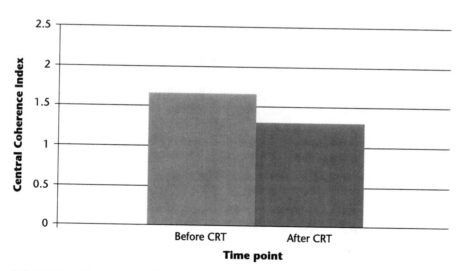

FIGURE 3.6   Change in Sarah's cognitive style, before and after CRT

Sarah's scores before and after CRT were similar to the average reported for healthy controls. It has been possible in previous studies to increase global processing using CRT in people with anorexia (e.g. Tchanturia et al., 2008; Tchanturia et al., 2013), but Sarah's results are not in line with these previous findings.

Self-report outcome measures

Sarah also completed the Cognitive Flexibility Scale (Martin and Rubin, 1995), a self-report measure of cognitive flexibility before and after CRT. Higher scores on this measure indicate greater cognitive flexibility. As shown in Figure 3.7, Sarah

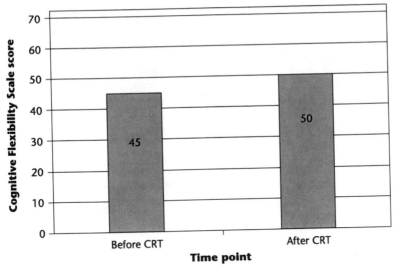

FIGURE 3.7 Sarah's self-report outcome measures, before and after CRT

reported having greater cognitive flexibility after, as compared to before the ten sessions of CRT. Compared to reported data for this self-report measure collected from 45 people with AN (Lounes, Khan, and Tchanturia, 2011), Sarah's scores are very similar to the mean of this AN inpatient population (mean = 45.4, SD = 9.6). After CRT, Sarah's self-rated cognitive flexibility was improving in the right direction towards the healthy control mean reported by Lounes *et al.* (2011) of 58.8 (SD = 4.59).

Finally, Sarah also completed a self-report measure of depression and anxiety, the Hospital Anxiety and Depression Scale (HADS: Zigmond and Snaith, 1983). An interesting qualitative outcome was that Sarah refused to complete this measure before treatment. However, after CRT, she found it much easier and was more willing to complete the measures. On this measure, higher scores relate to greater depression and anxiety symptoms. As can be seen in Figure 3.8, after CRT, her score for anxiety was below the clinical cut-off of 10 and her score for depression was at the clinical cut-off of 10.

Qualitative outcomes

There were several important qualitative outcomes associated with this case. Firstly, as mentioned, Sarah was more willing and able to complete the post-treatment outcome measures and this may relate to greater behavioural flexibility, in that she was willing to do more in her day. She also agreed to attend an assessment at a specialist residential OCD clinic which, before CRT, she resolutely said that she would not visit. This perhaps indicates greater flexibility in her thinking. She also reported feeling 'freer', as some tasks had become less cumbersome, perhaps because she had more options available to her. For example, she could now choose between

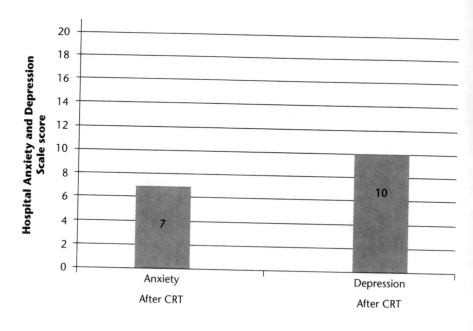

FIGURE 3.8 Hospital Anxiety and Depression Scale: Sarah's results after CRT

taking a bigger picture or detail-focused perspective when approaching her nutritional health.

In line with her goals to live independently, there were some small improvements in her behaviour in the community. For example, the experiments she had tried with the cutlery meant that she was more flexible in selecting cutlery, making it easier for her to eat out. Finally, she also reflected that she had an increased awareness of her thinking styles related to how she thought about the bullying she had experienced. She learnt that she could become stuck on the details of this experience very easily and this made her forget that she was currently safe and was not being bullied. Being able to remember the whole story, right through to the end rather than just small details, was an important skill which helped Sarah to move on more quickly from this topic during conversations. In the final session, Sarah explained that one thing she was going to take away from the sessions was the ability to step back and summarise, rather than being stuck in intricate details.

Discussion

Working with Sarah was an interesting experience, particularly because she brought rich information about her past experiences to the sessions, which we were able to use to explore thinking styles. This was one way in which the sessions were adapted. For example, she had a repetitive and highly detail-focused communication style and for this reason, the sessions often lasted an hour or an hour and a quarter (compared to the typical half- to three-quarters of an hour), but it was possible to use the material Sarah brought to the sessions (for example, the experience she had had of being bullied, which featured very strongly in much of her discourse) and to switch between exploring it from a detail-orientated, to a globally orientated perspective.

Furthermore, it was possible to use this material to practice set-shifting, as we practiced shifting attention from these experiences to other stimuli – for example, the CRT exercises. Initially, it was hypothesised that given Sarah's complex presentation, a greater number of sessions would be required. This does appear to be the case for bigger picture thinking, as the behavioural outcomes reported above do not indicate that ten sessions were sufficient to impact this thinking style.

However, it is important to mention that Sarah self-discharged herself from the inpatient unit after ten sessions had been completed. Nonetheless, it is notable that she was willing to remain an inpatient for the duration of all these sessions and agreed to visit an anxiety disorder residential unit which previously she had not considered. It may be that CRT contributed to her achieving this, as it allowed her to think more flexibly about other people's perspectives with regard to her treatment plan. This may have allowed her to access CBT for OCD for a longer period, which could have supported her response to CBT in the same way that Ayers *et al.* (2013) found cognitive rehabilitation for executive functioning combined with behavioural therapy resulted in a doubled response rate compared to behavioural therapy alone, for eleven older adults with hoarding disorder.

Finally, several other adaptations were made to support this complex presentation of illness. Information and new learning was written down to support verbal and visual memory function and difficulties in attention and concentration. This served to be very useful, as Sarah was able to share this with her family and a key worker on the ward, which may have added to greater repetition of the information and which perhaps increased the likelihood that this information was transferred into long-term memory.

In summary, it is possible to deliver CRT to an individual with complex comorbidities (depression and severe OCD) and to use this treatment to prolong engagement on the ward, support weight gain and nutritional improvement and increase cognitive and behavioural flexibility. As discussed above, CRT may have offered Sarah some additional ways of communicating with her mother and key workers in the ward, and her greater awareness of flexible, bigger picture thinking strategies may have supported the focused psychological work she was doing around her OCD. It is notable that despite very severe obsessions and compulsions around sugar avoidance, this patient was able to maintain her weight in the community for one month after discharge. It is hoped that CRT contributed to this important outcome.

References

Ayers, C. R., Saxena, S., Espejo, E., Twamley, E. W., Granholm, E. and Wetherell, J. L. (2013). Novel treatment for geriatric hoarding disorder: An open trial of cognitive rehabilitation paired with behavior therapy. *American Journal of Geriatric Psychiatry*, DOI: 10.1016/j.jagp.2013.02.010.

Barsaglini, A., Satori, G., Benetti, S., Pettersson-Yeo, W. and Mechelli, A. (2013). The effects of psychotherapy on brain function: A systematic and critical review. *Progress in Neurobiology*, DOI: 10.1016/j.pneurobio.2013.10.006.

Blinder, B. J., Cumella, E. J. and Sanathara, V. A. (2006). Psychiatric comorbidities of female inpatients with eating disorders. *Psychosomatic Medicine*, *68* (3), 454–462.

Bowie, C. R., Gupta, M., Holshausen, K., Jokic, R., Best, M. and Milev, R. (2013). Cognitive remediation for treatment-resistant depression: effects on cognition and functioning and the role of online homework. *The Journal of Nervous and Mental Disease*, *201* (8), 680–685.

Buhlmann, U., Deckersbach, T., Engelhard, I., Cook, L. M., Rauch, S. L., Kathmann, N. and Savage, C. R. (2006). Cognitive retraining for organizational impairment in obsessive-compulsive disorder. *Psychiatry Research*, *144* (2–3), 109–116.

Burgess, P. W. and Shallice, T. (1997). *The Hayling and Brixton Tests*. London: Thames Valley Test Company Limited.

Choi, J., Lisanby, S. H., Medalia, A. and Prudic, J. (2011). A conceptual introduction to cognitive remediation for memory deficits associated with right unilateral electroconvulsive therapy. *The Journal of ECT*, *27* (4), 286–291.

Douglas, K. M., Porter, R. J., Knight, R. G. and Maruff, P. (2011). Neuropsychological changes and treatment response in severe depression. *The British Journal of Psychiatry*, *198* (2), 115–122. DOI: 10.1192/bjp.bp.110.080713.

Elgamal, S., McKinnon, M. C., Ramakrishnan, K., Joffe, R. T. and MacQueen, G. (2007). Successful computer-assisted cognitive remediation therapy in patients with unipolar depression: a proof of principle study. *Psychological Medicine*, *37* (9), 1229–1238.

Harrison, A., Tchanturia, K. and Treasure, J. (2011). Measuring state trait properties of detail processing and global integration ability in eating disorders. *World Journal of Biological Psychiatry*, *12* (6), 462–472.

Kaye, W. H., Bulik, C. M., Thornton, L., Barbarich, N. and Masters, K. (2004). Comorbidity of anxiety disorders with anorexia and bulimia nervosa. *The American Journal of Psychiatry*, *161* (12), 2215–2221.

Kuelz, A. K., Hohagen, F. and Voderholzer, U. (2004). Neuropsychological performance in obsessive-compulsive disorder: a critical review. *Biological Psychology*, *65* (3), 185–236.

Kuelz, A. K., Riemann, D., Halsband, U., Vielhaber, K., Unterrainer, J., Kordon, A. and Voderholzer, U. (2006). Neuropsychological impairment in obsessive-compulsive disorder – improvement over the course of cognitive behavioral treatment. *Journal of Clinical and Experimental Neuropsychology*, *28* (8), 1273–1287.

Lewinsohn, P. M., Striegel-Moore, R. H. and Seeley, J. R. (2000). Epidemiology and natural course of eating disorders in young women from adolescence to young adulthood. *Journal of the American Academy of Child and Adolescent Psychiatry*, *39* (10), 1284–1292.

Lounes, N., Khan, G. and Tchanturia, K. (2011). Assessment of cognitive flexibility in anorexia nervosa – self-report or experimental measure? A brief report. *Journal of the International Neuropsychological Society*, *17* (5), 925–928.

Martin, M. M. and Rubin, R. B. (1995). A new measure of cognitive flexibility. *Psychological Reports*, *76* (2), 623–626.

McDermott, L. M. and Ebmeier, K. P. (2009). A meta-analysis of depression severity and cognitive function. *Journal of Affective Disorders*, *119* (1–3), 1–8.

McGurk, S. R., Twamley, E. W., Sitzer, D. I., McHugo, G. J. and Mueser, K. T. (2007). A meta-analysis of cognitive remediation in schizophrenia. *The American Journal of Psychiatry*, *164* (12), 1791–1802.

Menzies, L., Achard, S., Chamberlain, S. R., Fineberg, N., Chen, C., Campo, N., del Sahakian, B., Robins, T. and Bullmore, E. (2007). Neurocognitive endophenotypes of obsessive-compulsive disorder. *Brain*, *130* (12), 3223–3236.

Naismith, S. L., Diamond, K., Carter, P. E., Norrie, L. M., Redoblado-Hodge, M. A., Lewis, S. J. G. and Hickie, I. B. (2011). Enhancing memory in late-life depression: the effects of a combined psychoeducation and cognitive training program. *The American Journal of Geriatric Psychiatry*, *19* (3), 240–248.

Osterrieth, P. A. (1944). Le test de copie d'une figure complexe; contribution à l'étude de la perception et de la mémoire. [Test of copying a complex figure; contribution to the study of perception and memory.] *Archives de Psychologie, 30,* 206–356.

Porter, R. J., Bowie, C. R., Jordan, J. and Malhi, G. S. (2013). Cognitive remediation as a treatment for major depression: A rationale, review of evidence and recommendations for future research. *The Australian and New Zealand Journal of Psychiatry,* DOI: 10.1177/0004867413502090.

Santos, M., Richards, C. S. and Bleckley, M. K. (2007). Comorbidity between depression and disordered eating in adolescents. *Eating Behaviors, 8* (4), 440–449.

Shin, N. Y., Lee, T. Y., Kim, E. and Kwon, J. S. (2013). Cognitive functioning in obsessive-compulsive disorder: a meta-analysis. *Psychological Medicine,* 1–10. DOI: 10.1017/S0033291713001803.

Siegle, G. J., Ghinassi, F. and Thase, M. E. (2007). Neurobehavioral therapies in the 21st century: summary of an emerging field and an extended example of cognitive control training for depression. *Cognitive Therapy and Research, 31* (2), 235–262.

Simpson, H. B., Wetterneck, C. T., Cahill, S. P., Steinglass, J. E., Franklin, M. E., Leonard, R. C., Weltzin, T. E. and Riemann, B. C. (2013). Treatment of obsessive-compulsive disorder complicated by comorbid eating disorders. *Cognitive Behaviour Therapy, 42* (1), 64–76.

Tchanturia, K., Davies, H., Lopez, C., Schmidt, U., Treasure, J. and Wykes, T. (2008). Neuropsychological task performance before and after cognitive remediation in anorexia nervosa: a pilot case-series. *Psychological Medicine, 38* (9), 1371–1373.

Tchanturia, K., Davies, H., Roberts, M., Harrison, A., Nakazato, M., Schmidt, U., Treasure, J. and Morris, R. (2012). Poor cognitive flexibility in eating disorders: examining the evidence using the wisconsin card sorting task. *PLoS ONE, 7* (1), e28331.

Tchanturia, K., Harrison, A., Davies, H., Roberts, M., Oldershaw, A., Nakazato, M., Schmidt, U. and Treasure, J. (2011). Cognitive flexibility and clinical severity in eating disorders. *PLoS ONE, 6* (6), e20462.

Tchanturia, K., Lloyd, S. and Lang, K. (2013). Cognitive remediation therapy for anorexia nervosa: current evidence and future research directions. *The International Journal of Eating Disorders, 46* (5), 492–495.

Wells, A. (2011). *Metacognitive Therapy for Anxiety and Depression.* Guildford: Guildford Press.

Wykes, T. and Spaulding, W. D. (2011). Thinking about the future cognitive remediation therapy – what works and could we do better? *Schizophrenia Bulletin, 37* (2), S80–90.

Zaider, T. I., Johnson, G., J. and Cockell, S. J. (2002). Psychiatric disorders associated with the onset and persistence of bulimia nervosa and binge eating disorder during adolescence. *Journal of Youth and Adolescence, 31* (5), 319–329.

Zigmond, A. S. and Snaith, R. P. (1983). The Hospital Anxiety and Depression Scale. *Acta Psychiatrica Scandinavica, 67* (6), 361–370.

4

COGNITIVE REMEDIATION THERAPY (CRT) FOR ANOREXIA IN GROUP FORMAT: AN EVALUATION FROM AN ADULT POPULATION

Kate Tchanturia and Emma Smith

In general, the literature on CRT is extremely diverse, and forms of delivery of CRT vary greatly (options include individual, group, computerised, with or without therapist input). This chapter highlights one of the possible ways to implement CRT in eating disorders. At this stage, available studies and clinical reports are based on only the individual and group formats of the intervention. Further work is required in order to develop the computerised versions.

The main goal of CRT is to transfer cognitive knowledge and skills to everyday activities. We feel that the group format creates a appropriate and safe setting which is more similar to real life, in order for patients to practice their cognitive strategies with other people.

Background

Delivering psychological interventions in a group format can bring unique benefits that are not achievable when working individually with patients; these include sharing experiences and learning from others in a safe and therapeutic environment, becoming accustomed to being with other people and practising interpersonal skills. In the treatment of anorexia nervosa (AN) these therapeutic benefits also represent a challenge for group facilitators as it is exactly these interpersonal and relational demands that patients find difficult to tolerate (Richard, 1991). Facilitators are likely to be confronted with low motivation or worse, complete disengagement, as a result of the discomfort evoked by spending time in psychological groups. Nonetheless, when these difficulties are successfully overcome, the group setting can be effectively utilised to address the specific aims of a psychological intervention.

For example, in the context of a discussion regarding how AN might affect cognition, engaging in this task as a group enables the individual to explore if other patients have similar cognitive styles, how these cognitive styles impinge on everyday tasks and in which contexts they can become cognitive strengths; this gives group members the opportunity to hear others' perspectives on these issues. Patients attending cognitive remediation groups over the last three years have told us that, somewhat surprisingly, this was the first time they had had the opportunity to discuss these topics with their peer group.

In the current economic climate, mental health services in the UK are under pressure to provide brief but effective treatment for ever increasing numbers of patients. Mental health services differ between countries but the time pressure and demand for better tailored treatments are similar regardless of geography. Delivering interventions in a group format goes some way to meet these demands and group interventions are therefore common in inpatient settings; however there is a noticeable lack of research into group therapies for AN (recently we were only able to find twenty peer reviewed articles with mixed groups of patients and there was a variety of protocols including eating disorder patients; Tchanturia, in preparation). The few studies that have been published on group interventions with an eating disorder population vary greatly in terms of sample characteristics, setting and diagnosis, including our own studies (Genders and Tchanturia, 2010; Fleming et al., 2014).

In general, the evidence base for treatment in AN remains limited, with UK government guidelines describing a lack of directly applicable good quality studies (NICE, 2004). There is therefore a need to develop and evaluate clinically and cost effective psychological interventions for patients with AN. As a starting point, research investigating the cognitive, socio-emotional profile of individuals with eating disorders has yielded promising results and identified key areas for therapies to target.

In Chapters 1 and 3 we discussed neuropsychological functioning in eating disordered populations, which revealed that individuals with AN have difficulties in several cognitive domains. Studies from different research groups have reported problems in set-shifting, the ability to switch between strategies or rules (e.g. Tchanturia, Harrison et al., 2011; 2012; for a review, see Roberts et al., 2007), and weak central coherence, denoting a local rather than global information processing style (e.g. Lang, 2013, 2014; Lopez et al., 2008; Roberts et al., 2010; Harrison et al., 2012). In everyday tasks, this translates into inflexible and detail-focussed behaviours. cognitive remediation therapy (CRT) for AN is an intervention targeting these thinking styles (Tchanturia and Hambrook, 2009; Tchanturia and Lock, 2011; described in more detail in Chapters 1, 2 and 3). In the original format, CRT consists of ten individual sessions of cognitive exercises and behavioural experiments specifically designed to allow patients to practice skills in cognitive flexibility and global processing (bigger picture thinking).

Pilot work

Preliminary pilot work reported improvements on neuropsychological tasks and self reported cognitive flexibility along with increases in body mass index (see Tchanturia, Lloyd and Lang, 2013 for an overview of findings) which were maintained at six month follow up (Genders et al., 2008). Improvements in cognitive flexibility and global processing have been suggested as having a positive impact on a patient's ability to engage in more complex psychological therapies such as CBT which, amongst other things, requires patients to hold multiple perspectives and to view concepts or problems from a global position (Lock et al., 2013; see Chapters 6 and 7 which discuss CRT Randomized treatment trials conducted in Germany and the Netherlands).

Following the initial pilot work (Tchanturia et al., 2008), CRT has been implemented as part of the psychological intervention programme at our clinic which is a national eating disorders service at the Maudsley Hospital in London. Within this same service, a five session CRT group intervention has been developed (Genders and Tchanturia, 2010). This group maximises the number of patients able to access CRT within a time and resource limited service.

Early development of group sessions

The duration (four sessions) was influenced in part by the fact that the group was an unfunded pilot and also by the average length of inpatient admissions to the service at the time, which had been decreasing. The protocol was later expanded to five sessions after taking into account both patients' and therapists' feedback.

The aim of the group sessions was to practice global and flexible thinking, with the support of peer group members and group facilitators. This was predicted to have secondary benefits of increasing motivation, self-esteem and reducing social isolation. The clinical group designed the CRT group content that was both novel – as many participants were expected to have received individual CRT sessions – and interactive in nature to take advantage of the group setting. All sessions were designed to include the following elements: psycho-education, practical exercises, reflection and discussion within the session, and planning of homework tasks. As with individual CRT, continual discussion relating the exercises and homework tasks to real life thoughts and behaviours was defined as an essential part of the reflection process. However, the shorter group format necessitated incorporating reflections and discussions relating concepts to everyday life much earlier than the individual format. Fortunately, with several group members and two facilitators contributing to group discussions, these reflections tended to arise spontaneously in the early sessions.

The groups were designed to be delivered by multidisciplinary staff members with two facilitators per group (typically at least one from the Psychology team). The facilitators aimed to take a motivational and collaborative, rather than didactic, stance (as in the individual format) to explore the different thinking styles of the group members: there are no right or wrong ways of thinking but there are pros and cons for each.

The intervention was named 'Flexibility Group' (and this was later modified to 'Flexibility Workshop') to make it more accessible to patients who were not familiar with the term CRT. (See Appendix at the end of the chapter for more information on the protocol.)

Evaluation of CRT delivered in group format

As with an y novel intervention, it is essential to monitor and evaluate clinical outcomes as well as acceptability within the service. In terms of CRT (individual or group interventions), the therapeutic aim is to challenge inflexible and detailed thinking styles, therefore the primary outcome is cognitive flexibility and bigger picture thinking. In addition, poor motivation is recognised as a common challenge in AN (Vansteenkiste, Soenens and Vandereycken, 2005) and increased motivation has been shown to predict a reduction in eating disorder pathology after treatment (Wade, Frayne and Edwards, 2009). Motivation to change, and perceived ability to change are therefore also important outcomes to assess. Ideally, this data should be disseminated in order to inform other services and to contribute to the existing literature. There remain few high quality controlled studies of treatment for AN (Bulik, 2014; Hay, 2012) and even less evidence to suggest which type of intervention may be beneficial if offered in group format (Genders and Tchanturia, 2010). The aim of the current chapter was therefore to explore the benefits of CRT for AN in a group format, extending the pilot work, providing an update on the data collected since this initial study (Genders and Tchanturia, 2010) and outlining the current protocol, in order to assess the acceptability and feasibility of this intervention for service users and facilitators and to evaluate clinical effectiveness.

Summary of the first pilot results

A total of eighteen patients completed outcome questionnaires in the first and last session and provided written feedback after attending all four sessions. A quantitative analysis of questionnaire responses showed improvements in self-reported cognitive flexibility, self-esteem and motivation. These differences between the pre- and post-CRT group measures only reached statistical significance for patients' perceptions of their ability to change. A questionnaire specifically designed to obtain feedback on the CRT group indicated that, on average, participants enjoyed the sessions, found them useful and felt they learnt new skills. Open-ended questions asking patients what they liked most about the sessions and what could be improved revealed that the majority of group members valued being able to talk and share experiences. Other common responses included liking the practical approach; using tasks to demonstrate thinking and behavioural styles, the educational aspects, i.e. linking thinking styles to the brain, and homework tasks as a helpful way to practise new strategies. Of those that suggested improvements, half said they would like more sessions and further practice of the skills covered in sessions.

Revising the group sessions

From these preliminary results, it was concluded that the group content and format was acceptable and possibly beneficial for participants. The main recommendation which emerged was to increase the number of sessions. The clinical team agreed during the supervision group that a final session which consolidated ideas and learning points from the previous sessions, placing them in the context of the 'bigger picture' of 'recovery' and everyday life would improve the protocol and further make use of the unique benefits of the group format. An additional session was added accordingly.

Evaluation of the finalised protocol

The following sections will provide an overview of the data available following the implementation of the finalised protocol in our service in the Maudsley Hospital in London between January 2010 and May 2013. Measuring outcomes in inpatient settings, particularly at the evidence generating stage, is a huge challenge. The last part of this chapter summarises our attempt to gather data to evaluate the group format to the present date which will hopefully help to plan future work.

Finalised group protocol

Table 4.1 outlines the tasks and aims normally covered in five, hour long sessions.

The additional fifth session was added in response to patient feedback in the pilot study (Genders and Tchanturia, 2010). Both experiential exercises included in this session aim to consolidate the main messages of group CRT. Thinking styles are linked to everyday tasks as well as to longer term goals. In our experience, these tasks successfully engage patients in self-reflection and we suspect this is due to the simple but relevant content of the tasks which is easy to concentrate on and can be readily extended to their own lives.

Since modifying the protocol we have found this additional fifth session to be very helpful in improving communication between the patient and different members of the multidisciplinary team. For example, different members of the team are involved in different aspects of care: nurses deal with issues in the dining room, family therapists meet with the patient in the family context, and even within the psychology team, one person may deliver individual work while another is responsible for the flexibility group. We have found that mind maps provide concrete material to share (with the staff or family) what an individual has learnt and achieved in the flexibility workshop. It also helps to convey, during ward round or care plan meetings, the patient's perspective and level of insight gained from this piece of work. Psychologically, it is very powerful for the patient to 'own' and present the reflections they make through this process of 'thinking style' discovery and to apply this to other parts of their treatment.

TABLE 4.1 Tasks and aims for a five-session, group CRT

	Tasks	Aims
Session one	• Introduction to CRT • Psychoeducation about thinking styles and how the brain processes information • Figures-drawing task • Reflection, and an optional homework task	Familiarisation with concepts and approach of CRT Practising bigger picture thinking in pairs Relating learning in session to everyday tasks/events
Session two	• Visual illusions (taken from the internet) • Discussion • Brainstorming and homework	Practising cognitive flexibility, or 'switching' Relating this to how our brains work
Session three	• Card games and discussions in pairs • Reflection and optional homework	Focusing on switching and multi-tasking
Session four	• Recap • Occupation sorting task according to which thinking style they would use	Exploring how group sessions were different to individual CRT work Prompt discussion of pros and cons of different thinking styles. Relating concepts to real life; seeing that there are benefits of broadening repertoire of thinking skills
Session five	• Read and discuss 'the professor's story' • Draw 'mind maps' • Provide handout of motivational messages and mottos that reflect on CRT work	Prioritising the meaningful things in life Putting the central concept of 'cognitive styles' in the bigger picture of individual recovery Discussing the benefits of flexible thinking

Outcome measures

These included *Body Mass Index* (BMI: kg/m^2) which was obtained from the clinical records. The *Cognitive Flexibility Scale* (CFS: Martin and Rubin, 1995) consisting of twelve items that assess awareness of alternative ways of behaving and perceived willingness and ability to be flexible. Items are rated on a Likert scale from one (strongly disagree) to six (strongly agree), thus scores range from 12 to 72 with the higher scores representing greater cognitive flexibility. It has been used previously in an adult AN population (Lounes, Khan and Tchanturia, 2011). The *Motivational Ruler* (MR: Miller and Rollnick, 2002), a simple Likert scale measuring self reported importance and ability to change, was also administered. Higher scores indicate greater importance or ability respectively. Finally, a *Feedback Questionnaire* was developed specifically for the CRT group. It consists of three questions, asking patients: to rate how much they enjoyed the sessions, how useful the sessions were and whether they felt they had learnt new skills – both questions on a Likert scale of one to five (higher scores indicating a positive response) – and an additional question asking whether they thought the length of the group was too short (one) or too long (five). There were also two open-ended questions asking patients what they liked most about the sessions and what could be improved.

Results

A total of 59 patients attended the first session of a CRT group and 36 of these (61%) attended the final session. Specific reasons for non-attendance were not available. These groups remained 'open', which allowed patients to join despite having missed earlier sessions. However, in terms of the evaluation, this means the consistency of the outcome data is far from ideal. A comparison of baseline scores between patients who completed the CRT group and those not completing the group, did not reveal any significant differences in BMI, self reported cognitive flexibility assessment (CFS), importance to change or ability to change (see Table 4.2).

The vast majority of participants were female (97%) with a mean age of 27.57 years (SD = 10.48, Range = 18–69). Mean BMI at the first session was 15.65 (SD = 2.19, Range = 11.7–22.2). The average duration of illness was 8.83 years (SD = 6.76, Range = 1–32). Patients were receiving treatment in the inpatient Eating Disorders Unit (70.1%), Step Up to Recovery service (4.5%) and the Daycare service (25.4%).

BMI showed a significant increase between the first and last session. A comparison of pre- and post-treatment scores on the CFS and MR did not reveal significant changes over time (see Table 4.3).

Figure 4.1 summarises responses to the satisfaction questionnaire, which indicated that participants enjoyed the groups, found them useful and felt that they had learnt new skills. The final quantitative question asked participants about the appropriateness of the length of the groups and the results suggest that the majority

TABLE 4.2 Comparison of baseline scores for completers and non-completers

	Completers n = 45; M (SD)	Non-completers n = 14; M (SD)	t/U, Z	P	D
BMI	15.53 (1.91)	16.1 (2.18)	−0.92	0.36	0.3 Small
CFS	45.1 (9.68)	45.71 (11.57)	−0.2	0.84	0.06 Negligible
MR: Importance	7.77 (2.24)	8.07 (1.98)	293.5, −0.39	0.7	0.05 Negligible
MR: Ability	4.99 (2.63)	5.43 (2.44)	−0.56	0.58	0.17 Small

TABLE 4.3 Comparison of pre- and post-treatment scores

	Pre-treatment M (SD)	Post-treatment M (SD)	t/Z	P	D
BMI: n = 48	15.65 (2.21)	15.95 (1.93)	−3.1	0.003	0.15 Small
CFS: n = 34	44.97 (8.24)	46.47 (9.5)	−1.13	0.27	0.17 Small
MR: Importance n = 36	7.85 (2.43)	8.1 (1.83)	−0.46	0.65	0.12 Negligible
MR: Ability n = 36	5.07 (2.6)	5.83 (2.54)	−1.64	0.11	0.3 Small

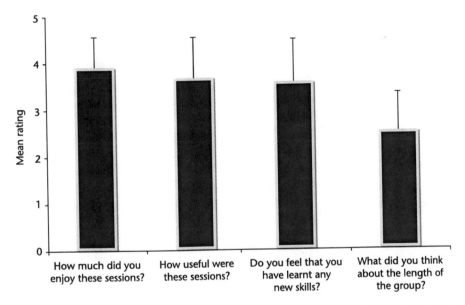

FIGURE 4.1 Responses to satisfaction questionnaire rated on a Likert scale of 1–5 for n = 45 patients.

were happy with the five session format. However, this contradicts the qualitative feedback somewhat, which included many comments recommending a greater number of sessions.

A thematic analysis was carried out on responses to the open-ended questions using the method described by Braun and Clarke (2006). This resulted in four main themes associated with eight sub-themes, as illustrated in Figure 4.2.

These themes are exemplified in the following quotes:

> I enjoyed the practical tasks; thinking about how one could use new techniques in everyday life. Also thinking about little things you could change to start with.

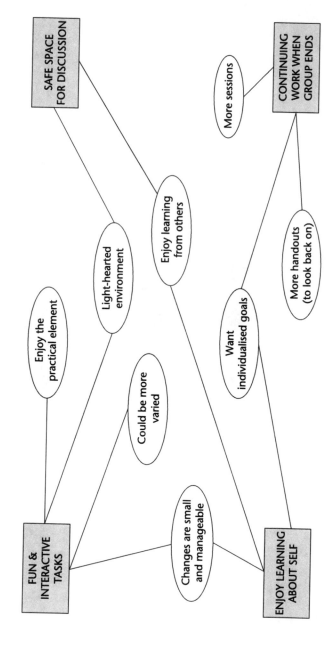

FIGURE 4.2 Thematic map illustrating main themes, and elicited from open-ended feedback questions

It was good hearing other patients' points of view and the areas in which they struggle and being able to relate, or realise my different ways of thinking to theirs.

I learned a lot about the things that I find difficult . . . I like having a greater understanding of why I do certain things. The realisation that I do get caught up in detail and so do many people. [I liked] being able to make slight adjustments to my routine, seeing how this can be ok.

I think it should run for a longer period of time as it is a major issue for most of the people on this ward as well as give [giving] more practical solutions and tools.

Reflections and conclusions: what we learned from the group format with adults

Up until now we have described how to deliver CRT in a group format (with adults) and have made an attempt to evaluate it using a minimal amount of self-report questionnaires and reflections from the patients. The results collected from groups following the finalised group protocol are consistent with the preliminary findings with adults (Genders and Tchanturia, 2010) and young people (Pretorius et al., 2012 [Chapter 9]) with AN, namely that CRT in a group format is both acceptable and enjoyable for patients in inpatient and day patient settings. It is worth noting that the feedback analysed in this evaluation was overwhelmingly positive. Patients' comments indicated that they valued the light-hearted approach to the introspective aspects of the sessions. This implies that they were able to engage in self-reflection in a gentle and safe way, perhaps unlike other groups that target eating disorder symptoms, behaviours or body image concerns more directly.

Furthermore, questionnaire measures assessing the clinical effectiveness of attending CRT groups, in terms of cognitive flexibility and motivation, showed changes in a positive direction. This corresponds well to the qualitative data which indicated that patients felt they were able to challenge themselves to make small changes and succeeded in being more flexible in everyday settings. It could be speculated that these small successes contributed to the small increases in perceived ability and importance to change. As previously mentioned, poor motivation is frequently associated with AN and improvements can predict recovery (Wade et al., 2009). Therefore, an intervention that can elicit comments from patients about challenging themselves to make changes certainly warrants further study.

Despite the positive feedback from patients, statistical analyses did not reveal significant differences. Therefore, on the one hand we have high satisfaction from the group members (and the clinical team, including group facilitators as well as staff not directly involved in the group; see Chapter 5 on the qualitative evaluation of CRT for more details), yet on the other hand, significant changes in self reported flexible thinking or motivation were not observed. What does this mean?

There are several potential explanations: it could reflect the minimal group dosage, indeed many patients commented on this; the outcome measures may not be ideal – for example, the flexibility questionnaire used was developed over fifteen years ago and does not correspond very well with more recently developed experimental measures of set-shifting (e.g. Lounes, Khan and Tchanturia, 2011); and finally motivation – particularly ability to change, which is closely linked to self esteem – is extremely difficult to change.

In general we also know that self evaluation is difficult, particularly so in a patient population. A recent review reported a relatively low correspondence between self-estimates and objectively measured cognitive abilities (Freund and Kasten, 2011).

In our individual CRT work, CFS (Cognitive Flexibility Scale) mean scores have been shown to be sensitive to change; for example, Tchanturia, Lloyd and Lang (2013) report statistically significant improvements with a larger sample (n = 46) and longer length of intervention (ten sessions of individual CRT). This may suggest that individual work with a longer duration results in more clinically significant change and larger effect sizes.

We could speculate that attending a greater number of sessions over a longer period of time may produce more substantial changes in quantitative clinical measures. This is supported by the thematic analysis of patients' feedback; one of the main themes reflected a desire to continue exploring and practising global and flexible thinking after the group sessions ended. Comments included requests for handouts to aid memory for the material covered in sessions and the suggestion that individual goals should be passed on to their keyworker or individual therapist. These are both feasible ideas. Unfortunately, the most obvious solution of extending the protocol to include more sessions is not possible at present given the aforementioned pressures on clinical time and resources. The authors feel that the five session protocol accompanied by material to facilitate ongoing self-directed work can achieve the balance of instigating change within realistic limits. It is worthwhile generating further evidence regarding optimal dose of individual and group therapy sessions, which will inform clinicians and help to decide priorities in terms of how to use available clinical time.

Another measure of acceptability is the rate of attrition from groups. In the data presented here, 39% of attendees at the beginning of the group did not attend the final session. Due to a lack of data it is not clear whether this high dropout rate is due to reasons unrelated to the group, such as discharge from the service, or dissatisfaction with the group. Examination of baseline responses for completers and non-completers show slightly, but not significantly, higher self-reported cognitive flexibility and motivation to change in the non-completers (see Table 4.2). This provides reassurance that the group is not actively dissuading a certain subset of the patient group from attending.

There are several strengths and limitations associated with the evaluation described in this chapter. Beginning with the positive aspects, the five sessions are well defined allowing different facilitators to adhere closely to the same protocol, ensuring that analyses of pooled results are valid. Secondly, collecting data from a variety of treatment settings indicates that the results are robust and applicable to varying levels of illness severity. However, it is possible that the heterogeneity of the sample could be masking a stronger treatment response from a specific subset. This is a salient point, as one of the benefits of CRT, noted by facilitators of the group (Genders and Tchanturia, 2010; Lock *et al.*, 2013; Dingemans *et al.*, 2014 [Chapter 6]) is that it is appropriate for patients with acutely low nutritional health, successfully engaging and preparing them for further psychological intervention work. In the future it will be interesting to compare patients at different stages of illness and recovery when a larger sample permits this subset analysis. A further limitation of the current evaluation stems from what is actually a positive aspect of the work, in that the groups were embedded in a treatment programme in a busy clinical environment. The clinicians facilitating the groups were responsible for collecting outcome measures therefore, inevitably their clinical tasks were prioritised, resulting on occasion in missing or incomplete data. Similarly, we were unable to conduct neuropsychological assessments as part of the pre- and post-group outcome measures due to limited time and resources. This would provide an objective measure of flexibility to complement the self-report data. More work is needed to develop outcome measures that can be administered easily in busy clinical settings. Recently, we developed a self report questionnaire which taps into both flexibility and detail-focused versus global thinking (Roberts *et al.*, 2011) but have not yet tested this as an outcome instrument.

Having run these groups several times over, facilitators report that it is very noticeable that people participate in CRT groups with great energy, curiosity, enthusiasm and interest. Group members are well engaged, talk to each other, make eye contact and continue conversations after the group. These observations in the clinic represent anecdotal evidence of clinical significance and the impact of this work, although self report improvements are not impressive. The findings reported in this chapter have clinical implications, demonstrating that individual therapy can be delivered in a group format in an acceptable manner. Importantly, this allows a greater number of patients to access treatment in a relatively short period of time. However, it is necessary to consider whether other interventions will translate as well – taking into account the similarities and differences with CRT – and whether the aims and content can be addressed in a group setting, and it will be important to investigate whether the positive aspects of the CRT group such as the interactive, practical nature of tasks and light-hearted discussions, as highlighted by patient feedback, can be utilised effectively in other groups.

In conclusion, the positive feedback elicited from patients with regard to the approach, the content and the aims of the finalised CRT group protocol are very encouraging. This evaluation goes some way to contribute to the limited evidence base for group interventions in AN; however, much more work in this area is required. A key message is that patients value and enjoy these groups and, given that poor motivation is recognised as a common challenge in AN, further research may help us to understand how this positive attitude to treatment can be fostered and maintained.

Acknowledgements

We would like to thank our colleagues Renata Stevens, Helen Davies and Becca Genders for their help with the development and implementation of this work.

References

Braun, V. and Clarke, V. (2006). Using thematic analysis in psychology. *Qualitative Research in Psychology, 3* (2), 77–101.

Bulik, C. (2014). The challenges of treating anorexia nervosa. *The Lancet, 383* (9912), 105–106. DOI: 10.1016/S0140-6736(14)60007-6.

Dingemans, A. E., Danner, U. N., Donker, J. M., Aardoom, J. J., van Meer, F., Tobias, K. and van Furth, E. F. (2014). The effectiveness of cognitive remediation therapy in patients with a severe or enduring eating disorder: A randomized controlled trial. *Psychotherapy and Psychosomatics, 83* (1), 29–36. DOI: 10.1159/000355240.

Fleming, C., Doris, E. and Tchanturia, K. (2014). Self-esteem group work for inpatients with anorexia nervosa. *Advances in Eating Disorders, 2* (3).

Freund, P. A. and Kasten, N. (2011). How smart do you think you are? A meta-analysis on the validity of self-estimates of cognitive ability. *Psychological Bulletin, 138* (2), 296–321.

Genders, R., Davies, H., St Louis, L., Kyriacou, O., Hambrook, D. and Tchanturia, K. (2008). Long-term benefits of CRT for anorexia. *British Journal of Healthcare Management, 14,* 105–9.

Genders, R. and Tchanturia, K. (2010). Cognitive remediation therapy (CRT) for anorexia in a group format: A pilot study. *Eating and Weight Disorders, 15* (4): e234–9.

Harrison, A., Tchanturia, K., Naumann, U. and Treasure, J. (2012). Social emotional functioning and cognitive styles in eating disorders. *British Journal of Clinical Psychology, 51* (3), 261–79.

Hay, P. J., Touyz, S. and Sud, R. (2012). Treatment for severe and enduring anorexia nervosa: A review. *Australian and New Zealand Journal of Psychiatry, 46* (12), 1136–1144. DOI: 10.1177/0004867412450469.

Lang, K., Stahl, D., Treasure, J. and Tchanturia, K. (2013). Set shifting abilities in children and adolescents with anorexia nervosa: An exploratory systematic review and meta-analysis. *IJED (IF=3),* DOI: 10.1002/eat.22235.

Lang, K., Lopez, C., Stahl, D., Tchanturia, K. and Treasure, J. (2014). Central coherence in eating disorders: An updated systematic review and meta-analysis. *World Journal of Biological Psychiatry, 1,* 1–14.

Lock, J., Agras, S., Fitzpatrick, K., Bryson, S., Booil, J. and Tchanturia, K. (2013). A Randomized assessment of novel treatment for anorexia nervosa addressing inefficient cognitive process. *International Journal of Eating Disorders,* DOI: 10.1002/eat.22134.

Lopez, C., Tchanturia, K., Stahl, D., Booth, R., Holliday, J. and Treasure, J. (2008). An examination of the concept of central coherence in women with anorexia nervosa. *International Journal of Eating Disorders, 42* (2), 143–52.

Lounes, N., Khan, G. and Tchanturia, K. (2011). Assessment of cognitive flexibility in anorexia nervosa – self-report or experimental measure? A brief report. *Journal of the International Neuropsychological Society, 17* (5), 925–8.

Martin, M. M., and Rubin, R. B. (1995). A new measure of cognitive flexibility. *Psychological Reports, 76,* 623–6.

Miller, W. R. and Rollnick, S. (2002). *Motivational interviewing: preparing people for change* (2nd edn). New York: Guilford Press.

National Institute for Health and Care Excellence (2004). Eating disorders: Core interventions in the treatment and management of anorexia nervosa, bulimia nervosa and related eating disorders. CG9. London: National Institute for Health and Care Excellence.

Pretorius, N., Dimmer, M., Power, E., Eisler, I., Simic, M. and Tchanturia, K. (2012). Evaluation of a cognitive remediation therapy group for adolescents with anorexia nervosa: Pilot study. *European Eating Disorder Review*, DOI: 10.1002/erv.2176.

Roberts, M. E., Barthel, S., Tchanturia, K., Lopez, C. and Treasure, J. (2011). Development and validation of the detail and flexibility questionnaire (DFlex) in eating disorders. *Eating Behaviours*, *12* (3), 168–174.

Roberts, M. E., Tchanturia, K., Stahl, D., Southgate, L. and Treasure, J. (2007). A systematic review and meta-analysis of set-shifting ability in eating disorders. *Psychological Medicine*, 37, 1075–1084.

Roberts, M. E., Tchanturia, K. and Treasure, J. (2010). Exploring the neurocognitive signature of poor set-shifting in anorexia and bulimia nervosa. *Journal of Psychiatric Research*, 44 (14), 964–970.

Richard, B. (1991). Group therapy in anorexia nervosa (apropos of a literature review). *Psychiatrie de l'Enfant*, *34* (1), 285–302.

Tchanturia, K., Davies, H., Harrison, A., Roberts, M., Nakazato, M., Schmidt, U., et al. (2012). Poor cognitive flexibility in eating disorders: Examining the evidence using the Wisconsin Card Sorting Task. *PLoS ONE*, 7 (1), e28331.

Tchanturia, K. and Hambrook, D. (2009). 'Cognitive remediation', in C. Grilo and J. Mitchell (Eds.), *The treatment of eating disorders; clinical handbook*. New York: Guilford Press.

Tchanturia, K., Harrison, A., Davies, H., Roberts, M., Oldershaw, A., Nakazato, M., et al. (2011). Cognitive flexibility and clinical severity in eating disorders. *PLoS ONE*, 6 (6), e20462.

Tchanturia, K. and Lock, J. (2011). Cognitive remediation therapy (CRT) for eating disorders: Development, refinement and future directions. *Current Topics in Behavioral Neurosciences*, 6, 269–287. PMID: 21243481.

Tchanturia, K., Davies, H., Lopez, C., Schmidt, U., Treasure, J. and Wykes, T. (2008). Neuropsychological task performance before and after cognitive remediation in anorexia nervosa: A pilot case series. *Psychological Medicine*, 38 (9): 1371–1373.

Tchanturia, K., Lloyd, S. and Lang, K. (2013). Cognitive Remediation in eating disorders. *International Journal of Eating Disorders*, *46* (5), 492–496.

Vansteenkiste, M., Soenens, B. and Vandereycken, W. (2005). Motivation to change in eating disorder patients: a conceptual clarification on the basis of Self-determination Theory. *International Journal of Eating Disorders*, 37: 207–219.

Wade, T. D., Frayne, A., Edwards, S. A., Robertson, T. and Gilchrist, P. (2009). Motivational change in an inpatient anorexia nervosa population and implications for treatment. *Australian and New Zealand Journal of Psychiatry*, *43*, 235–243.

Appendix: Flexibility Group Protocol

Aims:

- To educate patients on the brain and thinking styles.
- To promote more flexible and bigger picture thinking.
- To encourage social interaction and reduce social isolation.
- To contribute to the 'bigger picture of formulation'.
- To generate evidence for group interventions.

Criteria for attendance:

- Open to all patients on the ward who are willing and motivated to attend.
- Patients must be able and willing to stay for the whole session.
- Patients must be mindful of ground rules laid out in the first session and respectful of other group members.

Structure:

- Five-session format.
- Led by two facilitators.
- Any number of patients can attend.
- Closed group after first session to ensure continuity.
- Session lasts for forty-five minutes to one hour.
- Interactive exercises and group discussions that allow patients to practise and reflect on cognitive skills and share with other group members.
- Session topics include:
  - Psycho-education on thinking styles and the brain research in AN
  - Bigger picture vs. detail-focused thinking
  - Switching and flexibility, practising new routines
  - Multi-tasking
  - Doing things good enough vs. perfect
  - Creating own 'mind map' for what was learned through the group and how this contributes to recovery.

Evaluation:

- Outcome measures completed after first and last sessions.
- Written feedback form completed by patients on last session.
- Staff supervision.

5

CLINICIANS' EXPERIENCES OF COGNITIVE REMEDIATION THERAPY: A QUALITATIVE STUDY

Naima Lounes and Kate Tchanturia

Introduction

As has been highlighted elsewhere in this book (Chapters 2, 3, 6, 7 and 10) there is a lot of supportive evidence suggesting that CRT produces promising improvements in the cognitive domain, facilitates engagement in the treatment programme, and that it might have an impact on quality of life (Chapter 6). In early CRT studies, the acceptability and feasibility of CRT was assessed, where we carefully studied feedback from both patients and therapists (Davies and Tchanturia, 2005; Genders and Tchanturia, 2010) and two studies analysed CRT end-of-therapy letters for both patients and therapists (Whitney *et al.*, 2008; Easter *et al.*, 2011; see Table 5.1).

Whitney *et al.* (2008) first reported on patients' experiences of receiving CRT by analysing their feedback letters which were exchanged with their therapist at the end of the intervention. In total, the end-of-therapy letters for nineteen inpatients were analysed following ten sessions of CRT. A Grounded Theory approach was used so no pre-existing ideas were taken into consideration, and eight higher order themes were identified (see Table 5.1). Overall, the patients gave positive feedback, reported high levels of satisfaction with the intervention, and found CRT 'refreshing' and appreciated that the focus was not on food; they found CRT helpful in reducing perfectionistic tendencies and rigidity and also appreciated their increased ability to implement skills in real life. Patients also commented on their progression throughout the therapy and the stages of change; they also highlighted the differences between short-term and long-term outcomes of CRT. Finally, the patients made some suggestions regarding how CRT could be further developed: in particular they mentioned changes with regard to the levels of difficulty of the tasks and of having more guidance in implementing skills in everyday life.

In the second study (Easter and Tchanturia, 2011), therapists' experiences of CRT were explored by conducting a qualitative analysis of the therapists'

TABLE 5.1 Higher order themes from previous qualitative studies

Whitney, Easter and Tchanturia, 2008: Patients' experiences	Easter and Tchanturia, 2011: Therapists' experiences
Expectations and experiences of CRT at the beginning of treatment: • patients questioned the relevance of CRT at the beginning • difficult to understand purpose of the exercises • importance of discussing exercises in detail before linking to thinking styles and real life.	**1. Style and purpose of letters:** the letters were very motivational and aimed to summarise the patients' work in the individual sessions.
Targeted characteristics of anorexia nervosa: • characteristics of the illness, including their cognitive style and behavioural difficulties • perfectionist tendencies, need for precision; rigidity of thinking; difficulty being flexible • difficulty seeing the bigger picture; tendency to become obsessional.	**2. Reflection, and challenging thinking styles:** • discussion of the patients' metacognitive ability and their reflections on their cognitive strategies • acknowledgement of the patients' reflections on their thought processes and how they challenged them, such as by generating alternatives.
Stages of therapy: • progression through therapy; treatment must be 'at the right time' (i.e. in relation to motivation to change) • familiarisation at the beginning of therapy with linking the exercises to their thinking styles, then • connecting the exercises and real life experiences and behaviours • translating learnt skills into real life and everyday situations towards the end of therapy.	**3. Linking tasks with everyday life and patients' real life examples:** therapists reflected on how patients had related their thinking styles to everyday life situations; the therapists gave specific examples of this. **4. Applications of CRT and behavioural homework:** the therapists also outlined situations when patients had applied the skills, for example as part of CRT homework exercises as well as spontaneous applications.
Insight, skills and implementation: • discussion of insights and skills gained through CRT, namely gaining understanding about their thinking, the changes they had begun to make and risk-taking with rigid behaviours • sense of achievement through making small changes and increase in ability to multi-task and make decisions more easily.	**5. Therapists' suggestions for the future:** • the therapists highlighted key aspects for the patients to remember and suggestions relating to future implementation following the end of CRT • they also commented on the benefit of patients continuing to reflect on their thinking styles and behaviours in the future. **6. Praise and recognition of patients' achievements and progress:** • all the letters commented on patients' strengths, progress and achievements during CRT • therapists also praised patients' efforts in facing challenges and in pushing themselves.

Experience with CRT as compared to other therapies:

- CRT described as fun, enjoyable and psychologically interesting and refreshing
- viewed as less intense than other therapies
- helpful not to focus on rituals, beliefs, rules and behaviours related to anorexia.

Relationship with the therapist:

- positive relationship between the patients and the therapist; therapists viewed as warm, empathic, encouraging and knowledgeable
- acknowledgement of the importance of a good therapeutic relationship.

What patients did not like and suggestions for the future:

- some tasks were seen as too easy and their interest in them varied
- suggestion of gradual increases in difficulty levels for the tasks throughout therapy; suggestion of tailoring CRT for each patient
- some tasks were seen as too difficult and for some there was difficulty in linking tasks to real life, therefore needing more guidance and practice
- some felt that CRT may be more beneficial in an outpatient setting where patients are not as nutritionally compromised; some felt that there was a need for longer sessions, more tasks and a longer overall duration of therapy.

Overall satisfaction and importance of CRT:

- overall, CRT seen as a valuable and helpful therapy
- one patient expressed some scepticism about the benefits of CRT; one patient found the exercise 'tedious'
- several patients commented that they would recommend CRT to others
- one patient thought it could help people with obsessive compulsive disorder.

7. **Difficulties experienced by patients:**
   - some patients completed the tasks with ease; however, others experienced difficulties
   - difficulties were generally regarding reflecting on and challenging thinking, generating real life examples and on applying CRT principles in their homework.

8. **Patients' emotions and feelings:**
   - therapists acknowledged both positive and negative emotions
   - patients experienced enjoyment, fun and humour but some letters also commented on patients' confidence and self-esteem, as well as their bravery in challenging themselves; also commented on, was their anxiety in completing tasks and a concern about 'being judged'.

9. **Patients' characteristics that therapists found helpful:**
   comments were made about the patients' hard work and commitment over the course of the therapy, as well as their openness and honesty.

10. **Therapists' style and delivery of CRT tasks:**
    therapists were often creative with use of the tasks, thus encouraging further flexibility.

11. **Food, weight and body image:**
    some letters referred to core AN features (food, weight and body image); however, references to these were brief and not focused upon; reference to these were mainly to put CRT in the wider context of patients' difficulties.

end-of-treatment letters. Letters written by twelve therapists for twenty-three patients were analysed with the same Grounded Theory approach, using a constant comparison, data-driven method. They specifically looked at the structure and delivery of the intervention, the use of exercises and real-life links (ecologically valid examples) to everyday life, as well as specific considerations regarding the use of CRT with adolescents. Eleven higher order themes were identified (see Table 5.1), firstly regarding the processes and phases of the intervention, and secondly the specific aspects and content of CRT as experienced by patients. Three distinct stages of the intervention were commented on:

1   Reflecting on and challenging, cognitive styles.
2   Linking CRT tasks with everyday life situations and generating real life examples.
3   Carrying out behavioural homework tasks and applying CRT to everyday life.

Overall, therapists related how CRT was implemented, the patients' achievements and progress, and reflected on the application of the skills identified through the tasks to then make small behavioural changes. The majority of patients found the intervention useful and had little difficulty completing the tasks.

The two aforementioned papers provide an insight into both patients' and therapists' experiences of CRT. The end-of-therapy letters provided ecologically valid material as they were naturalistic data and were not from a self-selected sample. Despite this, as argued by the authors (Easter and Tchanturia, 2011), the therapist letters were all rather similar in style and aimed to be motivational and positive in summarising the work done in individual CRT sessions.

The qualitative analyses of patient and therapist letters gave us some useful insights and, to add to this, we wished to extend the study of therapist observations, to learn more about the active ingredients of CRT as well as to develop ideas for future developments of the intervention itself, training needs and other aspects of clinical and research developments in the context of CRT for AN.

The aims of this study were therefore to explore clinicians' experiences of delivering CRT in both individual and group format, and their perceptions with regard to the benefits of CRT and the ways it could be improved further.

Clinician interviews

Participants

Eleven clinicians who are involved in delivering individual and/or group CRT were interviewed. All of them had received training and supervision from the second author (KT) and worked in the South London and Maudsley NHS Foundation Trust specialist Eating Disorders service, in the inpatient programme. To contextualise the interviews, clinicians were asked for details regarding years of work experience in ED and in delivering CRT, including whether they had

TABLE 5.2 Interviewed clinicians' characteristics

Current position	Experience (in years) ED	CRT	Delivered individual CRT? (cases)	Delivered group CRT? (group runs)
Clinical Psychologist	5	3	Yes (5)	Yes (>20)
Clinical Psychologist	2	1	Yes (5)	Yes (1)
Clinical Psychologist	2	0.5	Yes (10)	No (2/10)★
Counselling Psychologist	15	2	Yes (10)	No (6/10)★
Counselling Psychologist	7	5	Yes (20)	Yes (20)
Counselling Psychologist	1	1	Yes (7)	Yes (4)
Trainee Clinical Psychologist	7	2	Yes (8)	Yes (2)
Trainee Clinical Psychologist	7	5	Yes (6)	No (7/10)★
Trainee Counselling Psychologist	0.5	0.5	Yes (5)	Yes (4)
Assistant Psychologist	1	1	Yes (4)	No (4/10)★
Assistant Psychologist	4	2.5	No (3/10)★	Yes (12)

★ If no experience of delivering CRT in the format, clinicians rated their perceived familiarity with it, out of ten.

delivered CRT in both formats and, if so, how many cases or group runs; clinicians who had not delivered CRT in a particular format were asked to rate their perceived familiarity (out of ten) with that format. See Table 5.2 for this information and for the duration of each interview. All the interviews, transcriptions and analyses were conducted by the first author (NL).

Interview schedule

A semi-structured interview schedule was developed (NL and KT) to explore clinicians' experiences of delivering CRT (see Table 5.3). Questions centred on their thoughts regarding the treatment of AN, what CRT might add to AN psychological treatment, and regarding the pros and cons of the formats of the intervention. Clinicians were also asked about future CRT research endeavours and their thoughts relating to CRT 'dosage' (individual, group or both) during a patient's admission. Clinicians' perspectives on contraindications were sought, and finally they were given the opportunity to make any further points or comments. The questions were open-ended and minimal promoting was used to encourage clarification or specific examples.

Procedure and methodology

The individual interviews were conducted during one-hour sessions: clinicians were shown the Information Sheet and written Informed Consent was sought; opportunities were given for any questions. The interviews were transcribed

TABLE 5.3 Interview questions and prompts

Question	Prompt
1. What, in your experience, are the ingredients of the more successful treatments for anorexia nervosa?	What works for whom, and how?
2. What does CRT bring that is not present in other treatments?	What do you see as the active ingredients of the CRT intervention? (e.g. engagement? motivation?)
3. What do you see as the advantages and disadvantages of CRT in individual format?	What do you see as the advantages and disadvantages of CRT in group format?
4. Which format of CRT (individual or group) do you believe would be best suited in a Randomized-controlled trial, to compare to other treatments for anorexia nervosa?	What intervention would you compare CRT to and why?
5. What do you think of the CRT 'dosage' during treatment? (By 'dosage' we mean patients receiving either no CRT, individual CRT or group CRT alone, or both individual and group CRT.)	Dosage (proportion, number of sessions . . .)
6. Are there any patients for whom CRT is contraindicated, or any phases of illness in which it is best not offered?	
7. Finally, are there any further points or comments you wish to make?	

verbatim and the qualitative software analysis tool NVivo 9 (QSR International, 2010) was used to facilitate the analysis. To analyse the interview data, the Thematic Analysis approach was used, as described by Braun and Clarke (2006). This method allows for the summary of key characteristics within large bodies of data: patterns or themes of meaning can be identified, analysed and reported. During the data analysis, a critical realist position was taken and the aim was to report the experiences, meanings and reality of the clinicians. A data-driven, inductive method of analysis was used and the data was coded without a pre-existing frame (Braun and Clarke, 2006).

Boyatzis (1998) argues that Thematic Analysis is more of a process than a method for encoding qualitative information and that a data-driven coding system should reduce the raw information and identify themes, and that the latter should then be compared across sub-samples and the original material re-read and the themes revised if necessary. As recommended (ibid.), to ensure reliability of the themes identified, a random selection of a third of the data (three interviews), was given to an independent researcher for an independent audit of the findings. Following a discussion, the themes were finalised and are reported below.

TABLE 5.4 Results of the Thematic Analysis – themes and sub-themes

Themes	*Sub-themes*
Theme 1: Anorexia and its treatment	How Anorexia patients present – factors affecting engagement in psychological work
	Treating Anorexia – how the therapeutic process can begin
Theme 2: CRT – its characteristics and delivery	CRT – A safe and gentle therapy
	CRT as an introduction to therapy, reflection and experimentation
	CRT and its delivery formats – a tailored intervention versus a group experience
	The therapist's confidence and role in promoting CRT
Theme 3: CRT and its effectiveness	CRT – an early intervention at the start of inpatient treatment
	How much CRT? Questions around meeting individuals' needs and how to combine the delivery formats
	Gaining insights, learning and celebrating small successes
	CRT research and testing – how to capture CRT's contribution to treatment

Thematic Analysis results

The Thematic Analysis of the data identified three main themes – shown in Table 5.4 – each accompanied by verbatim excerpts illustrating the theme and sub-theme.

Theme 1: anorexia and its treatment

The first theme relates to clinicians' thoughts related to AN patients' typical presentation on an inpatient unit and what seems to help treat the disorder, including the characteristics of the patient–therapist relationship and targets for treatment.

How anorexia patients present – factors affecting engagement in psychological work

With regard to how AN patients present, the majority of clinicians spoke of the resistance and motivation to change as areas to be considered for treatment and how best to engage the patients in therapy. They commented on patients' cognitive inefficiencies and rigidity, high levels of perfectionism and social difficulties which not only maintain the disorder but are appropriate targets for intervention.

AN patients' difficulty in managing emotions was also mentioned, particularly their reticence to engage in psychological work. Finally, the patients' low weight, especially on admission, was considered, due to its impact on cognitive ability and concentration levels; clinicians reported the difficulties of undertaking psychological work in the context of compromised physical states and the steps taken to engage patients in whatever psychological work they could manage.

> We know that therapeutic engagement with [these patients] is very difficult ... keeping that engagement going, to be able to [deliver therapy] is equally difficult ... this patient group who are very severely compromised nutrition-ally, ... we often get people arriving on the ward with a BMI 11, 12, 13, so cognitively they're not functioning at all at their usual capacity, strongly driven with rigid routine, can't think of alternative perspectives, have to follow this narrow single minded focus, ... and so we need to work with that before we can do anything else ...
>
> *(Clinician 4)*

Treating anorexia – how the therapeutic process can begin

Treating AN was seen as a very complex task though overall there was a consensus on the importance of a strong therapeutic relationship, and on tailoring the work to focus on the patients' personal goals, thus increasing motivation, building trust and increasing the sense of achievement, identity and self-esteem. Most of the therapists commented on the collaborative style, within a boundaried framework, which enables exploration of what the origins of the disorder may be and in engaging the patient. It was also discussed that low key interventions at the beginning of treatment can be helpful in starting this work, particularly due to the aforementioned reticence to change; some clinicians emphasised a more experiential style of learning as well as group work with other patients, to enable some of this work to begin.

> For me, the main components are something that tries to ... work on people's motivation to change ... that tries to help people make meaning of their experience. ... And I think something about doing rather than talking, so components of treatment that get people to just do things a bit differently.
>
> *(Clinician 8)*

> I've always thought there's something very important about, in some ways, modelling a relationship, ... there's a degree of curiousness, curiosity, playfulness, but also kind of a willingness to engage with really serious matters.
>
> *(Clinician 11)*

Theme 2: CRT – its characteristics and delivery

The second theme related to CRT's characteristics, its two delivery formats and how clinicians believe that it works. The clinicians were also able to reflect on their confidence in delivering CRT and their role in promoting the therapy.

CRT – A safe and gentle therapy

CRT therapists reflected on CRT's main characteristics, in particular the fact that is not related to core ED symptoms and foci such as weight and food, and that it does not demand much personal exposure from patients, meaning that it is thought of as non-threatening. CRT is viewed as a different kind of therapy: it is safe, fun, gentle and the therapists stress the importance of collaboration and play, which help patients explore the concepts with lightness and, at times, laughter. The therapists also comment on CRT's structure which is experienced as containing for both the patient and therapist.

> It's not around food, it's not around body image . . . it's more on a higher level, it's more about how you think, how you look at the world, how you approach tasks . . . I think it just takes that bit of pressure off [the patients], they can just try and look at, look at their sort of functioning in a broader way.
>
> *(Clinician 8)*

> It is very playful, very light, and it's a very gentle way of being able to look at something really serious.
>
> *(Clinician 11)*

> I think, because of the puzzles and the activities, it's almost like, a, a way to do therapy without them even realising that they're doing it . . .
>
> *(Clinician 1)*

CRT as an introduction to therapy, reflection and experimentation

With regard to what CRT might bring to AN treatment and how it works, the clinicians talked of CRT as an opportunity to introduce patients to therapy and reflection, and for patients to learn about themselves; CRT was considered to be a springboard for future work where the tasks were used as a tool for exploration and in eliciting reflections. CRT was seen as an experiential piece of work where patients could consider alternative ways of thinking and behaving, and practising them; in particular, the repetition of tasks was considered useful in consolidating new skills and in helping patients to practice being more flexible, thus targeting key disorder maintenance processes. Finally, clinicians reflected on CRT allowing therapists to work with what each patient can manage, thus facilitating the process.

> The tasks are a really good kind of starting point. . . . I've found that the . . . the more successful cases have probably been the ones where the tasks have been a platform for exploration . . .
>
> *(Clinician 2)*

I think that for the majority repetition is good because we need lots of repetition to get new learning so[,] kind of several examples of the same thing is really useful because it helps people to generalise . . .

(Clinician 8)

CRT is [very] experiential, . . . some of the other groups can sometimes be a little bit dry . . . whereas in CRT [we are] doing tasks, we're doing different activities, . . . they can actually see for themselves, [. . . and they] get to learn about their thinking style as well as what they're thinking.

(Clinician 5)

CRT and its delivery formats – a tailored intervention versus a group experience

The clinicians were invited to reflect on the CRT's two formats – individual and group – and to think about what each format might bring to AN treatment (see Table 5.5).

Individual CRT

Although it's standardised and it's the manual, once you get familiar with it you realise that you can individualise it hugely. . . . Sometimes you'll use the

TABLE 5.5 Individual versus group CRT

Individual CRT – flexibility within a manualised intervention	*CRT and group processes*
• the possibility of tailoring the work to the individual	• the group format allows patients to learn from others
• the benefit of creativity with the use of tasks to suit the individual patient	• patients can share the work with others in the group, thus getting support with tasks in the session as well as with homework tasks
• the therapist modelling flexibility in the sessions, for example with the use of the tasks or how sessions run	• the group can allow patients to discuss their thinking styles, thus normalising some of their experiences
• therapists recognising the variations in delivering CRT, mainly due to individualisation and therapist style	• the group format can be an additional opportunity for patients to experience social activities and can boost self-esteem
• therapists sometimes bringing other models into CRT to illustrate certain points	• therapists commented on the inevitable comparison to others in the group and the competitive aspects
• working from the Manual is seen as both an advantage and as restrictive: it is a helpful tool but can be restrictive, mainly in terms of what can be explored within the structure	• therapists have to manage group dynamics and processes which can be difficult
• therapists felt it may be safer for patients to open up in an individual setting, as opposed to a group setting	• less individual tailoring or focus is possible in the group

ethos of it rather than the actual exercises that are in the manual, so if it's about being flexible and spontaneous and not too achievement focussed, then I might do really playful things with people, . . . or get them to repeat the same task in very different ways.

(Clinician 3)

I found [the manual] quite constraining to begin with [. . . but now] I can see that they need [the structure . . .]. I do think there's something about having a physical manual that you both look at, that makes the whole thing less threatening

(Clinician 3)

Group CRT

I guess the pros are the shared sense of homework, 'cos they all get the same homework tasks set in each group so they could build up a good kind of, that sense of camaraderie and talk to each other in between about how they're getting on, and I know there's times when that's happened, there's a little buzz around for a couple of days . . .

(Clinician 3)

From my experience, CRT, one of the really helpful things is that it brings a kind of language to, to the other groups that we run . . . we hear language that is used in CRT . . . coming into different groups and also the dining room.

(Clinician 5)

The therapist's confidence and role in promoting CRT

CRT therapists reflected on their confidence in delivering CRT and how important it was for them to understand the rationale of CRT, to then be able to introduce it to patients in a way that highlights its key characteristics and to engage patients in the work; for example, therapists may present CRT as a fun distraction during what can be a difficult time on an inpatient unit. The therapists also commented that the small number of sessions was often an incentive, especially at the start of a patient's admission and that, despite patients' reluctance to engage in psychological work, they were able to ask some more difficult questions through CRT. Finally, therapists reflected on their own initial scepticism about CRT and how they had then seen the merits of the intervention.

Very often you can get people sitting there thinking how is this going to help? really . . . I was really sceptical myself . . . but it's not until you actually start doing it and you start working with it and using it and then you see how it's quite helpful and how it does work.

(Clinician 2)

I think as a therapist, on a very personal level, ... when we've got somebody coming into the room who really struggles to speak or engage in anything, very limited eye contact, very closed off, very trapped in their illness, ... it gives you something to focus on, I've got a tool, I've got a bit of a toolkit ... Some people are reticent to engage with it ... and it takes quite a lot of introduction and ... a lot of enthusiasm on the part of the therapist, because sometimes they can think these exercises are a bit pathetic, and pointless and stupid. ... That's when I do a lot more work with somebody about being really curious as to how their mind's working, ... then eventually you get them on board.

(Clinician 4)

Theme 3: CRT and its effectiveness

This theme encompasses who therapists felt CRT should be offered to, questions around what the optimal CRT 'dosage' might be, and finally about CRT outcomes and its future research and testing.

CRT – an early intervention at the start of inpatient treatment

All the therapists interviewed felt that CRT could be offered to anyone, that anyone can engage with it in their own way and no interviewee could think of any contraindications or detrimental effects of this intervention. Generally, the clinicians emphasised its use with more chronic and severely ill patients and highlighted its benefits in being an early and low key intervention for patients, despite very low weights at the start of an inpatient admission. The therapists also commented on the timing of the intervention, namely that it would generally be recommended as the first intervention that a patient engages in, before moving on to future work.

It's designed to be easily accessible for people who are severely underweight and ... sessions can be tailored in terms of time for, for, if people are having problems with paying attention for that amount of time ... and the sessions are quite short compared to other types of therapy ... I can't think of anyone off the top of my head for now who it would be contraindicated for.

(Clinician 9)

How much CRT? Questions around meeting individuals' needs and how to combine the delivery formats

CRT clinicians felt that there are different outcomes that are achieved depending on the format of the intervention; in particular, most therapists agreed that group CRT would raise patients' awareness of their thinking styles, whereas perhaps more change would be possible through individual CRT which can be tailored and focused to one patient. They emphasised however that the formats can certainly be used in combination, especially as having both can help to consolidate the learning and skills. With regard to which format may be advantageous, therapists commented that this would depend on each individual patient and there was also no general consensus regarding which would be the optimal order to deliver the formats, i.e. individual- or group CRT first, before the other. With regard to patients receiving both, the majority agreed that the 'dosage' required would depend on each individual and the complexities of each case.

> I've worked with some people who after seven sessions or six sessions had really got it, they'd made changes, they ... were much more aware of their thinking, of their tendencies and so on, whereas others I've worked with, particularly ones with more comorbid illness like OCD, social anxiety, I think they, it, it seemed to be they needed a bigger dose ... I guess they just had a more complex formulation, it felt like actually to have a big effect you needed a bit more.
>
> *(Clinician 8)*

> I know that for some patients, towards the end, the exercises are becoming less and less relevant and feel as though they're becoming repetitive, and with a patient like that I end up doing very much less of the exercises towards the end and a lot more reflection on the behavioural experiments that they've been practising in between sessions, so it becomes a lot more of a reflective process ...
>
> *(Clinician 4)*

Gaining insights, learning and celebrating small successes

The clinicians interviewed firstly felt that CRT is an opportunity for patients to acknowledge their strengths as well as their difficulties and to celebrate successes with behavioural changes, however small. CRT allows patients to gain an insight into themselves and this learning can be used for future work and in taking things further. The clinicians reflected on working within the limits of both what the patient can manage and what is possible within the structure of an inpatient unit, particularly in terms of real life testing. In terms of clinical outcomes, again the therapists felt that more actual change may be possible through individual CRT, and that the group – which requires patients to open up – may be more difficult for some. Finally, the clinicians wondered about the long-term effects of the intervention and thought about whether patients were able to maintain the gains achieved through CRT.

> I think in the individual work I've done, people have been able to change more, to try more things differently ... versus in the group, I think people have become more aware if you see what I mean, by seeing other people's approach, by seeing other people's perspectives, I guess their awareness of their thinking styles might have increased, whereas I think in the individual setting I think it is more about the practical, doing things, trying things out.
>
> *(Clinician 8)*

When somebody comes onto the ward, ... it's very ... limited what we can be asking somebody to do ... so, it's a way of enabling small changes to happen very ... early on in [their treatment ...] You can [also] use it at different stages of treatment with people, ... you can see where someone is cognitively and work within that.

(Clinician 4)

One thing I always wonder about is how much long term effect it has ... on people's actual functioning, ... people do seem to make changes and ... then you wonder how that translates into real life change later on, whether that can be sustained.

(Clinician 8)

I find that if I deliver CRT before going into a more in depth psychological therapy, the person stays engaged, we've developed that therapeutic engagement, we've started a process together, we've learned about collaborative understanding, we've learned about modelling, the, the therapist modelling [the] thinking styles for the patient, we're in a process together.

(Clinician 4)

Research and testing – how to capture CRT's contribution to treatment

Finally, with regard to CRT research and future testing, the therapists reflected on the practicalities of research, such as a Randomized controlled trial, and shared their thoughts about CRT formats, with no general consensus. To summarise, individual CRT may be more controlled; however, due to therapist variations and the individualisation of the work, more standardisation would be required. It was also commented on that it would be important to clarify what CRT does, in order to then choose a treatment comparison; although clinicians were clear on the rationale and aims of CRT, there was no consensus with regard to what comparison treatment may be best to test CRT's unique effect. Some clinicians felt that CRT could be tested as a 'pre-therapy', to assess its effect as an engagement tool and some also felt that, whatever control group is chosen, that it would need to be a non-specific, structured and manualised intervention. Finally, a few clinicians also commented about how much change it would be realistic to expect after this short intervention, in the context of nutritionally compromised patients and complex presentations.

For me there's a slight sort of tension between ... CRT shakes up that rigidity a lot but you have to make the treatment quite rigid in order to test it ...... How do you do [CRT] as a rigid standardised trial? How do you standardise playfulness and flexibility? (laugh) ... I would hate to think that CRT wouldn't perform well in a trial because of all that was seeped out of that when it got standardised ...

(Clinician 3)

I think maybe in individual format it's easier to deliver it, kind of, as the manual says, maybe in a group, managing the group dynamic, whether people are able to contribute, how safe people feel in the group environment and perhaps that's, that introduces a lot of potential confounds I guess, for an RCT.

(Clinician 8)

Discussion

Interviewing CRT clinicians on their experience of delivering CRT and on their perceptions with regard to what CRT offers to AN treatment was an opportunity to get an insight into first-hand experiences of CRT for AN, from the perspective of clinicians in an inpatient unit.

As mentioned in the Introduction, patient and therapist feedback had previously been analysed; however, the interview method had not been employed before. In our department, patient feedback is regularly sought following the intervention, as reported in the case study (Davies and Tchanturia, 2005) and in the group CRT study (Genders and Tchanturia, 2010), where patients commented on the short- and long-term benefits they noticed, and where they commented on finding CRT to be an acceptable and helpful intervention. Furthermore, the two studies looking at patient and therapist end-of-therapy letters (Whitney *et al.*, 2008, and Easter and Tchanturia, 2011) were an opportunity to analyse the patients' and therapists' thoughts in relation to specific pieces of work, and to generate ideas about how CRT is experienced and what could be considered in terms of future developments.

Content revision

For example, from patient feedback it was clear to us that an introductory script and a better explanation was needed at the beginning of CRT, and the revised manual (Tchanturia *et al.*, 2010) included more information for the rationale of CRT for AN. Patients were asking for a longer duration and more real life experience with cognitive styles, which stimulated us to develop the group format and take advantage of group-based exercises and the group dynamics. We also developed more homework for patients, including small challenges, to help patients to maintain the knowledge and skills obtained in the sessions.

The therapists' letters also informed further developments of CRT, for example with regard to the playful nature of the intervention and specific exercises helping with session flow and therapeutic engagement. The positive emotional atmosphere and encouragement to have fun was highly appreciated. This feedback stimulated us to strengthen the active ingredients of CRT, i.e. the playful, fun and positive nature of the intervention.

The clinician interviews were an additional opportunity to gain useful feedback and ideas about the current status and future developments of the individual and

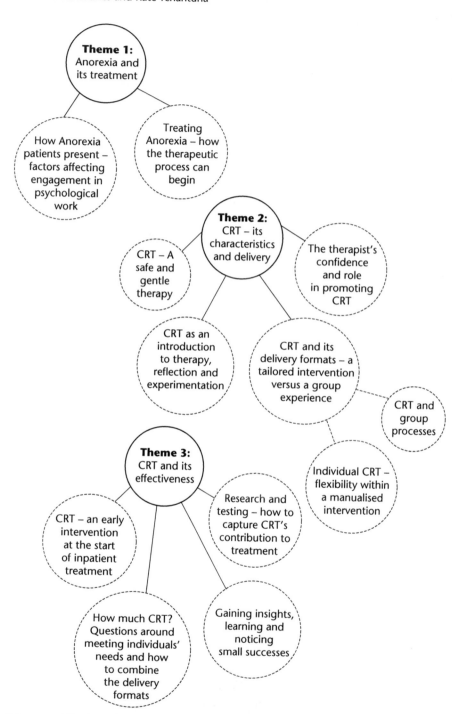

FIGURE 5.1 Thematic map

group formats. The interview method gave us the opportunity to explore clinicians' accounts of CRT, outside of the patient–therapist context, i.e. colleague to colleague reflections about the pros and cons of this novel approach for Anorexia.

This interview approach gave us new insights; for example, it was pretty clear from the analysis that clinicians identified a possible conflict between the therapeutic properties of CRT in the context of clinical use and in the context of CRT use. Most of them valued the flexible, engaging, playful nature of CRT and the ability to be creative and flexible as a therapist. A few of them expressed uncertainty with regard to how this strength can be maintained within an RCT – where clinicians are asked to be more structured and follow the manual.

Methodology and application

With regard to methodology, though the previous two exploratory studies were conducted using a Grounded Theory approach, a Thematic Analysis was chosen for this research, as its aim was to extend the previous findings, but was also informed by them; despite this, as mentioned above, a data-driven, inductive method of analysis was used and the data was coded without a pre-existing frame. Thus these interviews gave us more material to reflect on ideas for future developments.

Interestingly, several themes identified in this study were closely related to the previous findings through the analysis of the letters (Whitney *et al.*, 2008; Easter and Tchanturia, 2011), especially in terms of what helps treat AN and how CRT targets some of the key disorder maintenance processes. The interviews were also an opportunity for the clinicians to express their thoughts about CRT and its place within the wider treatment context, namely that CRT is seen as a springboard for future work, and enables patients to engage in psychological work even in nutritionally and physically compromised states. Furthermore, clinicians spoke of working with what the patients can manage, both in terms of limits placed by the inpatient setting but also with regard to tailoring the work to each individual's presentation and needs.

This study also provides insights into how the two formats of CRT work in combination, and additionally in terms of perceived different processes of change and outcomes. The clinicians were also very open about the challenges they face in delivering CRT, promoting engagement with it and in managing individual patients' scepticism (as well as their own initial scepticism), and also managing complex dynamics when delivering it in group format. Every clinician interviewed felt that CRT could be offered to anyone, would have no major detrimental effects, and that its adaptability to different presentations, complexity and need would mean it is an intervention that can be offered at the beginning of inpatient treatment, which is not necessarily the case for other psychological therapies.

One question that remains unanswered though, is what the optimal CRT 'dosage' would be, whether receiving individual or group CRT would be advantageous, and what intervention would be the ideal comparison in a trial, to continue to assess CRT's effectiveness.

Comment

This study benefited from a group of clinicians with varied levels of experience in eating disorders and of CRT, as well as being at different professional levels, from assistants to trainees to qualified psychologists. Furthermore, the triangulation through the involvement of an independent researcher ensures the reliability of the findings. All the therapists who were interviewed received training and supervision from the second author (KT), which is why the transcription and independent audit was undertaken independently to keep the data objective and anonymous. It is also acknowledged that the semi-structured interview schedule, though allowing the clinicians to answer open-ended questions, nevertheless meant that the structure of the questions may have led the interviews; future studies could use a case study approach, thus inviting clinicians to reflect in depth about particular CRT cases, which may further elucidate the specifics of how CRT works.

As well as the recommendations mentioned above and the suggestions made by the clinicians, it is important to highlight that there are many potential avenues for CRT research. At this stage, we are clear that CRT which is tailored to cognitive styles, improves cognition. In general, there is less research on the delivery of the therapy and, as CRT is a relatively novel tool in the context of AN, it is hugely important to hear the views of clinicians who are delivering this treatment.

Finally, the most noteworthy point for reflection from these interviews is the individual tailoring that clinicians report; this merits future research as it could not only inform future developments of CRT to meet patients' needs, but also needs to be considered in the context of any future controlled trials.

References

Boyatzis, R. E. (1998). *Transforming qualitative information. Thematic analysis and code development.* California: Sage.

Braun, V. and Clarke, V. (2006) Using thematic analysis in psychology. *Qualitative Research in Psychology*, 3 (2), 77–101. DOI: 10.1191/1478088706qp063oa.

Davies, H. and Tchanturia, K. (2005). Cognitive remediation therapy as an intervention for acute anorexia nervosa: A case report. *European Eating Disorders Review*, 13 (5), 311–316. DOI:10.1002/erv.655.

Easter, A. and Tchanturia, K. (2011). Therapists' experiences of cognitive remediation therapy for anorexia nervosa: Implications for working with adolescents. *Clinical Child Psychology and Psychiatry*, 16 (2), 233–246. DOI: 10.1177/1359104511401185.

Genders, R. and Tchanturia, K. (2010). Cognitive remediation therapy (CRT) for anorexia in group format: A pilot study. *Eating and Weight Disorders*, 15 (4), e234-e239.

QSR International (2010). *NVivo 9.* Victoria, Australia: QSR International Pty Ltd.

Whitney, J., Easter, A. and Tchanturia, K. (2008). Service users' feedback on cognitive training in the treatment of anorexia nervosa: A qualitative study. *International Journal of Eating Disorders*, 41 (6), 542–550. DOI: 10.1002/eat.20536.

PART II
Randomized controlled trials

6

COGNITIVE REMEDIATION THERAPY FOR PATIENTS WITH A SEVERE AND ENDURING EATING DISORDER

Alexandra Dingemans, Unna Danner and Eric van Furth

Severe and enduring eating disorders

Both anorexia nervosa (AN) and bulimia nervosa (BN) are chronic disorders with periods of symptom exacerbation and symptom remission (Herzog *et al.*, 1999). Fewer than half of the patients with AN fully recover whereas about one third recover only partially, and 20% remain chronically ill over a long term (Steinhausen, 2002). BN appears to have similar percentages (mean chronicity rate is 23%) (Steinhausen and Weber, 2009). However, the diagnostic stability of the subtypes of eating disorders is low (Anderluh *et al.*, 2009): there is a lot of migration (or cross-over) from one eating disorder subtype to another (Milos *et al.*, 2005). For example some individuals with a diagnosis of AN at some point in their lives, may be diagnosed with an eating disorder not otherwise specified (EDNOS) at a later moment. Patients with a severe and enduring eating disorder have high levels of disability, are often under- or unemployed or supported by health benefit plans (Touyz *et al.*, 2013). It has been suggested that after six or seven years of illness duration, the likelihood of people recovering from the eating disorder reaches – and more or less stays at – a plateau (Wonderlich *et al.*, 2012). Remission rates appear to be associated with duration of follow-up in the studies (Keel and Brown, 2010); if individuals are followed for a longer period of time the chances of recovering increase. There is some evidence that suggests that such a plateau does not appear until ten to twenty years after the onset of the disorder (Wonderlich *et al.*, 2012; Steinhausen, 2002). Individuals with a longstanding eating disorder have often experienced multiple treatment failures (Wonderlich *et al.*, 2012) and after many years of treatment full recovery is often no longer the ultimate goal. Treatment is then focused more upon retention, improved quality of life with harm minimization and avoidance of further failure experiences (Touyz *et al.*, 2013).

Neuropsychological inefficiencies: impact on severity and chronicity

One of the problems many individuals with longstanding eating disorders face is that they exhibit a trait of cognitive inflexibility as evident in their neuro-psychological functioning (Tchanturia *et al.*, 2012; Tchanturia *et al.*, 2011) (see Chapter 1 for more details). Not only does this influence pathology-related behaviours, but it also seems to hamper other aspects of their daily lives resulting in reduced quality of life. Evidence for these inefficiencies in neuropsychological functioning stems from a variety of studies (Tchanturia *et al.*, 2011; Lauer *et al.*, 1999; Tchanturia *et al.*, 2004a; Tchanturia *et al.*, 2004b; Roberts *et al.*, 2007; Abbate-Daga *et al.*, 2011; Van den Eynde *et al.*, 2011; Danner *et al.*, 2012). These inefficiencies may decrease both treatment motivation and the efficacy of psychological interventions, and may even perpetuate the illness (Tchanturia *et al.*, 2008; Lena *et al.*, 2004). It has been proposed that neuropsychological inefficiencies pre-exist, and underlie the etiology of eating disorders development and relapse (Lena, 2004). It is plausible that eating disorders are an expression of strategies such as rigid control and discipline to compensate for undiagnosed inefficiencies in cognitive functioning (Lena *et al.*, 2001).

Cognitive remediation therapy for patients with a severe and enduring eating disorder

Because of transdiagnostic nature of eating disorders (Herzog *et al.*, 1999; Fairburn, Cooper, and Shafran, 2003), the instability of eating disorder symptoms (Anderluh *et al.*, 2009) and the fact that neuropsychological inefficiencies are present across eating disorders (Roberts, Tchanturia, and Treasure, 2010), it was hypothesized that cognitive remediation therapy (CRT) might be suitable for patients with a severe or enduring eating disorder (Tchanturia, Lloyd, and Lang, 2013), since neuropsychological inefficiencies might play a role in the maintenance of the eating disorder (Chapter 1 Lena *et al.*, 2004). CRT was developed with the aim of improving cognition and thereby increasing the likelihood of improved functioning and quality of life (Wykes *et al.*, 2007). Case reports of severely ill adult patients with AN (Davies and Tchanturia, 2005; Tchanturia, Davies, and Campbell, 2007; Tchanturia *et al.*, 2008), as well as resent RCTs (Lock *et al.*, 2013; Brockmeyer *et al.*, 2014 (see Chapter 7)), showed that CRT improved the performance on cognitive tasks and that it is an acceptable and feasible therapy (Whitney, Easter, and Tchanturia, 2008) (see also Chapter 5). Lock *et al.* (2013) suggested that CRT might be most effective as an adjunctive training in the context of other therapies, to enhance treatment success (Chapter 8), and reported that CRT may reduce attrition from treatment in the short term. In a randomized controlled trial (RCT), Dingemans *et al.* (2014) aimed to explore the treatment-enhancing effectiveness of CRT for patients with a severe or enduring eating disorder by comparing intensive treatment-as-usual (TAU) *with* CRT, to TAU *without* CRT. Our study followed the publication of several case reports and uncontrolled studies of severely ill adult patients with AN and, the above mentioned, small RCT. The purpose of our study was to investigate the effectiveness of CRT in a real world treatment setting for patients with severe or enduring eating disorders. One of the strengths of the study was that the results might give us indications about the feasibility of CRT in everyday clinical practice.

Treatment as usual for patients with a severe and enduring eating disorder

We have conducted this trial in two large specialized centres for eating disorders in the Netherlands: Center for Eating Disorders Ursula, and Altrecht Eating Disorders Rintveld. Both centres provide specialized tertiary mental health care for patients with eating disorders, have a function of 'last resort', and treat the most severely ill patients in the Netherlands. Only patients within the inpatients units and within the units that treat patients with a chronic and enduring eating disorder were asked to participate in this study. TAU in both centres was an intensive treatment program. The patients who were included in the trial at the Center for Eating Disorders Ursula all received inpatient treatment (five to seven days a week). At the Altrecht Eating Disorders Rintveld half of the patients were inpatients and half received intensive day treatment one to four days a week. Within the Dutch health care systems, all treatments are reimbursed and the duration of treatment (TAU) is determined on clinical progress, which is different from many other countries.

The content of the treatment programs in the two centres was comparable and followed the guidelines for treatment for eating disorders in the Netherlands (Landelijke Stuurgroep Multidisciplinaire Richtlijnontwikkeling in de GGZ, 2006), which in turn are comparable to the NICE guidelines (National Collaborating Centre for Mental Health, 2004). Programs could consist of the following: a) normalization of eating behaviour; b) discussion of daily problems, goals, and evaluations; c) psychomotor therapy, d) art therapy, e) social skills training, f) psycho-education, and g) cognitive-behavioural therapy. Therapies could be conducted in groups or individually by therapists specialized in eating disorders. Sociotherapists and specialized psychiatric nurses were involved in normalizing eating behaviour during mealtimes and coffee breaks and discussed daily problems with patients. Also, appointments with a psychiatrist were scheduled if pharmacotherapy was provided. In total, participants who were inpatients received approximately thirty hours of treatment per week.

Both centres have highly specialized treatment units for patients with severe and/or enduring eating disorders. Treatment goals for the patients admitted to these units differed from each other, and are tailored more to the individual. For example, some patients are admitted for a few weeks for a booster in order to gain some weight, whereas others need special care because comorbid disorders like autistic spectrum disorders, anxiety disorders or diabetes, complicate the treatment for their eating disorder. Often treatment is more directed at the improvement of their quality of life and rehabilitation instead of full recovery of the eating disorder.

CRT in severe and enduring eating disorders

It has been suggested (Tchanturia and Lock, 2011) that CRT might be most effective as an adjunctive training in the context of other therapies to enhance treatment success. In our study (Dingemans *et al.*, 2014) patients in the CRT group received ten individual sessions of CRT as an adjunction to TAU within five or six weeks. We used the CRT manual, adapted for eating disorders by Tchanturia, Davies, Reeder and Wykes (2010). The manual was translated and a training was completed in London with the first two authors of the manual. The CRT sessions lasted approximately forty-five minutes depending on the physical state of the patients. CRT uses a range of cognitive (paper and pencil) exercises that are specifically aimed at improving cognitive flexibility and increasing global information processing – as opposed to detail-oriented processing (see www.national.slam.nhs.uk/wp-content/uploads/2014/04/Cognitive-remediation-therapy-for-Anorexia-Nervosa-Kate-Tchanturia.pdf for clarification; or for additional information, Tchanturia and Hambrook, 2009). The therapists did not have a fixed order in the exercises. Also, there was no fixed number of exercises: some patients only performed one or two and others performed many tasks. Overall, two or three exercises or tasks were chosen per session, which was decided upfront or in consultation with the patient. Some patients found particular tasks or exercises very easy whereas others did not. It was important to keep reminding patients that there is no right or wrong, since patients had a strong tendency to focus on their performance, but with practice it became easier for them to think of the tasks in terms of difficult or easy to do, instead of focusing on the outcome.

CRT aims to improve the awareness of ongoing thinking patterns. Reflection about thinking styles during these cognitive exercises is a crucial part of CRT. Similarly important, is the encouragement to find out how these thinking styles affect their daily life, by asking patients if they recognize using a particular thinking style in daily situations, and have them think about alternative ways to ease this situation. From about the sixth session onwards, the cognitive exercises are linked to real life behavioural tasks. These behavioural tasks are designed to allow patients to practice skills in daily life, thereby introducing more flexible behaviour in their everyday life. However, therapists should also be flexible in introducing these behavioural tasks.

Sometimes it might be more powerful and useful to introduce these behavioural tasks from the very beginning; by doing a behavioural task, patients increase awareness of their thinking styles. For others however, it is more useful and more secure to do the exercises during the sessions with the therapists, with only minor changes in daily life. Performing the tasks in a different way after a few sessions may already have become stressful, but the experience of actually being able to make a daily change is very motivating for patients. For example, one patient found changing a certain aspect in her daily routine too stressful, but together with the therapist she decided to practice changing the colour of the scarf that she wore daily and after doing so she told the therapist, feeling very proud of herself. Although this may seem to others a rather trivial change, for her it was a major step. One patient stated: '... because I know that these exercises are not about right or wrong and I am not judged by you [the therapist], I am less afraid and I feel up to do the task in a different way ...'. Another patient with severe comorbid OCD symptoms reported: '... the CRT sessions helped me to put things in perspective. I find it helpful to recognize my fear for a situation and to ask myself what am I afraid of and should I be? ...'

To put it briefly, CRT is suitable for patients with heterogeneous symptoms: whether you are quick or slow in performing the tasks or whether you have a global or an over-precise approach, reflecting on how you performed the tasks might give you insight in your specific thinking styles, and relating it to daily life makes it useful to learn about changing behaviours. Also CRT is well accepted, which was reflected in the high completion rate in our study: all but one patient completed all ten sessions. Reflections on thinking styles during cognitive exercises and implementation of behavioural changes in daily life seem to be a crucial part of CRT and might therefore be an explanation of how CRT achieves effects in functioning. That might also explain why CRT is effective as an additive training (at the beginning) of treatment. In the following, the experiences with CRT of three very different patients are given.

Examples

The first example is that of a 46-year-old woman with a history of anorexia nervosa. Her lowest BMI was 15. Recently she had a relapse. At the time of the study she fulfilled the DSM-IV diagnosis eating disorder NOS (resembling AN restrictive type). Her current BMI was 19.5. While doing the exercises she noticed that she found it difficult to do two tasks simultaneously. Also she noticed that she is not only focused on details with respect to eating but also with respect to other things like wrapping a present. At the end of the ten sessions she had learned that less focus on details made her less agitated. Further, she bought a science-fiction book which she thought she hated but it turned out to be fun. She learned to think more outside her box and to be more open to other suggestions. She found CRT challenging and fun to do.

The second example of the effect of CRT is that of a 35-year-old woman with a long history of AN (binge-purge subtype). Her current BMI was 13. She had two comorbid DSM-IV disorders: a depressive disorder and an obsessive compulsive disorder. The last ten years she had been in treatment ranging for outpatient treatment to intensive inpatient treatment. She had a lot of rituals not only related to food and had a very negative self-image. While doing the exercises she noticed that set-shifting was less difficult with a higher BMI. At first she found it very difficult to change her behaviours. One of the behavioural tasks was to choose which trousers to wear instead of taking the trousers on top of the pile. At first she felt very uncomfortable because she found herself not worthy to wear nice trousers. Also, she was not satisfied with her hair. Her task was to buy a new hairclip. At the end she did throw the old one away and wore a new one. She noticed that by repeating the tasks, she felt more comfortable, and the fact that during the CRT sessions, the therapist kept her reminding that CRT is not about good or wrong made her more at ease.

The third and last example is that of a 52-year-old woman with a longstanding AN (purging type using laxatives) and comorbid alcohol abuse. She had received treatment for the eating disorder in the past and had been able to control it for many years. However, after her husband died, it became worse, she lost her job and became socially isolated. Her strongest motivation for treatment was to prevent her children from becoming orphans. Her BMI at intake was approximately 18 and she had strong routines regarding eating and preparation of meals. During the first two sessions she was unsure what to expect from it but was willing to try something new.

Together with the therapist, she discovered that one of her problems was to try to do many things at once as quickly as possible, while she experienced difficulties switching between these tasks. She was unaware of this and with practice it became easier and she tried to do fewer things simultaneously. Regarding her social life, she found out that she had a tendency not to ask the opinion of others because she thought that she already knew the outcome. However, by practicing to ask the opinion of others, she was pleasantly surprised how people reacted and was able to reconnect with some old friends.

In the letter she wrote at the end of therapy, she stated how important it was to look beyond the first impression and take your time. The CRT sessions were a nice way to learn to understand and to gain insight in her own way of thinking and dealing with situations. Although practicing in daily life was somewhat difficult, it resulted in peace of mind and increased self-esteem.

Randomized controlled trial

In a randomized controlled trial (Dingemans et al., 2014) we investigated whether CRT plus TAU was more effective in reducing eating disorder psychopathology than TAU alone, and whether CRT plus TAU was also more effective in changing Body Mass Index (BMI), quality of life, depressive and anxiety symptoms, self-esteem, perfectionism, motivation to change, and neuropsychological functioning than TAU alone. However, the investigation of the general impact of CRT could mask individual differences in response to treatment. Some patients may strongly respond to CRT, while others may hardly benefit from this additional intervention. Moderator analyses can be used to specify such differential effects of treatment response within a population (Baron and Kenny, 1986; Kraemer et al., 2002). Successful identification of moderators could highly inform clinical practice and could optimize the intervention and its cost-effectiveness. Therefore, the current study also aimed to investigate moderators of treatment response.

The selection of potential moderators was based on previous research and theory. Regarding regular treatment (e.g. TAU), previous studies suggest that ED patients with more (severe) cognitive inefficiencies (Hamsher, Halmi, and Benton, 1981) and higher levels of perfectionism (Sutandar-Pinnock *et al.*, 2003) are more likely to demonstrate less favourable outcomes. Furthermore, lower self-esteem has been found to predict poor outcomes (Fichter, Quadflieg, and Hedlund, 2006). Finally, lower baseline levels of motivation to change, operationalized as readiness to change (Geller *et al.*, 2004) or perceived importance and ability to change (Wade *et al.*, 2009), have been found to predict poor treatment response among patients with an ED.

We approached all eligible patients who were admitted at our centres. About 50% fulfilled the inclusion criteria and agreed to participate. Forty-six percent ($n = 38$) had an enduring eating disorder (more than seven years of illness). Thirty-seven percent ($n = 30$) had a BMI below 15 and 93% ($n = 76$) had a history of AN (lowest BMI below 17.5). Only two patients did not meet the previously mentioned (Dingemans *et al.*, 2014) duration or severity criteria. However, their symptoms were rated as severe. The first patient was 20 years old and had a diagnosis of BN (BMI = 19.5). In the previous 28 days she had a frequency of self-induced vomiting of 50 times and reported to have misused laxatives 40 times. The other patient was 19 years old and had a diagnosis of AN EDNOS (BMI = 18.1). She reported self-induced vomiting on half of the previous 28 days. Both had received unsuccessful intensive treatment for their eating disorder in the past.

Fifty-six percent of the participants had AN restrictive type (or EDNOS resembling ANr), 33% had AN binge-purge type (or EDNOS resembling ANbp) and 11% had BN. More than 60% received a disability allowance or were currently out of work. About 70% received psychotropic medication and nearly 90% had received previous treatment for their eating disorder (for more details, see Dingemans *et al.*, 2014).

Our results (see Figures 6.1 and 6.2) showed that CRT in addition to TAU produced significantly more improvement in eating disorder-specific health-related quality of life at the end of treatment (T1), and more reduction of eating disorder psychopathology at six-months follow-up (T2) as compared to TAU alone.

Moreover, moderator analyses revealed that patients with poor baseline set-shifting abilities (as measured by the Trail Making Task – TMT) benefited significantly more from CRT than patients with no inefficiencies in set-shifting abilities at baseline. The eating disorder-specific quality of life in the CRT group for patients with poor set-shifting abilities was higher at follow-up. These results were not seen in the control group who only received TAU.

Conclusions

Both the results of our study and our personal clinical experiences demon-strated that CRT may be a promising novel additive training for patients with severe or enduring eating disorders, which confirms the findings from previous (un)controlled (case) studies (Davies and Tchanturia, 2005; Tchanturia *et al.*, 2007;

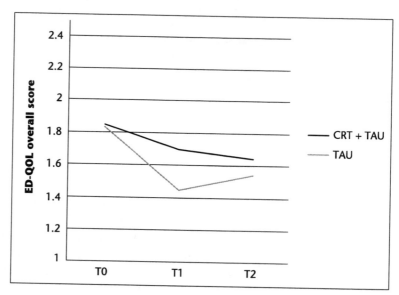

FIGURE 6.1 Eating disorder – specific health-related quality of life (ED-QOL overall score)

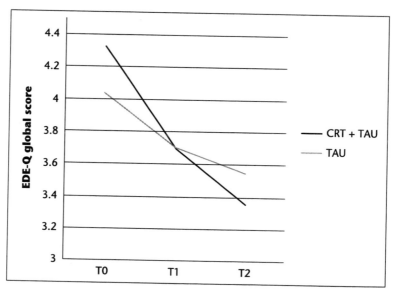

FIGURE 6.2 Eating disorder – psychopathology (EDE-Q global)

Tchanturia *et al.*, 2008; Lock *et al.*, 2013), that CRT is an acceptable and feasible therapy. There are some indications that CRT enhances the effectiveness of simultaneous and subsequent treatment with respect to eating disorder psychopathology and quality of life, particularly for patients with poor set-shifting abilities. Up until now, studies in which the effectiveness of CRT has been investigated, focused on patients with AN (ibid., except Lock) because AN is often associated with a rigid, inflexible and perfectionistic thinking style (Steinglass and Walsh, 2006; Baldock and Tchanturia, 2007). However, the results of this study might suggest that CRT could also be beneficial for patients with bulimic behaviours (purging and binging) because poor set-shifting abilities seem to be a transdiagnostic feature in women with ED (Roberts *et al.*, 2010).

References

Abbate-Daga, G., Buzzichelli, S., Amianto, F., Rocca, G., Marzola, E., McClintock, S. M. *et al.* (2011). Cognitive flexibility in verbal and nonverbal domains and decision making in anorexia nervosa patients: a pilot study. *BMC Psychiatry, 11,* 162.

Anderluh, M., Tchanturia, K., Rabe-Hesketh, S., Collier, D. and Treasure, J. (2009). Lifetime course of eating disorders: design and validity testing of a new strategy to define the eating disorders phenotype. *Psychological Medicine, 39,* 105–114.

Baldock, E. and Tchanturia, K. (2007). Translating laboratory research into practice: foundations, functions and future of cognitive remediation therapy for anorexia nervosa. *Therapy, 4,* 285–292.

Baron, R. M. and Kenny, D. A. (1986). The Moderator-Mediator variable distinction in Social Psychological research: Conceptual, strategic, and statistical considerations. *Journal of Personality and Social Psychology, 51,* 1173–1182.

Brockmeyer, T., Ingenerf, K., Walther, S., Wild, B., Hartmann, M., Herzog, W. *et al.* (2014). Training cognitive flexibility in patients with anorexia nervosa: A pilot randomized controlled trial of cognitive remediation therapy. *International Journal of Eating Disorders, 47,* 24–31.

Danner, U. N., Sanders, N., Smeets, P. A. M., van Meer, F., Adan, R. A. H., Hoek, H. W. *et al.* (2012). Neuropsychological weaknesses in anorexia nervosa: Set-shifting, central coherence, and decision making in currently ill and recovered women. *International Journal of Eating Disorders, 45,* 685–694.

Davies, H. and Tchanturia, K. (2005). Cognitive remediation therapy as an intervention for acute anorexia nervosa: A case report. *European Eating Disorders Review, 13,* 311–316.

Dingemans, A. E., Danner, U. N., Donker, J. M., Aardoom, J. J., van Meer, F., Tobias, K. *et al.* (2014). The effectiveness of cognitive remediation therapy in patients with a severe or enduring eating disorder: a randomized controlled trial. *Psychotherapy and Psychosomatics, 83,* 29–36.

Fairburn, C. G., Cooper, Z. and Shafran, R. (2003). Cognitive behaviour therapy for eating disorders: A 'transdiagnostic' theory and treatment. *Behaviour Research and Therapy, 41,* 509–528.

Fichter, M. M., Quadflieg, N. and Hedlund, S. (2006). Twelve-year course and outcome predictors of anorexia nervosa. *International Journal of Eating Disorders, 39,* 87–100.

Geller, J., Drab-Hudson, D. L., Whisenhunt, B. L. and Srikameswaran, S. (2004). Readiness to change dietary restriction predicts outcomes in the eating disorders. *Eating Disorders, 12,* 209–224.

Hamsher, K. S., Halmi, K. A. and Benton, A. L. (1981). Prediction of outcome in anorexia nervosa from neuropsychological status. *Psychiatry Research, 4,* 79–88.

Happé, F. G. E. and Booth, R. D. L. (2008). The power of the positive: Revisiting weak coherence in autism spectrum disorders. *Quarterly Journal of Experimental Psychology*, *61*, 50–63.

Herzog, D. B., Dorer, D. J., Keel, P. K., Selwyn, S. E., Ekeblad, E. R., Flores, A. T. *et al.* (1999). Recovery and relapse in anorexia and bulimia nervosa: A 7.5-year follow-up study. *Journal of the American Academy of Child and Adolescent Psychiatry*, *38*, 829–837.

Keel, P. K. and Brown, T. A. (2010). Update on course and outcome in eating disorders. *International Journal of Eating Disorders*, *43*, 195–204.

Kraemer, H. C., Wilson, G. T., Fairburn, C. G. and Agras, W. S. (2002). Mediators and moderators of treatment effects in randomized clinical trials. *Archives of General Psychiatry*, *59*, 877–883.

Landelijke Stuurgroep Multidisciplinaire Richtlijnontwikkeling in de GGZ (2006). *Multidisciplinaire Richtlijn Eetstoornissen.* Trimbos instituut, the Netherlands.

Lauer, C. J., Gorzewski, B., Gerlinghoff, M., Backmund, H. and Zihl, J. (1999). Neuropsychological assessments before and after treatment in patients with anorexia nervosa and bulimia nervosa. *Journal of Psychiatric Research*, *33*, 129–138.

Lena, S. M., Chidambaram, U., Panarella, C. and Sambasivan, K. (2001). Cognitive factors in anorexia nervosa: a case history. *International Journal of Eating Disorders*, *30*, 354–358.

Lena, S. M., Fiocco, A. J. and Leyenaar, J. K. (2004). The role of cognitive deficits in the development of eating disorders. *Neuropsychology Review*, *14*, 99–113.

Lock, J., Agras, W. S., Fitzpatrick, K. K., Bryson, S. W., Jo, B. and Tchanturia, K. (2013). Is outpatient cognitive remediation therapy feasible to use in randomized clinical trials for anorexia nervosa? *International Journal of Eating Disorders*, Sep, *46* (6), 567–75. DOI: 10.1002/eat.22134.

Lopez, C., Tchanturia, K., Stahl, D. and Treasure, J. (2008). Central coherence in eating disorders: a systematic review. *Psychological Medicine*, *38*, 1393–1404.

Milos, G., Spindler, A., Schnyder, U. and Fairburn, C. G. (2005). Instability of eating disorder diagnoses: prospective study. *British Journal of Psychiatry*, *187*, 573–578.

National Collaborating Centre for Mental Health (2004). *Eating disorders: core interventions in the treatment and management of anorexia nervosa, bulimia nervosa and related eating disorders.* London: National Institute for Clinical Excellence.

Roberts, M. E., Tchanturia, K., Stahl, D., Southgate, L. and Treasure, J. (2007). A systematic review and meta-analysis of set-shifting ability in eating disorders. *Psychological Medicine*, *37*, 1075–1084.

Roberts, M. E., Tchanturia, K. and Treasure, J. L. (2010). Exploring the neurocognitive signature of poor set-shifting in anorexia and bulimia nervosa. *Journal of Psychiatric Research*, *44*, 964–970.

Steinglass, J. and Walsh, B. T. (2006). Habit learning and anorexia nervosa: A cognitive neuroscience hypothesis. *International Journal of Eating Disorders*, *39*, 267–275.

Steinhausen, H. C. (2002). The outcome of anorexia nervosa in the 20th century. *American Journal of Psychiatry*, *159*, 1284–1293.

Steinhausen, H. C. and Weber, S. (2009). The outcome of bulimia nervosa: findings from one-quarter century of research. *American Journal of Psychiatry*, *166*, 1331–1341.

Sutandar-Pinnock, K., Blake, W. D., Carter, J. C., Olmsted, M. P. and Kaplan, A. S. (2003). Perfectionism in anorexia nervosa: a 6-24-month follow-up study. *International Journal of Eating Disorders*, *33*, 225–229.

Tchanturia, K., Anderluh, M. B., Morris, R. G., Rabe-Hesketh, S., Collier, D. A., Sanchez, P. *et al.* (2004a). Cognitive flexibility in anorexia nervosa and bulimia nervosa. *Journal of the International Neuropsychology Society*, *10*, 513–520.

Tchanturia, K., Davies, H., Reeder, C. and Wykes, T. (2010). www.national.slam.nhs.uk/wp-content/uploads/2014/04/Cognitive-remediation-therapy-for-Anorexia-Nervosa-Kate-Tchanturia.pdf.

Tchanturia, K., Davies, H. and Campbell, I. C. (2007). Cognitive remediation therapy for patients with anorexia nervosa: preliminary findings. *Annals of General Psychiatry*, *6*, 14.

Tchanturia, K., Davies, H., Lopez, C., Schmidt, U., Treasure, J. and Wykes, T. (2008). Neuropsychological task performance before and after cognitive remediation in anorexia nervosa: a pilot case-series. *Psychological Medicine, 38,* 1371–1373.

Tchanturia, K., Davies, H., Reeder, C. and Wykes, T. (2010). www.katetchanturia.com, publication subsection.

Tchanturia, K., Davies, H., Roberts, M., Harrison, A., Nakazato, M., Schmidt, U. *et al.* (2012). Poor cognitive flexibility in eating disorders: Examining the evidence using the Wisconsin Card Sorting Task. *PLoS One, 7,* e28331.

Tchanturia, K. and Hambrook, D. (2009). 'Cognitive Remediation', in C. Grilo and J. Mitchell (Eds.), *The Treatment of Eating Disorders: Clinical Handbook,* pp. 130–150. New York: Guilford Press.

Tchanturia, K., Harrison, A., Davies, H., Roberts, M., Oldershaw, A., Nakazato, M. *et al.* (2011). Cognitive flexibility and clinical severity in eating disorders. *PLoS One, 6,* e20462.

Tchanturia, K., Lloyd, S. and Lang, K. (2013). Cognitive remediation therapy for anorexia nervosa: current evidence and future research directions. *International Journal of Eating Disorders, 46,* 492–495.

Tchanturia, K. and Lock, J. (2011). Cognitive remediation therapy for eating disorders: development, refinement and future directions. *Current Topics in Behavioural Neurosciences, 6,* 269–287.

Tchanturia, K., Morris, R. G., Anderluh, M. B., Collier, D. A., Nikolaou, V. and Treasure, J. (2004b). Set-shifting in anorexia nervosa: an examination before and after weight gain, in full recovery and relationship to childhood and adult OCPD traits. *Journal of Psychiatric Research, 38,* 545–552.

Tenconi, E., Santonastaso, P., Degortes, D., Bosello, R., Titton, F., Mapelli, D. *et al.* (2010). Set-shifting abilities, central coherence, and handedness in anorexia nervosa patients, their unaffected siblings and healthy controls: exploring putative endophenotypes. *The World Journal of Biological Psychiatry, 11,* 813–823.

Touyz, S., Le, G. D., Lacey, H., Hay, P., Smith, R., Maguire, S. *et al.* (2013). Treating severe and enduring anorexia nervosa: a randomized controlled trial. *Psychological Medicine, 43* (12), 2501–11. DOI: 10.1017/S0033291713000949.

Van den Eynde, F., Guillaume, S., Broadbent, H., Stahl, D., Campbell, I. C., Schmidt, U. *et al.* (2011). Neurocognition in bulimic eating disorders: a systematic review. *Acta Psychiatrica Scandinavica, 124,* 120–140.

Wade, T. D., Frayne, A., Edwards, S. A., Robertson, T. and Gilchrist, P. (2009). Motivational change in an inpatient anorexia nervosa population and implications for treatment. *Australian and New Zealand Journal of Psychiatry, 43,* 235–243.

Whitney, J., Easter, A. and Tchanturia, K. (2008). Service users' feedback on cognitive training in the treatment of anorexia nervosa: a qualitative study. *International Journal of Eating Disorders, 41,* 542–550.

Wonderlich, S., Mitchell, J. E., Crosby, R. D., Myers, T. C., Kadlec, K., LaHaise, K. *et al.* (2012). Minimizing and treating chronicity in the eating disorders: A clinical overview. *International Journal of Eating Disorders, 45,* 467–475.

Wykes, T., Reeder, C., Landau, S., Everitt, B., Knapp, M., Patel, A. *et al.* (2007). Cognitive remediation therapy in schizophrenia: Randomized controlled trial. *British Journal of Psychiatry, 190,* 421–427.

7

COMPREHENDING AND FOSTERING COGNITIVE-BEHAVIOURAL FLEXIBILITY IN ANOREXIA NERVOSA

Timo Brockmeyer and Hans-Christoph Friederich

Introduction

Patients with anorexia nervosa (AN) typically show obsessive preoccupations with food, body shape and weight as well as ritualized behaviours such as body checking, counting calories, and excessive exercising (Davis and Kaptein, 2006; Halmi *et al.*, 2003). Beyond these food- and body-related compulsions, AN patients commonly show rigid cognitions and behaviours in many other domains. Indeed, AN has considerable overlaps with obsessive-compulsive disorder (OCD) and obsessive-compulsive personality disorder (OCPD) (for a comprehensive review, see Serpell *et al.*, 2002) (see also Chapter 3). About half of AN patients have a lifetime diagnosis of either OCD or OCPD and there is some evidence that these obsessive-compulsive features and temperament traits, including perfectionism, precede the onset of AN and persist after recovery in a considerable number of patients (for reviews see Lilenfeld *et al.*, 2006; Serpell *et al.*, 2002).

Accordingly, obsessive-compulsive features are assumed to play an important role in the development and maintenance of the disorder and have been shown to negatively impact treatment outcome (Serpell *et al.*, 2002; Treasure *et al.*, 2010; Crane *et al.*, 2007). Thus, it is of great interest to improve our understanding of the specific components of obsessive-compulsiveness that are linked to the development and course of AN, their underlying neurocognitive and neurobiological mechanisms, and interventions that have the potential to ameliorate them.

In the first part of this chapter we will focus on one specific facet of obsessive-compulsiveness that is thought to be particularly relevant for the low responsiveness to treatment in AN patients: resistance to change. Next, we will briefly review the current evidence for inefficient flexibility in AN, from neuropsychological studies. Thereafter, we will elaborate on a previous neuroimaging study in which we have compared AN patients and healthy controls in terms of neural activation during a flexibility task. Then, we will report on a recently published randomized-controlled trial examining the efficacy and effectiveness of an adapted and intensified version of cognitive remediation therapy (CRT) for severe AN patients. Finally, we will present ten research questions concerning cognitive-behavioural flexibility in AN that should be addressed by future studies.

Resistance to change as a facet of cognitive inflexibility in daily life

In daily life, AN patients oftentimes stick to their routines and feel stressed when plans or rules are to be changed (Roberts *et al.*, 2011; Lounes *et al.*, 2011). And so, there is growing evidence that AN patients feature high levels of intolerance of uncertainty (Frank *et al.*, 2012; Sternheim *et al.*, 2011a; Sternheim *et al.*, 2011b; Konstantellou *et al.*, 2011). They commonly feel overly uncomfortable with uncertain or less predictable situations and typically try to avoid these feelings by thinking and planning ahead and trying to be in control at all times (Sternheim *et al.*, 2011a). This over-controlling behaviour may represent an attempt to compensate for a perceived lack of control over interpersonal and general life stressors and to alleviate corresponding negative effect (Frank *et al.*, 2012; Brockmeyer *et al.*, 2013a; Sternheim *et al.*, 2011a). This compensatory mechanism may be rooted in experiences of physical and emotional abuse in childhood which is more often reported by AN patients than by healthy individuals (Jaite *et al.*, 2013; Tagay *et al.*, 2010).

Against this background, it appears well understandable that the disorder of AN itself represents a reinforcing condition by providing a sense of safety (Serpell *et al.*, 2003, 1999 and 2004). Thus, it can be assumed that strong resistance to change stemming from early adverse life-experiences represents a stable trait that makes people more vulnerable to develop and maintain a disorder like AN.

Methodology

Based on these notions, we conducted a cross-sectional study in which we examined whether women with acute AN (ac-AN) and those recovered from AN (rec-AN) would exceed healthy women in terms of their self-reported resistance to change. Within a larger project, 30 ac-AN were compared to 20 rec-AN and 30 healthy control women (HC). Ac-AN and rec-AN were recruited consecutively from the inpatient and outpatient units as well as from the registers of a university hospital. HC were recruited from the university campus and the community. All participants were Caucasian, and between 17 and 44 years of age. HC had a normal body mass index (BMI) in the range 18.5 to 25 kg/m² and neither a history of, or a current DSM-IV diagnosis. Rec-AN had a history of AN according to DSM-IV, a current BMI >18.5 kg/m², regular menstruation, and no more dietary restraint for at least one year as well as no other current DSM-IV diagnosis. In the AN group, 17 women had a comorbid depressive disorder and four had an anxiety disorder.

Diagnosis

DSM-IV diagnoses (APA, 1994) were obtained using the German version of the *Structured Clinical Interview for DSM-IV* (SCID) – Wittchen *et al.*, 1997. Resistance to change was assessed using the *Resistance to Change scale* (RTC) – Oreg, 2003. The RTC is a 17-item self-report scale which consists of 4 distinct but inter-correlated subscales that are thought to reflect behavioural, affective, and cognitive facets of the construct. The behavioural facet focuses on an individual's tendency to adopt routines in daily life (subscale 'routine seeking'). The affective facet includes two subcomponents: The subscale 'emotional reaction' captures the degree of an individual's stress and uneasiness when faced with change, whereas the subscale 'short-term focus' appraises the extent to which an individual is so distracted by temporary inconveniences associated with change that he or she refrains from valued long-term goals. The subscale 'cognitive rigidity', indexes the frequency and ease with which people change their minds in general. Participants rate their resistance to change on a 6-point Likert Scale. Responses may range from 1 (*strongly disagree*) to 6 (*strongly agree*). Previous studies supported the factorial structure, the construct validity as well as an excellent internal consistency for the total scale. Furthermore, the scale showed acceptable to good internal consistencies for the subscales (Oreg, 2003; Oreg *et al.*, 2008).

Group profile

In this study, the mean ages were 23.47 years (SD = 5.79 years) in the ac-AN group, 28.70 years (SD = 5.58 years) in the rec-AN group, and 24.97 years (SD = 3.23 years) in the HC group. Ac-AN and HC were significantly younger than rec-AN ($p < 0.001$ and $p = 0.010$, respectively) but did not differ from each other in this regard ($p = 0.242$). By definition, ac-AN had lower BMI levels than rec-AN and HC (both $p < 0.001$) whereas rec-AN did not differ from HC ($p = 0.189$). The mean BMI (kg/m^2) were: ac-AN – 14.91 (SD = 1.31); rec-AN – 20.73 (SD = 2.53), and HC – 21.52 (SD = 1.72).

Analysis

A multivariate analysis of variance (MANOVA) was conducted with subject group as independent variable and the RTC total score and subscale scores as dependent variables. MANOVA results indicated significant differences between the groups, *Pillai's trace* = 0.29, $F(8, 150) = 3.16$, $p < 0.01$. Follow-up one-way ANOVAs revealed significant group differences in terms of the RTC total score and subscale scores except for the subscale 'cognitive rigidity'. Post-hoc comparisons with Bonferroni corrections revealed that ac-AN reported greater routine seeking, emotional reaction, short-term focus, and greater overall resistance to change than HC. Rec-AN reported greater short-term focus and greater overall resistance to change than HC. Rec-AN did not differ from ac-AN, neither in the total score nor in any of the subscale scores. Results are summarized in Table 7.1.

TABLE 7.1 Resistance to change in women with acute anorexia nervosa (ac-AN), women recovered from anorexia nervosa (rec-AN), and healthy control women (HC)

	ac-AN (n = 30)	rec-AN (n = 20)	HC (n = 30)	ANOVA	p	Cohen's d
	M (SD)	M (SD)	M (SD)	F (2, 77)		
Resistance to change – total score	61.80 (13.30)[a]	58.20 (9.15)[a]	49.43 (7.73)[b]	10.90	< 0.001	ac-AN vs. HC: 1.14 rec-AN vs. HC: 1.04 ac-AN vs. rec-AN: 0.32
Subscale: routine seeking	16.10 (4.84)[a]	14.75 (3.91)[a,b]	12.80 (3.13)[b]	5.05	0.009	ac-AN vs. HC: 0.81 rec-AN vs. HC: 0.55 ac-AN vs. rec-AN: 0.31
Subscale: emotional reaction	15.63 (4.54)[a]	14.15 (3.67)[a,b]	12.13 (3.65)[b]	5.74	0.005	ac-AN vs. HC: 0.85 rec-AN vs. HC: 0.55 ac-AN vs. rec-AN: 0.36
Subscale: short-term focus	14.93 (4.04)[a]	13.70 (4.44)[a]	10.03 (2.98)[b]	13.32	< 0.001	ac-AN vs. HC: 1.38 rec-AN vs. HC: 0.97 ac-AN vs. rec-AN: 0.29
Subscale: cognitive rigidity	15.13 (4.41)[a]	15.60 (4.71)[a]	14.47 (2.86)[a]	0.51	0.601	ac-AN vs. HC: 0.18 rec-AN vs. HC: 0.29 ac-AN vs. rec-AN: 0.10

Note: different superscripts denote significant differences between groups

As hypothesized, ac-AN and rec-AN showed greater resistance to change than HC. These findings are in line with previous findings that women with AN report heightened intolerance of uncertainty and reduced cognitive-behavioural flexibility in their daily lives (Sternheim *et al.*, 2011a, 2011b; Frank *et al.*, 2012; Konstantellou *et al.*, 2011; Lounes *et al.*, 2011). Particularly, the high levels of emotional reactions to change reported by ac-AN, support the assumption that cognitive-behavioural rigidity may serve to decrease negative affect that may be associated with changes in the environment (Frank *et al.*, 2012; Brockmeyer *et al.*, 2013a; Sternheim *et al.*, 2011a).

The higher levels of resistance reported by rec-AN as compared to HC and the finding of comparable levels of resistance in rec-AN and ac-AN corresponds to previous findings of reduced self-reported cognitive flexibility in women with a lifetime diagnosis of an eating disorder (Roberts *et al.*, 2011). Together, these findings suggest that resistance to change (as a facet of limited cognitive-behavioural flexibility in daily life) may be a stable trait marker in women with a lifetime diagnosis of AN and thus may form a potential vulnerability factor. Alternatively, resistance to change may represent a 'scar' of the disorder that persists after recovery.

In the present study, the differences in resistance to change were limited to the emotional and behavioural facets of the construct. There were no group differences regarding 'cognitive rigidity'. In contrast, studies using the Detail and Flexibility Questionnaire (D-Flex – Roberts *et al.*, 2011) did find elevated levels of cognitive rigidity in AN as compared to HC (Lounes *et al.*, 2011; Roberts *et al.*, 2011). This discrepancy is probably due to the different item formulations in the two measures and their different conceptualization of 'cognitive rigidity'. Whereas the D-Flex assesses cognitive rigidity with items like 'I get upset when people disturb my plans for the day' (which is quite similar to the items of the RTC 'emotional reaction' subscale), a typical cognitive rigidity item in the RTC is 'My views are very consistent over time'. The latter may rather describe the degree of temporal stability in personal attitudes which is rather not specifically linked to AN phenomenology.

The neurocognitive imprint of cognitive flexibility

Self-reports are limited to the patient's subjective impressions and are sensitive to memory biases and demand characteristics. Neuropsychological tests offer a way to assess inefficiencies in cognitive functions on a more basic and objective level. Although AN show lower levels in both self-reported and objectively measured cognitive flexibility, previous research suggests that these are two distinct dimensions of the global construct of cognitive flexibility, as there has been only poor correspondence between self-report measures and performances in neuropsychological tests (Lounes *et al.*, 2011).

At a neuropsychological level, obsessive-compulsiveness may appear as inefficient set-shifting which is defined as the ability to easily move back and forth between multiple tasks, operations, or mental sets in response to changing goals or environmental experiences (Miyake *et al.*, 2000). People with poor set-shifting abilities instead are characterized by resistance to changing rules and perseverative thinking and behaviour (Friederich and Herzog, 2011; Tchanturia et al., 2004). Using specific neuropsychological tests that require some shift in cognitive set, rules, or behavioural responses, several studies have demonstrated inefficient cognitive set-shifting in adults (e.g., Tchanturia et al., 2011), adolescents (e.g., Shott et al., 2012) currently-ill with AN, and their first-degree relatives (e.g., Holliday et al., 2005), as well as in women recovered from AN (e.g., Roberts et al., 2010) (for a review see also Chapter 1). Together, these findings suggest that inefficient cognitive set-shifting constitutes a trait marker which may contribute to the development and maintenance of AN.

The neural signature of inefficient cognitive-behavioural flexibility

Neuroimaging research has the potential to contribute to our understanding of this neurocognitive inefficiency observed in AN by providing insight into its neurobiological signature.

Previous studies with non-clinical samples have demonstrated that striatocortical pathways play a pivotal role in shifts of cognitive-set and behavioural response: Corticosubcortical reentrant circuits can be differentiated in ventral (e.g., ventral striatum, the amygdala, anterior insula, ventral ACC and OFC) and dorsal (e.g., dorsal striatum, dorsolateral prefrontal cortex, parietal cortex, dorsal insular region) striatocortical pathways (Alexander et al., 1990; Heimer 2003). Whereas the ventral circuit is involved in motivational processing and reinforcement learning, the dorsal circuit reflects effortful cognitive functions of goal-directed behaviour. Functional neuroimaging studies found the lateral prefrontal cortex and the anterior cingulate/ventromedial prefrontal cortex were involved in cognitive set-shifting and inhibitory control (Aron et al., 2003; Cools et al., 2004; Shafritz et al., 2005). Furthermore, subcortical regions (e.g., thalamus, subthalamic nucleus, and striatum) facilitate shifts in behavioural responses mediated by the prefrontal cortex (Block et al., 2007; Monchi et al., 2006). In addition, the dorsal parietal cortex is involved in shifts of attention and in detecting salient target stimuli (Hampshire et al., 2007; Snyder et al., 2000).

To gain more insight into the neural signature of cognitive-behavioural flexibility in AN we conducted a functional magnetic resonance imaging (fMRI) study (Zastrow et al., 2009). In this study, poor cognitive-behavioural flexibility in AN was associated with altered metabolism in the ventral fronto-striatal network. More precisely, in AN patients poor shifting performance in a behavioural task was associated with hypoactivations in the frontostriatothalamic network (i.e., in the thalamus, the ventral striatum, and the rostral anterior cingulate cortex). The anterior cingulate cortex is known to be involved in performance monitoring, conflict detection, and emotional processing to initiate and control behaviour. This finding of the present study corresponds to previous morphometric and functional brain imaging studies showing an altered anterior cingulate cortex function in AN patients (Muhlau et al., 2007; Naruo et al., 2001; Uher et al., 2003). Also, AN patients showed preserved neural metabolism in the right ventral frontoparietal network (i.e., in the right middle frontal gyrus and the temporoparietal junction bilaterally). This was specific to AN patients and not observed in healthy controls. The ventral frontoparietal network plays an important role in allocating and directing the individual's attention towards salient stimuli (Corbetta and Shulman, 2002). Correspondingly, during correct responses in incongruent trials of a Simon spatial incompatibility task, adolescent and adult BN patients showed less activation in frontostriatal circuits, particularly in the inferior frontal gyrus, the anterior cingulate cortex, the dorsolateral prefrontal cortex and the putamen than healthy controls (Marsh et al., 2011 and 2009).

However, in this study we did not find an increased metabolism in the dorsal striatum of AN patients as a central structure of the dorsal striatocortical network. Such a result would have further strengthened the notion of an imbalance between the ventral and dorsal striatocortical system in AN patients (Kaye et al., 2009). In line with this idea, studies using positron emission tomography have demonstrated an altered striatal activity in AN patients in the resting state (Herholz et al., 1987; Delvenne et al., 1997).

In a nutshell, neuroimaging studies so far suggest that inefficient cognitive-behavioural flexibility in AN is closely associated with functional disturbances in striatocortical circuits. The AN patients' preserved neural metabolism in the right fronto-parietal network may indicate a predominant effortful and supervisory top-down control over altered ascending motivational processing. Currently, we are investigating changes in brain metabolisms after CRT as compared to a non-specific cognitive training. These results will be reported elsewhere.

Remediating cognitive flexibility – testing an adapted and intensified version of CRT

As already described in introduction of this book, there is a lack of evidence-based, successful, and sizable treatments for adult AN patients (NICE, 2004; Hay et al., 2003). One reason for this unsatisfactory state may lie in the patients' cognitive inflexibility and strong resistance to change which we have outlined in the first parts of this chapter. Inefficient cognitive-behavioural flexibility is an expression of obsessive-compulsive personality traits (Schmidt and Treasure, 2006; Schmitz et al., 2006; Tchanturia et al., 2004) that seem to play an important role in the development and maintenance of the disorder and that negatively impact treatment outcome (Serpell et al., 2002; Treasure et al., 2010; Crane et al., 2007).

In order to translate these findings from basic research into a specific clinical intervention, Tchanturia and colleagues have adapted CRT for the specific needs of AN patients (see Chapters 1, 2, 3, 4, 5, 11). Initially, this approach was developed for treating patients with brain lesions and schizophrenia. CRT for AN specifically aims at improving basic neurocognitive functions that are thought to underlie rigid and perseverative behaviours in AN (Tchanturia et al., 2007, 2008, 2013). As described in detail in Chapters 2, 3 and 5, several case reports, non-controlled trials, and one randomized controlled trial so far suggested that CRT is effective in improving cognitive set-shifting. However, some limitations of these previous studies were the confined comparability or lack of control conditions (Abbate-Daga et al., 2012; Lock et al., 2013; Tchanturia et al., 2008), the restriction to relatively well functioning AN outpatients (Lock et al., 2013), and a lack of outcome variables that are different from the tasks that are used in the training (Lock et al., 2013).

Questions to be answered

Thus, some questions concerning the efficacy and effectiveness of CRT remained open: 1 – How effective is CRT for more severe AN patients in lower weight conditions? 2 – To what degree are improvements in cognitive flexibility during CRT specifically attributable to genuine CRT interventions? 3 – Do CRT training effects on cognitive set-shifting generalize to set-shifting tasks, other than those used in the training? Furthermore, Tchanturia and colleagues recently (2013) outlined some issues concerning CRT practice that should be also examined (Chapters 5, 9); 4 – the efficacy of more intense forms of CRT as the optimal dosage of the program is not yet known, and 5 – What is the feasibility of CRT programs that involve homework sessions which are to be accomplished by the patients on their own? Finally: 6 – to gain more insight into how CRT unfolds its beneficial effects on cognitive control capacities, a closer look at stepwise changes in cognitive set-shifting during the application of CRT might be helpful.

In order to address these questions, we conducted a randomized-controlled trial to estimate the efficacy and feasibility of an adapted and intensified form of CRT for severe AN patients (Brockmeyer et al., 2013b). In this study we tested CRT against a control treatment of non-specific neurocognitive therapy (NNT) that resembled CRT in the dosage, structure, and form of treatment but only differed from CRT in the focus of interventions. Whereas CRT focused solely on cognitive flexibility, NNT focused on other cognitive functions such as attention, memory, and logical deduction. Participants were recruited from two specialized inpatient units for eating disorders (CRT: 65%; NNT: 61%) and from an outpatient centre of a university hospital. They were randomly assigned to receive either CRT ($n = 20$) or NNT ($n = 20$) as an add-on to treatment as usual (TAU). Both treatments comprised 30 sessions of computer-based (21 sessions) and face-to-face (9 sessions) training, delivered over a three week period. Each session lasted approximately 45 minutes.

In this study, a modified version of CRT was used. The principles, structure and main components of the original CRT manual were kept with respect to cognitive flexibility training. However, we intentionally omitted the central coherence component of the training – to reduce the influence of potentially confounding factors, and to focus specifically on cognitive set-shifting. In addition, this version differed from the original CRT in the number of sessions (30 instead of 10) and the use of computer-assisted homework tasks to intensify cognitive flexibility training.

Tasks – protocols and controls

The computer-based homework comprised a *Simon task* (Simon and Rudell, 1967) and a *Flanker task* (Eriksen and Eriksen, 1974). Both tasks require participants to focus on one specific aspect of several presented stimuli and to ignore another aspect which requires a shift between two cognitive sets. In the *Simon task*, participants view arrows that are presented at the left hand or right hand side on a computer screen and which either point to the left- or right hand side. Subjects are asked to respond via button press as to the direction of the arrow and to ignore the position of the arrow on the screen. This operation requires a switch between two cognitive sets (location vs. direction) which is even more difficult in incongruent trials where left-pointing arrows are presented on the right hand side, and vice versa.

In the *Flanker task*, participants view a number of arrows that are simultaneously presented side by side on a computer screen. However, participants are asked to only attend to one of these arrows (marked by a cross above this one arrow). The other arrows surrounding the index arrow can be either distracting (i.e., incongruent: pointing in the opposite direction) or facilitating (i.e., congruent: pointing in the same direction as the index arrow). Thus, incongruent trials demand a switching between two cognitive sets (i.e., direction of target vs. non-target arrows). Whereas the difficulty level in the *Simon task* was kept stable to allow for a monitoring of training progress, difficulty levels in the *Flanker task* gradually increased (e.g., by presenting more items at the same time).

As already stated, the control condition resembled CRT in all aspects except that training tasks focused solely on attention, memory, and logical deduction instead of flexibility. In face-to-face sessions, the participants were, for example, asked to solve arithmetic problems, word puzzles, matchstick riddles, memory games, and so on. The computer-assisted homework sessions comprised selected tasks and games from commercial software packages.

TAU consisted of common multimodal inpatient and day clinic programs in Germany, composed of medical assessments, weekly individual- and group psychodynamic psychotherapy, body therapy, art therapy, nutrition management, symptom-oriented behavioural interventions (e.g., food diaries, weight-contracts, meal plans), and family interventions. However, during the three-week period of the training, a maximum of three individual and group therapy sessions were offered. The participants in the CRT and NNT groups currently receiving weekly outpatient psychotherapy were 35% and 39% respectively.

Reaction times during shift runs in a cued task-switching paradigm (Monsell, 2003) were considered the main outcome measure and an indication of cognitive flexibility. Note that this task was different from the training tasks. We controlled for potentially confounding insufficiencies in other cognitive functions by also administering the d2 test of attention (Brickenkamp, 2002), the digit-span forward and backward subtests of the Wechsler Memory Scale III (Wechsler, 1997) and the Multiple-Choice Vocabulary Intelligence Test (Lehrl, 2005).

Analysis

Analyses were based on the data available from 25 treatment completers. At baseline there were no differences between participants in the CRT and in the NNT condition regarding any demographic, clinical, or neuropsychological variable. Likewise, groups did not differ in the proportion of non-completers. Completers and non-completers likewise did not differ regarding any demographic, clinical, or dependent variable. Participants dropped out of treatment due to transferral to a different site or patient discharge. Cognitive flexibility was not correlated with attention, working memory, or premorbid intelligence.

As expected, mean cognitive set-shifting as measured by the cued task-switching paradigm at post-assessment was better in the CRT group than in the NNT group, even when controlling for cognitive set-shifting performance at pre-assessment. The between-groups effect size of Cohen's $d = 0.61$ underscores that cognitive set-shifting at post-assessment was more efficient in the CRT group than in the NNT group. In order to provide a finer-grained picture of how cognitive flexibility improved over time, participants' performances in the *Simon task* were recorded during the 21 homework sessions. The means of the percentages of correct responses in the *Simon task* are indicative of cognitive flexibility, and analyses showed that scores significantly increased over the three weeks of training.

To also gain an impression of the participants' subjective view on the training, they were asked to give feedback on a structured evaluation form. Eighty per cent of participants in the CRT group and 57% of participants in the NNT group found that the training matched well with their problems in daily life. Sixty per cent of the CRT group and 43% of the NNT group felt they were more flexible in their daily routines after the training. Similarly, 60% in the CRT group and 43% in the NNT group agreed that they were less afraid of general changes after the training. Eighty per cent in the CRT group and 71% in the NNT group stated that they would try out new ways of thinking and feeling after the training. Ninety per cent in the CRT group and 43% in the NNT group felt that they had gained some insight into their ways of thinking and feeling. Ninety per cent in the CRT group and 71% in the NNT group found that they benefited from the training. Finally, 90% in the CRT group and 86% in the NNT group liked the training, and would recommend the training to others.

Summary

This study was the first to examine whether specifically-tailored neurocognitive training for AN is more effective than non-specific neurocognitive training. With a medium effect size, CRT led to greater improvements in cognitive flexibility than NNT. This result provides evidence that limited cognitive flexibility in AN can be effectively reduced by CRT and that these effects are attributable to the specific contents of CRT and not to more general factors which may be present in any kind of cognitive training. The study furthermore illustrates how cognitive flexibility was gradually improving over time. Furthermore, the study demonstrated that an adapted, intensified, computer-assisted version of CRT including homework sessions, is feasible for severe AN patients. According to the qualitative feedback of participants, CRT does not only foster performance in neuropsychological tests of cognitive flexibility but also unfolds beneficial effects on participants' flexibility in their daily lives which supports the ecological validity of the training.

Whether improving such basic functions of cognitive control in AN patients increases their responsiveness to parallel/consecutive psychotherapeutic treatments has to be examined further. In a recently published pilot study with AN outpatients (Lock *et al.*, 2013), no differences were found between a) CRT + CBT (Cognitive Behavioural Therapy) and, b) CBT alone, in terms of eating disorder psychopathology. From a different point of view, the reduction of cognitive inefficiencies itself represents a discrete and justifiable goal of an add-on treatment like CRT, apart from any impact on eating disorder psychopathology.

Future directions

In our view, a number of research questions concerning CRT for AN remain open and need to be addressed by well-conducted studies in the future. Here we give ten examples for what in our opinion it would be important to clarify:

1. Common neuropsychological tests of cognitive set-shifting/cognitive flexibility do not merely assess cognitive set-shifting but also capture a range of other cognitive functions. Therefore, it would be of great interest to disentangle the core inefficiencies in cognitive control in AN patients by utilizing broader sets of neuropsychological tests that allow us to gather a finer-grained picture of the specific neurocognitive inefficiencies in AN patients that are involved in, or may co-occur with inefficient set-shifting. Such hierarchical test batteries may differentiate between:

    a) motor inhibition (i.e., stopping already initiated psychomotor responses),
    b) behavioural inhibition (i.e. withholding psychomotor responses that have not yet been initiated),
    c) cognitive inhibition (i.e., withholding prepotent, interferential cognitive processes),
    d) shifting of behavioural responses in the absence of rule changes,
    e) set-shifting (i.e., shifting of behavioural response to a rule change),
    f) reversal learning (i.e., shifting of behavioural response to a covert rule change).

Greater insight into the precise architecture of AN patients' neurocognitive system may help to refine CRT interventions and to also implement cognitive domains other than cognitive set-shifting (as can be seen in the context of schizophrenia research and treatment). Such an approach may also help to specifically tailor CRT interventions for individual patients corresponding to their key cognitive concerns – as already done in the context of schizophrenia (Franck *et al.*, 2013).

2. On the other hand, if we knew that CRT effects spread to other domains of cognitive functioning, it may not be necessary to implement separate exercises for each and every domain of cognitive functioning. Thus, we need to examine whether and to which degree CRT effects generalize to other cognitive domains (cf. Murthy *et al.*, 2012; Dickinson *et al.*, 2010).

3. In addition, it would help us to refine CRT treatment modules if we knew which elements/exercises of CRT have the greatest impact on cognitive set-shifting or other cognitive inefficiencies.

4. In order to adequately organise the structure and frequency of CRT interventions, we need to know more about the sustainability of CRT effects (cf. Wykes *et al.*, 2003). For example, it may be necessary to implement CRT brush-up sessions in long-term psychological treatments instead of providing CRT only in the beginning of a treatment.

5. One of the most crucial points belongs to whether CRT unfolds any direct or indirect (e.g., via increased responsiveness to psychotherapy) effects on eating disorder symptoms. At this point, CRT for schizophrenia and CRT for AN somewhat differ in their direction, as the first one directly addresses symptoms of the respective disorder whereas the latter addresses potentially underlying mechanisms or epiphenomena of the respective disorder (cf. Gharaeipour and Scott, 2012). Furthermore, with respect to long-term outcomes it is important to examine whether CRT for AN has potential to reduce relapse rates, as shown for CRT for schizophrenia (Trapp *et al.*, 2013).

6. With respect to its ecological validity, it is of interest whether CRT also affects broader domains of functioning such as self-esteem, quality of life, and real-world functioning, as demonstrated for CRT for schizophrenia (Garrido *et al.*, 2013; Bowie *et al.*, 2012).

7. Considering that not all patients may benefit to the same degree from one specific treatment, we need to find out which patients benefit most from CRT. As some preliminary evidence suggests, those patients with poor baseline set-shifting, benefit more from CRT than those with no significant problems in this area (see Chapter 6). In addition, moderator analyses in larger trials could examine whether, for instance, AN subtype, weight status, or comorbidity influence the effects of CRT for AN.

8. Furthermore, as previous studies have demonstrated set-shifting inefficiencies, not only in AN but also in BN and partly in BED and obesity (see Chapters 6 and 12), the obvious question is if we can adopt CRT also for patients with BN, BED, and EDNOS.

9. Referring to studies on resistance to change and intolerance of uncertainty, it would be interesting to examine the potential link between cognitive-behavioural inflexibility, adverse childhood events, and emotion regulation capacities in AN patients. This would be of great relevance, particularly for

comprehensive treatment packages which do not only focus on cognitive remediation but also on socio-emotional functioning (Schmidt *et al.*, 2012; Davies *et al.*, 2012).

10. Finally, it is of great interest to better understand the neurobiological mechanisms underlying cognitive flexibility and also, which changes in these processes are associated with successful CRT. This may help us to further tune CRT elements (cf. Penades *et al.*, 2013).

References

Abbate-Daga, G., Buzzichelli, S., Marzola, E., Amianto, F. and Fassino, S. (2012). Effectiveness of cognitive remediation therapy (CRT) in anorexia nervosa: A case series. *Journal of Clinical and Experimental Neuropsychology, 34*, 1009–1015.

APA (1994). *Diagnostic and statistical manual of mental disorders* (4th edn). Arlington, VA: American Psychiatric Publishing, Inc.

Aron, A. R., Fletcher, P. C., Bullmore, E. T., Sahakian, B. J. and Robbins, T. W. (2003). Stop-signal inhibition disrupted by damage to right inferior frontal gyrus in humans. *Natural Neuroscience, 6*, 115–116.

Block, A. E., Dhanji, H., Thompson-Tardif, S. F. and Floresco, S. B. (2007). Thalamic-prefrontal cortical-ventral striatal circuitry mediates dissociable components of strategy set shifting. *Cereb Cortex, 17*, 1625–1636.

Bowie, C. R., McGurk, S. R., Mausbach, B., Patterson, T. L. and Harvey, P. D. (2012). Combined cognitive remediation and functional skills training for schizophrenia: effects on cognition, functional competence, and real-world behavior. *American Journal of Psychiatry, 169*, 710–718.

Brickenkamp, R. (2002). Test d2, *Aufmerksamkeits-Belastungs-Test*. Göttingen: Hogrefe.

Brockmeyer, T., Holtforth, M. G., Bents, H., Kämmerer, A., Herzog, W. and Friederich, H.-C. (2013a). Interpersonal motives in anorexia nervosa: The fear of losing one's autonomy. *Journal of Clinical Psychology, 69*, 278–289.

Brockmeyer, T., Ingenerf, K., Walther, S., Wild, B., Hartmann, M., Herzog, W., Bents, H. and Friederich, H.-C. (2013b). Training cognitive flexibility in patients with anorexia nervosa: A pilot randomized controlled trial of cognitive remediation therapy. *International Journal of Eating Disorders, 47* (1), 24–31.

Cools, R., Clark, L. and Robbins, T. W. (2004). Differential responses in human striatum and prefrontal cortex to changes in object and rule relevance. *The Journal of Neuroscience, 24*, 1129–1135.

Corbetta, M. and Shulman, G. L. (2002). Control of goal-directed and stimulus-driven attention in the brain. *Nature Reviews. Neuroscience, 3*, 201–215.

Crane, A. M., Roberts, M. E. and Treasure, J. (2007). Are obsessive-compulsive personality traits associated with a poor outcome in anorexia nervosa? A systematic review of randomized controlled trials and naturalistic outcome studies. *International Journal of Eating Disorders, 40*, 581–588.

Davies, H., Fox, J., Naumann, U., Treasure, J., Schmidt, U. and Tchanturia, K. (2012). Cognitive remediation and emotion skills training for anorexia nervosa: An observational study using neuropsychological outcomes. *European Eating Disorders Review, 20*, 211–217.

Davis, C. and Kaptein, S. (2006). Anorexia nervosa with excessive exercise: A phenotype with close links to obsessive-compulsive disorder. *Psychiatry Research, 142*, 209–217.

Delvenne, V., Goldman, S., de Maertelaer, V., Wikler, D., Damhaut, P. and Lotstra, F. (1997). Brain glucose metabolism in anorexia nervosa and affective disorders: influence of weight loss or depressive symptomatology. *Psychiatry Research, 74*, 83–92.

Dickinson, D., Tenhula, W., Morris, S., Brown, C., Peer, J., Spencer, K., Li, L., Gold, J. M. and Bellack, A. S. (2010). A randomized, controlled trial of computer-assisted cognitive remediation for schizophrenia. *American Journal of Psychiatry, 167*, 170–180.

Eriksen, B. A. and Eriksen, C. W. (1974). Effects of noise letters upon the identification of a target letter in a nonsearch task. *Perception and Psychophysics, 16*, 143–149.

Franck, N., Duboc, C., Sundby, C., Amado, I., Wykes, T., Demily, C., Launay, C., le Roy, V., Bloch, P., Willard, D., Todd, A., Petitjean, F., Foullu, S., Briant, P., Grillon, M.-L., Deppen, P., Verdoux, H., Bralet, M.-C., Januel, D., Riche, B., Roy, P. and Vianin, P. (2013). Specific vs general cognitive remediation for executive functioning in schizophrenia: A multicenter randomized trial. *Schizophrenia Research, 147*, 68–74.

Frank, G. K. W., Roblek, T., Shott, M. E., Jappe, L. M., Rollin, M. D. H., Hagman, J. O. and Pryor, T. (2012). Heightened fear of uncertainty in anorexia and bulimia nervosa. *International Journal of Eating Disorders, 45*, 227–232.

Friederich, H.-C. and Herzog, W. (2011). 'Cognitive-behavioral flexibility in anorexia nervosa', in Adan, R. A. H. and Kaye, W. H. (Eds.), *Behavioral Neurobiology of Eating Disorders.* New York, NY: Springer-Verlag Publishing.

Garrido, G., Barrios, M., Penadés, R., Enríquez, M., Garolera, M., Aragay, N., Pajares, M., Vallès, V., Delgado, L., Alberni, J., Faixa, C. and Vendrell, J. M. (2013). Computer-assisted cognitive remediation therapy: Cognition, self-esteem and quality of life in schizophrenia. *Schizophrenia Research, 150*, (2–3), 563–569.

Gharaeipour, M. and Scott, B. J. (2012). Effects of cognitive remediation on neurocognitive functions and psychiatric symptoms in schizophrenia inpatients. *Schizophrenia Research, 142*, 165–170.

Halmi, K. A., Sunday, S. R., Klump, K. L., Strober, M., Leckman, J. F., Fichter, M., Kaplan, A., Woodside, B., Treasure, J., Berrettini, W. H., al Shabboat, M., Bulik, C. M. and Kaye, W. H. (2003). Obsessions and compulsions in anorexia nervosa subtypes. *International Journal of Eating Disorders, 33*, 308–319.

Hampshire, A., Duncan, J. and Owen, A. M. (2007). Selective tuning of the blood oxygenation level-dependent response during simple target detection dissociates human frontoparietal subregions. *The Journal of Neuroscience, 27*, 6219–6223.

Hay, P., Bacaltchuk, J., Claudino, A., Ben-Tovim, D. and Yong, P. Y. (2003). Individual psychotherapy in the outpatient treatment of adults with anorexia nervosa. *The Cochrane database of systematic reviews*, CD003909.

Herholz, K., Krieg, J. C., Emrich, H. M., Pawlik, G., Beil, C., Pirke, K. M., Pahl, J. J., Wagner, R., Wienhard, K., Ploog, D. *et al.* (1987). Regional cerebral glucose metabolism in anorexia nervosa measured by positron emission tomography. *Biological Psychiatry, 22*, 43–51.

Holliday, J., Tchanturia, K., Landau, S., Collier, D. and Treasure, J. (2005). Is impaired set-shifting an endophenotype of anorexia nervosa? *The American Journal of Psychiatry, 162*, 2269–2275.

Jaite, C., Pfeiffer, E., Lehmkuhl, U. and Salbach-Andrae, H. (2013). Traumatische kindheitserlebnisse bei jugendlichenmit anorexia nervosa im vergleich zu einer psychiatrischen und einer gesunden kontrollgruppe. *Zeitschrift für Kinder- und Jugendpsychiatrie und Psychotherapie, 41*, 99–108.

Kaye, W. H., Fudge, J. L. and Paulus, M. (2009). New insights into symptoms and neurocircuit function of anorexia nervosa. *Nature Reviews. Neuroscience, 10*, 573–584.

Konstantellou, A., Campbell, M., Eisler, I., Simic, M. and Treasure, J. (2011). Testing a cognitive model of generalized anxiety disorder in the eating disorders. *Journal of Anxiety Disorders, 25*, 864–869.

Lehrl, S. (2005). *Mehrfachwahl-Wortschatz-Intelligenztest.* Balingen: Spitta.

Lilenfeld, L. R. R., Wonderlich, S., Riso, L. P., Crosby, R. and Mitchell, J. (2006). Eating disorders and personality: A methodological and empirical review. *Clinical Psychology Review, 26*, 299–320.

Lock, J., Agras, W. S., Fitzpatrick, K. K., Bryson, S. W., Jo, B. and Tchanturia, K. (2013). Is outpatient cognitive remediation therapy feasible to use in randomized clinical trials for anorexia nervosa? *International Journal of Eating Disorders*, *46*, (6), 567–575.

Lounes, N., Khan, G. and Tchanturia, K. (2011). Assessment of cognitive flexibility in anorexia nervosa—Self-report or experimental measure? A brief report. *Journal of the International Neuropsychological Society*, *17*, 925–928.

Marsh, R., Horga, G., Wang, Z., Wang, P., Klahr, K. W., Berner, L. A., Walsh, B. T. and Peterson, B. S. (2011). An FMRI study of self-regulatory control and conflict resolution in adolescents with bulimia nervosa. *American Journal of Psychiatry*, *168*, 1210–1220.

Marsh, R., Steinglass, J. E., Gerber, A. J., Graziano O'Leary, K., Wang, Z., Murphy, D., Walsh, B. T. and Peterson, B. S. (2009). Deficient activity in the neural systems that mediate self-regulatory control in bulimia nervosa. *Archives of General Psychiatry*, *66*, 51–63.

Miyake, A., Friedman, N. P., Emerson, M. J., Witzki, A. H. and Howerter, A. (2000). The unity and diversity of executive functions and their contributions to complex 'frontal lobe' tasks: A latent variable analysis. *Cognitive Psychology*, *41*, 49–100.

Monchi, O., Petrides, M., Strafella, A. P., Worsley, K. J. and Doyon, J. (2006). Functional role of the basal ganglia in the planning and execution of actions. *Annals of Neurology*, *59*, 257–264.

Monsell, S. (2003). Task switching. *Trends in Cognitive Sciences*, 7, 134–140.

Muhlau, M., Gaser, C., Ilg, R., Conrad, B., Leibl, C., Cebulla, M. H., Backmund, H., Gerlinghoff, M., Lommer, P., Schnebel, A., Wohlschlager, A. M., Zimmer, C. and Nunnemann, S. (2007). Gray matter decrease of the anterior cingulate cortex in anorexia nervosa. *American Journal of Psychiatry*, *164*, 1850–1857.

Murthy, N. V., Mahncke, H., Wexler, B. E., Maruff, P., Inamdar, A., Zucchetto, M., Lund, J., Shabbir, S., Shergill, S., Keshavan, M., Kapur, S., Laruelle, M. and Alexander, R. (2012). Computerized cognitive remediation training for schizophrenia: an open label, multi-site, multinational methodology study. *Schizophrenia Research*, *139*, 87–91.

Naruo, T., Nakabeppu, Y., Deguchi, D., Nagai, N., Tsutsui, J., Nakajo, M. and Nozoe, S. (2001). Decreases in blood perfusion of the anterior cingulate gyri in anorexia nervosa Restricters assessed by SPECT image analysis. *BMC Psychiatry*, *1*, 2.

NICE (2004). Core interventions for the treatment and management of anorexia nervosa, bulimia nervosa and related eating disorders. *NICE Clinical Guideline No. 9*. National Institute for Clinical Excellence, UK.

Oreg, S. (2003). Resistance to change: Developing an individual differences measure. *Journal of Applied Psychology*, *88*, 680–693.

Oreg, S., Bayazit, M., Vakola, M., Arciniega, L., Armenakis, A., Barkauskiene, R., Bozionelos, N., Fujimoto, Y., Gonzalez, L., Han, J., Hrebickova, M., Jimmieson, N., Kordacova, J., Mitsuhashi, H., Mlacic, B., Feric, I., Topic, M. K., Ohly, S., Saksvik, P. O., Hetland, H., Saksvik, I. and van Dam, K. (2008). Dispositional resistance to change: Measurement equivalence and the link to personal values across 17 nations. *Journal of Applied Psychology*, *93*, 935–944.

Penades, R., Pujol, N., Catalan, R., Massana, G., Rametti, G., Garcia-Rizo, C., Bargallo, N., Gasto, C., Bernardo, M. and Junque, C. (2013). Brain effects of cognitive remediation therapy in schizophrenia: a structural and functional neuroimaging study. *Biological Psychiatry*, *73*, 1015–1023.

Roberts, M. E., Barthel, F. M. S., Lopez, C., Tchanturia, K. and Treasure, J. L. (2011). Development and validation of the Detail and Flexibility Questionnaire (DFlex) in eating disorders. *Eating Behaviors*, *12*, 168–174.

Roberts, M. E., Tchanturia, K. and Treasure, J. L. (2010). Exploring the neurocognitive signature of poor set-shifting in anorexia and bulimia nervosa. *Journal of Psychiatric Research*, *44*, 964–970.

Schmidt, U., Oldershaw, A., Jichi, F., Sternheim, L., Startup, H., Mcintosh, V., Jordan, J., Tchanturia, K., Wolff, G., Rooney, M., Landau, S. and Treasure, J. (2012). Out-patient psychological therapies for adults with anorexia nervosa: Randomized controlled trial. *The British Journal of Psychiatry, 201,* 392–399.

Schmidt, U. and Treasure, J. (2006). Anorexia nervosa: Valued and visible. A cognitive-interpersonal maintenance model and its implications for research and practice. *British Journal of Clinical Psychology, 45,* 343–366.

Schmitz, N., Rubia, K., Daly, E., Smith, A., Williams, S. and Murphy, D. G. M. (2006). Neural correlates of executive function in autistic spectrum disorders. *Biological Psychiatry, 59,* 7–16.

Serpell, L., Livingstone, A., Neiderman, M. and Lask, B. (2002). Anorexia nervosa: Obsessive-compulsive disorder, obsessive-compulsive personality disorder, or neither? *Clinical Psychology Review, 22,* 647–669.

Serpell, L., Neiderman, M., Haworth, E., Emmanueli, F. and Lask, B. (2003). The use of the Pros and Cons of anorexia nervosa (P-CAN) Scale with children and adolescents. *Journal of Psychosomatic Research, 54,* 567–571.

Serpell, L., Teasdale, J. D., Troop, N. A. and Treasure, J. (2004). The development of the P-CAN, a measure to operationalize the pros and cons of anorexia nervosa. *International Journal of Eating Disorders, 36,* 416–433.

Serpell, L., Treasure, J., Teasdale, J. and Sullivan, V. (1999). Anorexia nervosa: Friend or foe? *International Journal of Eating Disorders, 25,* 177–186.

Shafritz, K. M., Kartheiser, P. and Belger, A. (2005). Dissociation of neural systems mediating shifts in behavioral response and cognitive set. *Neuroimage, 25,* 600–606.

Shott, M. E., Filoteo, J. V., Bhatnagar, K. A. C., Peak, N. J., Hagman, J. O., Rockwell, R., Kaye, W. H. and Frank, G. K. W. (2012). Cognitive set-shifting in anorexia nervosa. *European Eating Disorders Review, 20,* 343–349.

Simon, J. R. and Rudell, A. P. (1967). Auditory SR compatibility: The effect of an irrelevant cue on information processing. *Journal of Applied Psychology,* 51, 300–304.

Snyder, L. H., Batista, A. P. and Andersen, R. A. (2000). Intention-related activity in the posterior parietal cortex: a review. *Vision Research, 40,* 1433–1441.

Sternheim, L., Konstantellou, A., Startup, H. and Schmidt, U. (2011a). What does uncertainty mean to women with anorexia nervosa? An interpretive phenomenological analysis. *European Eating Disorders Review, 19,* 12–24.

Sternheim, L., Startup, H. and Schmidt, U. (2011b). An experimental exploration of behavioral and cognitive–emotional aspects of intolerance of uncertainty in eating disorder patients. *Journal of Anxiety Disorders, 25,* 806–812.

Tagay, S., Schlegl, S. and Senf, W. (2010). Traumatic events, posttraumatic stress symptomatology and somatoform symptoms in eating disorder patients. *European Eating Disorders Review, 18,* 124–132.

Tchanturia, K., Davies, H. and Campbell, I. C. (2007). Cognitive remediation therapy for patients with anorexia nervosa: Preliminary findings. *Annals of General Psychiatry, 6,* 14.

Tchanturia, K., Davies, H., Lopez, C., Schmidt, U., Treasure, J. and Wykes, T. (2008). Letter to the Editor: Neuropsychological task performance before and after cognitive remediation in anorexia nervosa: A pilot case-series. *Psychological Medicine, 38,* 1371–1373.

Tchanturia, K., Harrison, A., Davies, H., Roberts, M., Oldershaw, A., Nakazato, M., Stahl, D., Morris, R., Schmidt, U. and Treasure, J. (2011). Cognitive flexibility and clinical severity in eating disorders. *PLoS ONE, 6.*

Tchanturia, K., Morris, R. G., Anderluh, M. B., Collier, D. A., Nikolaou, V. and Treasure, J. (2004). Set shifting in anorexia nervosa: An examination before and after weight gain, in full recovery and relationship to childhood and adult OCPD traits. *Journal of Psychiatric Research, 38,* 545–552.

Trapp, W., Landgrebe, M., Hoesl, K., Lautenbacher, S., Gallhofer, B., Gunther, W. and Hajak, G. (2013). Cognitive remediation improves cognition and good cognitive performance increases time to relapse – results of a 5 year catamnestic study in schizophrenia patients. *BMC Psychiatry, 13,* 184.

Treasure, J., Claudino, A. and Zucker, N. (2010). Eating disorders. *The Lancet, 375,* 583–593.

Uher, R., Brammer, M. J., Murphy, T., Campbell, I. C., Ng, V. W., Williams, S. C. and Treasure, J. (2003). Recovery and chronicity in anorexia nervosa: brain activity associated with differential outcomes. *Biological Psychiatry*, *54*, 934–942.

Wechsler, D. (1997). *Wechsler memory scale (3rd edn.)*. San Antonio, TX, US: Psychological Corporation.

Wittchen, H. U., Zaudig, M. and Fydrich, T. (1997). *Structural Clinical Interview for DSM-IV (SKID-I and SKID-II)* [in German]. Göttingen: Hogrefe.

Wykes, T., Reeder, C., Williams, C., Corner, J., Rice, C. and Everitt, B. (2003). Are the effects of cognitive remediation therapy (CRT) durable? Results from an exploratory trial in schizophrenia. *Schizophrenia Research*, *61*, 163–174.

Zastrow, A., Kaiser, S., Stippich, C., Walther, S., Herzog, W., Tchanturia, K., Belger, A., Weisbrod, M., Treasure, J. and Friederich, H. C. (2009). Neural correlates of impaired cognitive-behavioral flexibility in anorexia nervosa. *American Journal of Psychiatry*, *166*, 608–616.

PART III

Adaptations of CRT
in young people with AN

8

COGNITIVE REMEDIATION THERAPY WITH CHILDREN AND ADOLESCENTS

Kathleen Kara Fitzpatrick and James D. Lock

Given the increasing interest in the use of cognitive remediation or cognitive rehabilitation programs with adults (Chapters 1, 2, 3, 4, 5, 6), it is hardly surprising that efforts have been made to modify programs for use with children and adolescents. Protocols for the use of CRT exist for such disparate challenges as traumatic brain injury, post-chemotherapy cognitive challenges, Attention Deficit Hyperactivity Disorder (ADHD), Obsessive-Compulsive Disorder (OCD) and eating disorders (EDs). While the use of these protocols is based on similar characteristics – targeting specific areas of neurocognitive inefficiencies or injury, with a goal of generalizing behaviour change over time – work with children and adolescents is also marked by specific challenges (see Chapter 9). Most importantly, brain development in this group is ongoing, and protocols must be sensitive both to rehabilitation of skills that may have been lost, as well as training nascent skills in development. Symptoms associated with psychopathology may also vary with age (e.g. effects of chemotherapy at younger ages is distinctly different from those encountered in adulthood).

Finally, children and adolescents may lack the metacognitive skills necessary to independently implement and practice skills gained in treatment. This chapter will outline the challenges facing those who are adapting CRT protocols for use with children and adolescents, particularly in relation to anorexia nervosa (AN).

Background

Childhood and adolescence have long been assumed to be a period of significant neuroplasticity, with the brain responding to environmental and maturational demands to shape development towards more efficient 'adult' brain processes (Casey and Jones, 2010; Casey *et al.*, 2011; Blakemore and Chowdhury, 2006). This maturation occurs though a combination of apoptosis (cell death) and synaptic proliferation (synaptogenesis), which enable the brain to be responsive to environmental challenges while refining and maximizing important connections. Synaptogenesis provides the basis for reinforcing cognitive processes – such that what 'fires together wires together', making these connections stronger (Lask and Frampton, 2011; Jetha and Segalowitz, 2012; Seigel, 2012). Further, adolescent brains are at the peak of myelination, increasing speed and efficiency of existing connections. All of this sets the stage for impressive changes in cognitive functioning across childhood and adolescence.

These neurological changes are reflected in significant behavioural changes across adolescence (Somerville *et al.*, 2013; Casey and Jones, 2010; Casey *et al.*, 2011; Blakemore and Chowdhury, 2006). The advent of greater attention to emotionally salient stimuli, the decreased salience of risk versus the increased drive towards reward and generally greater impulsivity, combine to make adolescence a time of increasing independence and exploration. Not surprisingly, this corresponds to an increased risk of injury, substance use and psychopathology during the period of ages twelve to twenty-four. Although most adolescents manage the transition to adulthood without the development of psychopathology, the changes and challenges in maturation make adolescence an ideal time to also solidify health and wellness behaviours. Among these are consolidating the executive functions that underlie the transition from an adolescent to an 'adult' brain.

Cognitive rehabilitation or remediation models, (as described throughout this chapter) have been developed to target challenges in neurocognitive processes following injury, illness or in the presence of specific neurocognitive deficits, such as those seen in schizophrenia. These therapies aim to assist the brain with 'rewiring' and addressing areas of cognitive deficits through skilled practice (Moore and Mateer, 2001; Moore Sohlberg and Turkstra, 2011). CRT draws inspiration from a range of disciplines including psychology, speech/language pathology, occupational and physical therapy (Moore and Mateer, 2001; Moore Sohlberg and Turkstra, 2011). Within the realm of psychopathology, the purpose is not symptom abatement through direct remediation, but rather support for more targeted development of skills and development of cognitive processes that support health-related behaviours. This may take the form of work with basic perception up to development of more sophisticated tasks that address executive functioning challenges.

Adults vs adolescents

Inconsistencies

Although it would appear that neurocognitive rehabilitation should be ideal for use with children and adolescents, the literature demonstrates a paucity of approaches using these tenets in younger ages. Articles exist outlining the use of CRT in children following chemotherapy (Nazemi and Butler, 2011; Masneri and Bolis, 2011), cerebral palsy (Akhutina *et al.*, 2003), Attention-Deficit Hyperactivity

Disorder (ADHD) (O'Connell *et al.*, 2006), and schizophrenia (Wykes *et al.*, 2007, 2009; Oie *et al.*, 2011; Ueland and Rund, 2004, 2005). Further, evaluation of neuropsychological functioning and, to a lesser extent, inefficiencies, have been documented in a wide range of psychopathology in children and adolescents, most within the area of eating disorders, mood disorders and obsessive-compulsive disorders (Bowie *et al.*, 2013a, 2013b; Brown *et al.*, 2012; Casey *et al.*, 2011; Casey and Jones, 2010). Interestingly, the data on neurocognitive features in adolescents appears to demonstrate greater resiliency and intact cognitive functioning compared to adults with the same disorder (Dahlgren *et al.*, 2013b, 2013c; Fitzpatrick *et al.*, 2012; Tenconi *et al.*, 2010; Stedal *et al.*, 2012; Rose *et al.*, 2011, 2012, 2013).

However, given the significant variability in executive functioning presentation amongst adolescents, this population may not demonstrate the same degree of cognitive challenges associated with psychopathology as adults (Lang *et al.*, 2013 and Chapter 1 for more details). The presence of specific neurocognitive profiles may be obscured when looking at group means, which include those who will recover during adolescence as well as those with risk for greater chronicity. Additionally, there is the possibility of a sensitive period for the development of these skills by late adolescence. Failure to practice and secure neurocognitive skills by adulthood may contribute to illness chronicity. Insufficient sample sizes and lack of longitudinal data make it challenging to explore the relationship between neurocognitive development and psychopathology more explicitly.

Available data

The discrepancy between adults and adolescents in cognitive functioning is particularly evident in the eating disorders. While mounting evidence indicates that adults with AN have challenges with excessive inhibition (Lask and Frampton, 2011), set-shifting (Chapter 1; Holliday *et al.*, 2005; Lounes *et al.*, 2011; Roberts *et al.*, 2007; Tchanturia *et al.*, 2011, 2012) and central coherence (Lang *et al.*, 2014; Fonville *et al.*, 2013; Harrison *et al.*, 2011; Lopez *et al.*, 2008a, 2008b, 2009), similar data looking at adolescents has failed to uniformly replicate these inefficiencies (Chapter 1; Fitzpatrick *et al.*, 2012; Stedal *et al.*, 2012; Lang *et al.*, 2013). Virtually no work has been done with children, given the paucity of cases that present below age 10. Adolescents may differ from adults for several reasons.

Adolescence is a peak age of onset for these disorders, particularly AN, and only a subset of those who have AN in adolescence will go on to have a chronic eating disorder. Given that these features are in development and there may be a sensitive period of the development of a chronic form of AN, adolescents may represent distinct groups in which cognitive endophenotypes (see Chapter 1) may distinguish between those with a greater risk for chronicity. It could also be that intervention during adolescence may prevent cases from developing greater chronicity. Thus, there is significant utility in rehabilitation models for the development of 'everyday' attention memory and executive functioning behaviours amongst adolescents with

AN, even in the absence of specific neurocognitive profiles suggesting some inefficiencies.

Despite the lack of evidence for consistent group-based difficulties in neuropsychological functioning in adolescents, there is considerable clinical observation of these traits, which appear to map well on to adult manifestations of AN. Adolescents present with the same cognitive rigidity, overly-detailed focus, perseverative attentional difficulties and limitations in metacognitive ability that adults with AN also demonstrate in a therapeutic setting. It may be that the traditional paper-and-pencil measures of assessment that accurately capture neurocognitive inefficiencies in adults with AN are not as sensitive to the challenges presented to adolescents (Bodnar et al., 2007; Schmitter-Edgecombe and Chaytor, 2003; McAuliffe et al., 2006).

Finally, when comparing profiles of adults to adolescents with AN, it has been noted that adolescents often have a significant discrepancy between their IQ and their executive functioning skills (Strauss et al., 2006). Thus, while both may be falling at or above the 'average' range, this may be obscuring actual challenges, as executive skills have been seen to be well below IQ scores, indicating individual weaknesses. Thus, despite the clinical evidence for specific group weaknesses in these skills for adolescents, it is likely that challenges exist in at least a subset of these participants.

Developmental modifications for CRT-AN for adolescents

CRT protocols for adolescents with AN have been developed for inpatient use (Fitzpatrick, unpublished manual; Dahlgren et al., 2013a), for outpatient use (Fitzpatrick, op. cit.), group (Chapter 9) and family use (Chapter 10). These manuals present with similar principals and structure (Chapter 1) and some significant departures from those originally developed with adults (Tchanturia et al., 2007, 2010 (clinical) manuals). Generally speaking, the principles guiding CRT for eating disorders are based on clinical observations and data from translational neuroscience assessments which indicate challenges in set-shifting, central coherence, inhibition and emotional awareness (described in Chapters 1, 6, 7, 8, 10). The principles guiding CRT focus on the implementation of tasks that address these underlying challenges without a specific focus on symptoms. Rather, the focus is on tasks that present sufficient challenges with the process of thinking, which are then practiced in an engaging, interactive fashion until such skills progress. CRT is designed to be adaptive, in that it allows for different levels of entry for participants based specifically upon their skill levels and advancement based upon skill-acquisition. All tasks were developed to target skill acquisition in the realms described above and are aligned with the principles of adult CRT. Modifications between adult and adolescent protocols addressed developmental differences between these groups and focused largely on supporting metacognitive skill acquisition for younger patients.

Modifications for adolescent AN CRT were supported from a series of assessments of adolescents on an inpatient unit. Tasks were piloted with 52 adolescents, all of whom were diagnosed with AN or Eating Disorder Not Otherwise Specified with significant dietary restriction and weight loss (ED NOS AN). Participants were hospitalised due to medical instability secondary to their eating disorder. In the first set of 25 participants tasks were delivered without any specific ordering or expectations for task performance. At times several of the 'levels' of a task were presented in succession and rated by participants for difficulty. In other sessions tasks were presented in differing order to understand whether ordering of presentation made a difference for participants in their approach to the tasks. Feedback was also solicited regarding task difficulty and prompts, with an eye towards improving our wording and addressing development.

Different measures

Another seminal difference was the use of different measures to assess intellectual functioning and executive functioning. We utilized the Ravello Profile to select most of these tasks. As a screening task for executive functioning we utilized the Delis-Kaplan Executive Functioning System (DKEFS) which provides standardized tests of traditional neuropsychological assessments that are normed for ages 8–80. The wide age range for this assessment allowed us to evaluate children, adolescents and adults on tasks with the same structure, administration and norming properties. Additionally, test selection focused on tasks that had norms for younger ages (e.g. WCST, Hooper, Rey Complex Figure Task). Some assessment tools not normed for adolescents (e.g. Brixton, Hayling) were also utilized but are not reported until a sufficient norming sample of healthy controls can be presented to provide comparison data.

Differences

In our development, several critical change parameters were identified: first, adolescents varied considerably in their presentation, much more so than the adults who completed similar studies of CRT in an outpatient setting using a similar manual (Lock *et al.*, 2013). This translated into the need to create 'stepped tasks' which presented material at increasing levels of difficulty, which also had multiple opportunities for practice at each level. For example, simple line illusions were often familiar to our adolescents: they had been exposed to them at school or through social media. As a result of this familiarity, knowing both how to complete the task and knowing what the alternate image would be mean they could complete the task, often without being able to identify and switch between the two elements.

Second, adolescents often were quite quick at both understanding the tasks and typically approached the tasks with much greater speed than is evident in our experience with adults. This was true even when neuropsychological assessments had identified fairly profound psychomotor slowness on the Delis-Kaplan Executive Functioning System (DKEFS) motor speed task of the trails. The familiarity with paper-and-pencil tasks completed in a more 'academic' setting (e.g. interactive, need for completion before moving to the next task) likely led to greater ease of production in a setting such as this. This was marked compared to our adult patients, who often expressed worries about their production or used the time in what they identified as more 'therapeutic' activities – most often talking about interpersonal difficulties. In some cases, adults worked to make CRT more like traditional psychotherapy, while adolescents approached CRT more as though it was school-work.

The tendency to approach a task more as a 'school based task' often made the use of metacognitive strategy induction more challenging. As students, our participants were familiar and comfortable with producing work, but less confident in identifying and sharing the ways in which they approached the tasks, highlighting an emphasis on outcome instead of process. These difficulties are also strongly influenced by development, as individual differences in metacognition are wide-ranging. Metacognition emphasizes an ability to both be aware of thought processes underlying behaviour, including aspects of planning and management, as well as thought monitoring. As such, metacognition necessarily develops in the context of expanding breadth and depth of executive skills. While adolescents were often clearly adopting a strategy (e.g. skipping a challenging problem, returning to complete it at a later time), and could recognize their use of strategy when presented with options, they often had difficulty generating a description of their approach.

Assistance

Several steps were necessary to assist adolescents in developing metacognitive skills. First, therapists provided direct instruction around metacognition, providing education on what this is and why such strategies are important. Several different explanations were provided, allowing therapists flexibility in helping participants understand: some focusing on mindfulness (metacognition is the 'noticing' that goes on when one meditates, you notice your thoughts and can think about them without doing anything about them), more traditional 'thinking about your thinking, stepping back from what you are thinking to notice patterns about your thoughts or your behaviour, like when you feel rushed you might notice that your thoughts are faster, more rushed, but when you are calm they may be slower and 'lazier.' We also modelled metacognition in early sessions, for those having more difficulty engaging with these skills. This typically involved the therapist completing a task and then disclosing the relevant process of thinking and self-observation of cognition and performance. The manual was developed with specific queries to guide awareness and metacognitive processing. These ranged from prompts to explicit questioning and guidance in adopting different approaches to tasks. The latter were only used for participants who struggled in applying these skills with less guidance. Finally, we found our adolescent sample to rely heavily on their intact, often superior, verbal abilities to compensate for performance on many tasks. Teens were comfortable with the verbal 'back and forth' of ideas and didactics, but far less comfortable with verbalizing self-generated observations.

Practice choices

There remains a question of the issue of spaced versus massed practice for maximum benefit from CRT. For skill acquisition, there is a most definite emphasis on the use of massed practice until the skill reaches threshold competence, then spaced practice to maintain these skills. In an outpatient setting, however, massed practice presents greater challenges, given the time commitment for patients and families and the disruption of tasks of everyday living. These are naturally suspended during an inpatient admission and, in such a setting, an emphasis on massed practice is ideal. This is also true based on the differences in symptom acuity, with hospitalised patients generally presenting with greater acuity and benefiting from more frequent practice. Our implementation of CRT on an inpatient unit underscored the benefits of this approach in such a setting, as the modular, individualized approach was particularly well-suited to a setting where participants had significant time to work on these tasks while the ability to stop/start these tasks allowed for interruptions during meals and medical monitoring. We addressed these concerns by presenting both groups with 'homework' with a greater emphasis in outpatient treatment on the daily practice of these skills in a setting that would maximize their ecological validity. For example, for those with central coherence difficulties, applying concepts directly to writing assignments proved beneficial.

Finally, adolescents presented some unexpected challenges. One of the most significant was that adolescents frequently expressed a belief that the tasks had a 'hidden meaning' or that they were being tricked in some way. Despite assurances that this was not the case, indeed it became part of our introduction of CRT, adolescents frequently asked 'so what was the *real* purpose of that task?' or 'What was the hidden meaning?' Additionally, once exposed to tasks, adolescents also used social media and internet tools to attempt to solve tasks or anticipate future tasks. At times this became competitive between patients and their friends or family and removed some of the playfulness of the tasks. Participants often inquired about the performance of other adolescents in a more general way, 'Did I do this task better than other people my age?' in a way that was less pronounced and persistent in our experience with adult patients.

Sample CRT exercises

We have provided an overview of the session schedules for 18 sessions of CRT for adolescents, in our outpatient model (see Table 8.1 – a table of tasks presented by sample session). Tasks are presented successively, but not all tasks are presented in each session (see Figure 8.1 – sample session 4). One significant adaptation was the development of several 'layers' for each task, such that participants could practice tasks of similar levels of difficulty until they reached a level of mastery. For example, although 'geometric figures' are scheduled for each session, if a participant had difficulty with early figures, several alternate forms of comparable levels of difficulty could be presented for some of the following sessions, until the participant was

TABLE 8.1 CRT Task presentation across sessions

Task presentation by session number	1	2	3	4	5	6	7	8	9	10	11	12	13	14
Geometric Figures	X	X	X	X	X	X	X	X	X	X	X	X	X	X
Illusion Task	X	X	X	X	X	X	X	X	X	X	X	X	X	X
Stroop Task	X	X	X	X	X	X	X	X	X	X	X	X	X	X
Manipulations	X	X	X	X	X									
Line Bisection	X	X	X	X	X	X	X	X	X	X				
Infinity Signs	X	X	X	X	X	X	X	X	X	X				
Set Game	X	X	X	X	X	X				X	X	X	X	X
Hand Tasks	X	X	X	X	X	X	X	X	X					
Qbitz	X	X	X	X	X	X	X	X	X	X				
Rebus		X	X	X	X	X								
Switching Attention					X									
The Main Idea							X	X	X	X	X	X		
Embedded Words							X	X	X	X	X	X	X	X
Maps							X	X	X	X	X	X	X	X
Behavioral Tasks	X	X	X	X	X	X	X	X	X	X	X	X	X	X

X indicates a task is performed in that session

- *Review behavioral tasks*
- *Geometric figure*
  - 1 task from Set 4 of Geometric figures
    - Note: If task was challenging at the previous session, use one from the last set that was completed with moderate difficulty
    - Note: You may present more than one figure if these are completed quickly
- *Illusion task*
  - Rotation illusion: magician/rabbit
- *Stroop*
  - Odds/evens
  - Note: if task was challenging at the previous session, return to the exact same task and repeat before presenting Odds/evens; if the repeated task remains difficult, do not present Odds/evens
- *Line Bisection*
  - Vertical design lines (dashed, dotted)
- *Infinity Signs*
- *Set*
  - Set puzzle book Puzzle 15
  - Note: If task was challenging at the previous session can do any previous puzzle that was not already completed
- *Hand Tasks*
  - All fingers tapping
    - Note: if all fingers tapping is completed easily, no further presentations of this task are necessary
  - Hand flip
- *Qbitz*
  - 2 cards from Qbitz-pack #2
  - Note: Continue to present cards from packs that present the participant with a moderate challenge
- *Rebus*
  - Choose 3 cards from pack #1

FIGURE 8.1 Sample session 4 for Outpatient 15 session CRT with adolescent AN

ready to move on to the next figure. Alternatively, if a task presented was completed effortlessly, more challenging materials could also be provided for practice in later sessions. This flexibility in development was necessary to address the variability in presentation amongst our adolescent patient population. In our experience, while this was present in the adult manual, adolescents presented with greatly discrepant skills and challenges in metacognitive ability in processing the tasks. The revisions made are described in more detail below.

CRT for Adolescent AN involves a number of different tasks and games, and efforts were made to streamline the use and production of these. In early iterations, we handmade many tasks, which presented challenges in expanding and replicating CRT across different therapists and settings. A major goal was streamlining administration and use of easily obtainable tools. Many of the tasks described here can be purchased online or through local retailers (where feasible, ordering information is provided below). When tasks that have been adapted directly from the adult CRT manuals (www.katetchanturia.com/#!publications/c1y51) are not reported here – even when there are modifications to these tasks for adolescents – these tasks are explained elsewhere in great detail. The novel tasks however, specifically added for adolescent version, are described here in more detail.

Novel tasks

SET® game – a widely available card game (Set Enterprises, Inc.; www.setgame. com) that focuses on matching by shading, colour, figure, number of elements presented in a set of cards. This can be played with multiple players and is similar to the principles behind the Wisconsin Card Sort Task (WCST). Problem-solving, organization and memory are all critical elements. Unlike the WCST, the organizing principles do not shift, but the participant needs to be able to shift their thinking to find all of the possible ways of sorting a limited number of cards using the principles listed above. In early tasks we utilized the New York Times SET® Puzzle Book (2010) with participants, to allow for an element of 'teaching the task.' In the puzzle book format, cards are presented together and there is a space below to write down each of the possible sets that can be created from the cards presented. After session 6, participants use the SET® card game – a faster, dynamic, interactive set-creating task – with the therapist. This task is also available for purchase as an app for most mobile phones and tablets, which allows for more individualized practice and play.

Adolescents reported finding this game quite enjoyable, and appreciated the iterative development of the task. Almost uniformly, adolescents reported being overwhelmed by the WCST (which they completed at baseline) and immediately recognized the similarities between SET® and the WCST. They noted that beginning with a more limited range of stimuli (a limited card set) for matching, and only four to six total sorts available helped them to think through their choices and develop strategies and patterns which could then be applied to more challenging materials. As a result, this task was also very useful in developing metacognitive strategies, such as how one might break a task down when presented with 'too much' information, identifying patterns in responses and where they struggled with matching principles, and taking the opportunity to practice more challenging sorts before the easier sorts. Additionally, with increases in task complexity, many participants were able to verbalize their response to frustration and feeling 'stuck', which provided opportunities to practice different skills when facing challenging emotional reactions.

Q-bitz™ – manufactured by MindWare™ (www.mindware.com/p/Q-bitz/44002), this provides an excellent visual–constructional task mapping well on to the Wechlser Block Design tasks. Q-bitz provides a set of blocks with coloured or white squares, squares that are half coloured and half white, and ones with a coloured background with a white dot or a white background with a coloured dot. They are presented in a nine-block matrix. The goal is to learn to identify patterns or integration of elements, solve visual–spatial problems and practice some visual motor integration without excessive fine motor demands (as seen in the Rey-Osterrieth Complex Figures). This task also allows for evaluation of planning, as some people approach the figure by working from the outside in, others work from one corner or break the design down into interrelated parts. This task has the 'answer' right in front of the participant, but the cards have been separated to tap increasing levels of ambiguity. The early cards use lines to demarcate each of the blocks in the design while later designs make extensive use of white space and do not show the discrimination between the individual blocks. This requires a higher level of integration and planning. Additional card sets are available for purchase. Tasks were divided to present increasing difficulties with perceptual challenge, and also decrease cues to discriminating between blocks.

In the first set of tasks, the target cards start with clear delineation between each square block. The next set increases the integration of simple shapes (blocks, diamonds) clearly made from single blocks and in a replicated pattern. This decreases demand, as once a pattern is 'figured out' it can be reproduced to achieve the remainder of the task. The third set has more complex, integrated shapes that still have a replicated pattern. The fourth set uses more white space and develops specific elements that 'twist' or spin and require integration of blocks in a way that may not be clear on the first assessment (white spaces may join in non-linear or unexpected ways). The fifth set continues to develop this theme, utilizing more 'cross bars' which are harder to make as they require using half-blocks to create the image. The sixth set uses random elements, lots of white space, and non-replicating patterns – although these may seem easier at first blush, getting the elements placed correctly is more challenging and the full pictures take longer to develop. The increasing use of 'white space' across the card sets means there is less segmentation between the blocks, much like later items in WISC/WAIS Block Design tasks that are more challenging for this population (Roberts *et al.*, 2013; Lopez *et al.*, 2008b).

Rebus – this task uses visual or graphical images to represent a word, idiom, common expression or saying. While these are tied to culture, such tasks can be created in almost any language. The goal is to use what you see, to think of the saying or phrase that is captured by the image. This is a verbal set-shifting task, as the common rules (e.g. reading the words) must be sacrificed for the goal of understanding how they work together in this context. In many ways this is like a verbal 'illusion' task. Once the answer is understood, it becomes quite clear and one should be able to move easily between the image itself and the 'meaning' of the image.

This can be useful for our sample, particularly given the relatively strong verbal skills in AN and the comparatively weaker perceptual skills. This is a way of introducing some set-shifting tasks into a domain at which our patients may be more facile. This is also ideal, as participants can try to work it out by saying strategies out loud, helping you identify those that they may be using. There are several strategies for solving these tasks: Some of the cards are set up so that the way the font/words are written provides the clue to the answer; the placement on the card may be the answer; the number of times an element is written might provide a clue; and finally, the way one would pronounce or describe the image ('a pair of dice' would be 'paradise') is a cue to solving the puzzle.

Alternate Uses – this is a verbal set-shifting task that challenges the participant(s) to identify alternative uses for common objects. The goal is to think 'outside the box' to identify unique ways objects can be used, based on their shape, size, colour or other properties. In this case, the common rules (e.g. eating an apple) are set aside to think of an uncharacteristic approach (e.g. cut it in half and use it as a way to stamp paint on fabric). This allows for creativity, brainstorming, and problem-solving skills. These aspects are all higher order executive functioning aspects and rest upon the ability to break set. This task starts by 'teaching the task,' with the therapist participating directly, taking turns in identifying common uses and providing target items that can generate multiple alternate uses.

For participants who find this task easy, more complex objects can be used (e.g. uses for a laptop); for those who find it harder, working through the task with them may be helpful. Task complexity can be increased by switching back and forth between two items (pencils, then oranges). There are several ways to identify alternative uses: based on the shape of the object (a laptop could be a serving tray, they are both rectangular); based on the colour of the object (a red bandana could also be a red flag); based in imagination (something you would like to see, but do not have, or an object that doesn't really exist, such as a pencil being used as a magic wand); or based on a derivation of a typical use (drawing in the sand with a pencil, rather than on paper).

Rush Hour™ – made by ThinkFun (www.thinkfun.com/rushhour), the purpose of this task is for the participant to develop problem-solving skills and balance inhibition with speed. This task also relies on memory. Puzzles start off with few items and increase in intensity until they are quite challenging and have many elements. Additionally, items often need to be moved 'backwards' rather than making progress towards the 'exit'. Reversals can be challenging, particularly for adolescent patients, as they tend to view movement towards a particular goal as critical and moving away from this goal as challenging. This task does not specifically fall under set-shifting or central coherence, but rather problem-solving and abstract thinking, being able to anticipate movements over time and 'plan ahead' in a visual–spatial manner. In many ways, this is a more complex version of the Towers task but it also includes the potential for perseverative responding – it is important to identify this and to work towards stopping it, in what is called an 'errorless learning' paradigm. If the same movement is made three times in a row, it is important to stop and suggest a different course of action, with a goal of breaking perseverative actions. This task requires the use of a tablet, and downloading the full version of the 'Rush Hour' application. Adolescents reported enjoying the use of a tablet-delivered task, and reported that this modality was both familiar and challenging. For those for whom technology is a limitation, a board game version of this game is also available and provides different levels of challenge cards to replicate the increasing difficulty of the computerized version.

Inpatient/outpatient

In the outpatient model described, the goal is repeated practice with tasks with increasing challenge, 'teaching the task' when necessary, and providing an array of tasks that tap verbal, non-verbal and motor processes. Outpatient sessions tend to be longer in length and focus on a variety of tasks. In contrast, inpatient CRT models, while utilizing the same tasks, are generally shorter in length and may provide more detailed practice on specific tasks. The latter change allows for greater adaptability, necessary with shorter lengths of stay in the hospital setting – at least among patients in US hospitals. Behavioural tasks are often more limited among inpatients, given the more restricted environment. Inpatients are, by definition, more acutely ill and thus are likely to fatigue more quickly than patients who are sufficiently stable for outpatient treatment. The modular nature of the tasks assists with this flexibility, allowing for doing only one task repeatedly, gaining skill with repetition or choosing a limited number of tasks.

Currently, the 18-session outpatient CRT protocol is being studied in a randomized clinical trial and data is not yet available. The study compares CRT to an ART therapy protocol specifically developed for adolescent AN. Participants are randomly assigned to either ART or CRT, all completing Family Based Therapy (FBT) and having AN or sub-threshold AN, and scoring above one standard deviation on measures of obsessionality (YBC-ED).

STUDY BACKGROUND AND PROTOCOL

KF was trained in *London workshop for CRT for Anorexia* (www.katetchanturia. com), and two additional workshops in Stanford were provided by Dr. Tchanturia. Pilot evaluations of inpatient CRT have been conducted, undergoing several revisions (Fitzpatrick, unpublished manual). This data included feasibility and acceptability data. On the inpatient unit, the goal was daily administration of forty minutes of CRT – administered by the first author (KF), and two advanced graduate students. Graduate students observed the first author in conducting sessions, then were observed themselves until it was felt that they reached fidelity to the model. In addition, these students also had the opportunity to train with Dr. Tchanturia during her visits to the site and were also required to view tapes of sessions conducted by Dr. Fitzpatrick. Neuropsychological assessments were conducted prior to initiating CRT.

On average there was a delay of 48 hours from the date of admission to starting testing. These delays were typically due to the time taken in gathering consent from parents (for patients under 18) and assent from the patient. Due to short hospital stays in the United States, an average of 7 sessions of CRT were administered, with a range of 4–10 sessions. This meant that patients were often discharged before completion of a 10-session inpatient CRT protocol, despite efforts of the administrators to provide daily sessions, including weekends.

Participant sample was of 54 adolescent females, with a mean age = 15.4 (SD = 1.93) years. Body weight was reflective of their diagnosis of restricting eating disorders with a mean % IBW = 82.13% (SD = 8.97) with 13.6% presenting with primary amenorrhoea, 59.1% with secondary amenorrhoea. Consent was obtained from parents/guardians and signed assent gathered from participants. Study was approved by our IRB and all participants were aware that they were participating in a study trial, and that participation was entirely voluntary.

Patient evaluations of CRT

CRT received generally positive reviews from patients, families and hospital staff in our case series and implementation studies with adolescents. Feedback was assessed both verbally and with questionnaires. One participant approached declined to participate, two more families declined: The participant declined as she felt she had 'sufficient treatment' without the need to complete additional training; one family declined due to concerns that their child would 'enjoy time in the hospital' and this would work against efforts towards a prompt discharge; the second family declined to state the reason for not participating. No participants discontinued treatment for any reason other than discharge.

On the Patient Satisfaction with Treatment (PST) measure, a combination of a Likert-type measure, rating treatment, as well as free response measure, participant responses indicated treatment was both perceived as useful (also described as 'positive' response to treatment) and effective. On the 10-point Likert scale, treatment was described positively (mean = 8; SD = 2.00) and effective (mean = 7.33; SD = 3.05). Participants also rated number and length of sessions as being 'just right' (mean = 6.5; SD = 2.12; and mean = 6; SD = 0, respectively).

Free response section comments on the PST included: 'This was very fun and helped me learn to think differently', 'I didn't think playing "games" could help my thinking but I can see that they can', and 'this helped me to think about my thinking and I can see how this can help me in school as well as maybe with my eating disorder.'

Comments

Participants and parents

Participants also provided direct feedback on tasks – both during and at the end of treatment – and on CRT generally, and many also suggested task modifications, such as rotating the Infinity Signs task to include 'figure eights'. Although initially there were concerns about the ability of this patient population to generalise these tasks to their everyday life, comments by participants reflected that tasks were similar to those they might complete in school. Additionally, participants felt that guided metacognitive strategy instruction was useful and of benefit in the treatment. General evaluation of the tasks tended to lean towards them being easy to average in difficulty. As a result, the protocols described above included more complex and comprehensive tasks.

Family comments were available from four parents of participants. The low response rate was typically due to therapists not being present for discharge and being unable to 'catch' parents while they were at the unit visiting their children (Note: efforts were made to provide therapy in a manner that did not interfere with parent visits). Parent reports indicated scepticism that tasks could be beneficial for the participant at the outset of treatment. End of treatment assessments indicated that these four parents felt that they learned about their child's thinking and that the participants had shared the tasks with them. This is consistent with Lask *et al.*'s work with families (Chapter 10), which underscored the interest in families, of learning and engaging in these tasks together. One parent, present but not participating during treatment, reported CRT was tremendously helpful in understanding eating disorder challenges as well as more general behaviour difficulties.

Staff

Staff comments, from attending psychiatrists, physicians and nursing staff, were highly favourable. The psychiatric team described patients as interested and enthusiastic about CRT treatment. Care team members also felt that information generated from the baseline assessment and subsequent skills follow-up were useful in case formulation. Nursing staff reported that participants would discuss tasks during meals or free choice time and would share their experiences with each other. Indeed, this led to patients requesting CRT, even if they did not qualify for study inclusion.

Overall, CRT as implemented in this and other studies (Chapters 5, 6, and Tchanturia *et al.*, 2013) appears to be feasible and acceptable to patients and their families. Further, reports from these studies also indicate that participants felt therapy was useful to them and could be applied both to specific eating disorder symptoms as well as more general quality of life issues (Chapter 6). Additional studies evaluating the relationship between CRT – both inpatient and outpatient – to neurocognition and eating disorder symptoms are necessary.

Future directions

As CRT with adolescents advances, several points are worth examining. First, identifying neurocognitive profiles associated with illness chronicity will help further refine and target treatments (see Chapter 1; Tchanturia and Lock, 2011). Refining the role of CRT as an adjunctive treatment is another area for further study. This is well-suited to child and adolescent eating disorders, given the availability of empirically supported treatments for this group; evaluating whether CRT sufficiently enhances treatment to increase recovery rates or resolution of specific symptoms. Additionally, given the state of flux of adolescent brain development, the efficacy of CRT protocols may be assessed not only by symptom resolution, but by resumption of a more typical neurocognitive trajectory. The expansion of CRT protocols to address other eating disorder diagnoses, such as Bulimia Nervosa, or as a preventative approach amongst those designated as being at-risk are important areas for further development.

References

Akhutina, T., Foreman, N., Krichevets, A., Matikka, L., Narhi, V., Pylaeva, N. and Vahakuopus, J. (2003). Improving spatial functioning in children with cerebral palsy using computerized and traditional game tasks. *Disability and Rehabilitation, 25*, 1361–1371.

Blakemore, S., and Chowdhury, S. (2006). Development of the adolescent brain: implications for executive function and social cognition. *Journal of Child Psychology and Psychiatry, 47*, 269–312.

Bodnar, L. E., Prahme, M. C., Cutting, L. E., Denckla, M. B. and Mahone, E. M. (2007). Construct validity of parent ratings of inhibitory control. *Child Neuropsychology, 13*, 345–362.

Bowie, C. R., Gupta, M. and Holshausen, K. (2013a). Cognitive remediation therapy for mood disorders: rationale, early evidence, and future directions. *Canadian Journal of Psychiatry, 58*, 319–325.

Bowie, C. R., Gupta, M., Holshausen, K., Jokic, R., Best, M. and Milev, R. (2013b). Cognitive remediation for treatment-resistant depression: effects on cognition and functioning and the role of online homework. *Journal of Nervous and Mental Disorders, 201*, 680–685.

Brown, T. T., Kuperman, J. M., Chung, Y., Erhart, M., McCabe, C., Hagler, D. J. Jr., Venkatraman, V. K., Akshoomoff, N., Amaral, D. G., Bloss, C. S., Casey, B. J., Chang, L., Ernst, T. M., Frazier, J. A., Gruen, J. R., Kaufmann, W. E., Kenet, T., Kennedy, D. N., Murray, S. S., Sowell, E. R., Jernigan, T. L. and Dale, A. M. (2012). Neuroanatomical assessment of biological maturity. *Current Biology, 22*, 1693–1698.

Casey, B., Jones, R. M. and Somerville, L. H. (2011). Braking and accelerating of the adolescent brain. *Journal of Research on Adolescence, 21*, 21–33.

Casey, B. J. and Jones, R. M. (2010). Neurobiology of the adolescent brain and behaviour: implications for substance use disorders. *Journal of the American Academy of Child and Adolescent Psychiatry, 49*, 1189–1201; quiz 1285.

Casey, B. J., Ruberry, E. J., Libby, V., Glatt, C. E., Hare, T., Soliman, F., Duhoux, S., Frielingsdorf, H. and Tottenham, N. (2011). Transitional and translational studies of risk for anxiety. *Depression and Anxiety, 28*, 18–28.

Dahlgren, C. L., Lask, B., Landrø, N. I. and Rø, Ø. (2013a). Developing and evaluating cognitive remediation therapy (CRT) for adolescents with anorexia nervosa: A feasibility study. *Clinical Child Psychology and Psychiatry*, PMID: 23761592.

Dahlgren, C. L., Lask, B., Landrø, N. I. and Rø, Ø. (2013b). Neuropsychological functioning in adolescents with anorexia nervosa before and after cognitive remediation therapy: a feasibility trial. *International Journal of Eating Disorders, 46*, 576–581.

Dahlgren, C. L., Lask, B., Landrø, N. I. and Rø, Ø. (2013c). Patient and parental self-reports of executive functioning in a sample of young female adolescents with anorexia nervosa before and after cognitive remediation therapy. *European Eating Disorders Review, 22*(1), 45–52.

Delahunty, A., Reeder, C., Wykes, T., Morice, R. and Newton, E. (2002). Cognitive remediation therapy: cognitive shift module.

Fitzpatrick, K. K., Darcy, A., Colborn, D., Gudorf, C. and Lock, J. (2012). Set-shifting among adolescents with anorexia nervosa. *International Journal of Eating Disorders, 45*, 909–912.

Fonville, L., Lao-Kaim, N. P., Giampietro, V., Van den Eynde, F., Davies, H., Lounes, N., Andrew, C., Dalton, J., Simmons, A., Williams, S. C., Baron-Cohen, S. and Tchanturia, K. (2013). Evaluation of enhanced attention to local detail in anorexia nervosa using the embedded figures test; an FMRI study. *PLoS One, 8*, e63964.

Harrison, A., Tchanturia, K. and Treasure, J. (2011). Measuring state trait properties of detail processing and global integration ability in eating disorders. *The World Journal of Biological Psychiatry, 12*, 462–472.

Holliday, J., Tchanturia, K., Landau, S., Collier, D. and Treasure, J. (2005). Is impaired set-shifting an endophenotype of anorexia nervosa? *The American Journal of Psychiatry, 162*, 2269–2275.

Jetha, M. and Segalowitz, S. (2012). *Adolescent Brain Development: Implications for Behaviour.* Waltham, MA: Academic Press.

Lang, K., Stahl, D., Espie, J., Treasure, J. and Tchanturia, K. (2013). Set shifting in children and adolescents with anorexia nervosa: an exploratory systematic review and meta-analysis. *International Journal of Eating Disorders, 47* (4), 394–399.

Lask, B. and Frampton, I. (Eds.) (2011). *Eating Disorders and the Brain.* West Sussex: Wiley-Blackwell.

Lock, J., Agras, W. S., Fitzpatrick, K. K., Bryson, S. W., Jo, B. and Tchanturia, K. (2013). Is outpatient cognitive remediation therapy feasible to use in randomized clinical trials for anorexia nervosa? *International Journal of Eating Disorders, 46*, 567–575.

Lopez, C., Tchanturia, K., Stahl, D., Booth, R., Holliday, J. and Treasure, J. (2008a). An examination of the concept of central coherence in women with anorexia nervosa. *International Journal of Eating Disorders, 41*, 143–152.

Lopez, C., Tchanturia, K., Stahl, D. and Treasure, J. (2008b). Central coherence in eating disorders: a systematic review. *Psychological Medicine, 38*, 1393–1404.

Lopez, C., Tchanturia, K., Stahl, D. and Treasure, J. (2009). Weak central coherence in eating disorders: a step towards looking for an endophenotype of eating disorders. *Journal of Clinical and Experimental Neuropsychology, 31*, 117–125.

Lounes, N., Khan, G. and Tchanturia, K. (2011). Assessment of cognitive flexibility in anorexia nervosa – self-report or experimental measure? A brief report. *Journal of the International Neuropsychological Society, 17*, 925–928.

Masneri, S. and Bolis, T. (2011). Late neurocognitive effects in children and adolescents who have undergone oncological treatment: a rehabilitation model. *Giornale Italiano di Medicina del Lavoro ed Ergonomia, 33*, A37–40.

McAuliffe, M. D., Hubbard, J. A., Rubin, R. M., Morrow, M. T. and Dearing, K. F. (2006). Reactive and proactive aggression: stability of constructs and relations to correlates. *Journal of Genetic Psychology, 167,* 365–382.

Moore, S. M. and Mateer, C. (2001). *Cognitive Rehabilitiation: An Integrative Neuropsychological Approach.* New York: Guilford Press.

Moore Sohlberg, M. and Turkstra, L. S. (2011). *Optimizing Cognitive Rehabilitation: Effective Instructional Methods.* New York, NY: Guilford Press.

Nazemi, K. J. and Butler, R. W. (2011). Neuropsychological rehabilitation for survivors of childhood and adolescent brain tumors: a view of the past and a vision for a promising future. *Journal of Pediatric Rehabilitation Medicine, 4,* 37–46.

O'Connell, R. G., Bellgrove, M. A., Dockree, P. M. and Robertson, I. H. (2006). Cognitive remediation in ADHD: effects of periodic non-contingent alerts on sustained attention to response. *Neuropsychological Rehabilitation, 16,* 653–665.

Oie, M., Sundet, K. and Ueland, T. (2011). Neurocognition and functional outcome in early-onset schizophrenia and attention-deficit/hyperactivity disorder: a 13-year follow-up. *Neuropsychology, 25,* 25–35.

Roberts, M. E., Tchanturia, K., Stahl, D., Southgate, L. and Treasure, J. (2007). A systematic review and meta-analysis of set-shifting ability in eating disorders. *Psychological Medicine, 37,* 1075–1084.

Roberts, M. E., Tchanturia, K. and Treasure, J. L. (2013). Is attention to detail a similarly strong candidate endophenotype for anorexia nervosa and bulimia nervosa? *World Journal of Biological Psychiatry, 14,* 452–463.

Rose, M., Davis, J., Frampton, I. and Lask, B. (2011). The Ravello Profile: development of a global standard neuropsychological assessment for young people with anorexia nervosa. *Clinical Child Psychology and Psychiatry, 16,* 195–202.

Rose, M., Frampton, I. and Lask, B. (2012). A case series investigating distinct neuropsychological profiles in children and adolescents with anorexia nervosa. *European Eating Disorders Review, 20,* 32–38.

Rose, M., Frampton, I. J. and Lask, B. (2013). Central coherence, organizational strategy, and visuospatial memory in children and adolescents with anorexia nervosa. *Applied Neuropsychology. Child.,* DOI: 10.1080/21622965.2013.775064.

Schmitter-Edgecombe, M. and Chaytor, N. S. (2003). Self-ordered pointing performance following severe closed-head injury. *Journal of Clinical and Experimental Neuropsychology, 25,* 918–932.

Seigel, D. J. (2012). *The Developing Mind: How Relationships and the Brain Interact to Shape Who You Are.* New York: Guilford Press.

Somerville, L. H., Jones, R. M., Ruberry, E. J., Dyke, J. P., Glover, G. and Casey, B. J. (2013). The medial prefrontal cortex and the emergence of self-conscious emotion in adolescence. *Psychological Science, 24,* 1554–1562.

Stedal, K., Rose, M., Frampton, I., Landro, N. I. and Lask, B. (2012). The neuropsychological profile of children, adolescents, and young adults with anorexia nervosa. *Archives of Clinical Neuropsychology, 27,* 329–337.

Strauss, E., Sherman, E. and Spreen, O. (2006). *A Compendium of Neuropsychological Tests: Administration, norms and commentary.* Oxford: Oxford University Press.

Tchanturia, K., Davies, H. and Campbell, I. C. (2007). Cognitive remediation therapy for patients with anorexia nervosa: preliminary findings. *Annals of General Psychiatry, 6,* 14.

Tchanturia, K., Davies, H., Roberts, M., Harrison, A., Nakazato, M., Schmidt, U., Treasure, J. and Morris, R. (2012). Poor cognitive flexibility in eating disorders: examining the evidence using the Wisconsin Card Sorting Task. *PLoS One, 7,* e28331.

Tchanturia, K., Harrison, A., Davies, H., Roberts, M., Oldershaw, A., Nakazato, M., Stahl, D., Morris, R., Schmidt, U. and Treasure, J. (2011). Cognitive flexibility and clinical severity in eating disorders. *PLoS One, 6,* e20462.

Tchanturia, K., Lloyd, S. and Lang, K. (2013). Cognitive remediation in eating disorders. *International Journal of Eating Disorders, Special Issue, 46* (5), 492–496.

Tchanturia, K. and Lock, J. (2011). Cognitive remediation therapy for eating disorders: development, refinement and future directions. *Current Topics in Behavioral Neurosciences*, 6, 269–87.

Tenconi, E., Santonastaso, P., Degortes, D., Bosello, R., Titton, F., Mapelli, D. and Favaro, A. (2010). Set-shifting abilities, central coherence, and handedness in anorexia nervosa patients, their unaffected siblings and healthy controls: exploring putative endophenotypes. *World Journal of Biological Psychiatry*, 11, 813–823.

Ueland, T. and Rund, B. R. (2004). A controlled randomized treatment study: the effects of a cognitive remediation program on adolescents with early onset psychosis. *Acta Psychiatrica Scandinavica*, 109, 70–74.

Ueland, T. and Rund, B. R. (2005). Cognitive remediation for adolescents with early onset psychosis: a 1-year follow-up study. *Acta Psychiatrica Scandinavica*, 111, 193–201.

Wykes, T., Newton, E., Landau, S., Rice, C., Thompson, N. and Frangou, S. (2007). Cognitive remediation therapy (CRT) for young early onset patients with schizophrenia: an exploratory randomized controlled trial. *Schizophrenia Research*, 94, 221–230.

Wykes, T., Reeder, C., Landau, S., Matthiasson, P., Haworth, E. and Hutchinson, C. (2009). Does age matter? Effects of cognitive rehabilitation across the age span. *Schizophrenia Research*, 113, 252–258.

9

EVALUATION OF A COGNITIVE REMEDIATION THERAPY GROUP FOR ADOLESCENTS WITH ANOREXIA NERVOSA IN A DAY PATIENT SETTING

Natalie Pretorius, Jonathan Espie and Mima Simic

Background

The typical onset of anorexia nervosa (AN) in adolescence, a time of major biological, social, and cognitive change, can have severely negative consequences for many areas of the young person's life (Smink *et al.* 2012). The current recommended treatment for anorexia nervosa (AN) in children and adolescents in the UK is family therapy (NICE 2004), based on empirical findings that involve the family in treatment, and is effective in combating the AN symptoms and in facilitating recovery (Eisler *et al.* 1997). This differs from treatment for adult AN for which there is no single recommended treatment (NICE 2004). Despite this, however, most people do not access specialist treatment (Hoek and van Hoeken 2003). Of those who do, 10–20% of young people who develop AN will not respond to family therapy and will need alternative methods of treatment in order to recover from the illness (Smink *et al.* 2012). A subset of these young people are often admitted to inpatient or day patient settings. Developing new, innovative, and effective early interventions for these young people with AN is crucial in order to prevent disruption to development, a poor prognosis, and long-term difficulties that persist into adulthood. As well as the invaluable positive impact on the lives of young people and their families, there are considerable implications from the perspective of health economics.

Group interventions for adolescents are commonly used in inpatient and day-patient settings for a variety of different psychiatric disorders. The benefits of providing therapeutic interventions in a group context include enhancing social skills and relationships, sharing and normalising difficulties/symptoms, and generating a diversity of ideas and solutions from different perspectives. Children and adolescents in particular may be familiar with groups from school settings. Carrying out therapeutic groups within inpatient or day patient settings also provides the opportunity to provide effective treatments to larger numbers of people.

Cognitive remediation therapy (CRT), described in previous chapters (2, 3, 4, 5), has been developed and piloted in adult inpatient populations, and is based on findings that adults with AN have difficulties in set-shifting, resulting in a tendency towards rigid thinking and behaviours (e.g. Tchanturia *et al.* 2011, 2012; Roberts *et al.* 2007). There is also a tendency in a group of adult patients with AN, towards a predominance of a detail-focused style of thinking often at the expense of more gistful, holistic thinking, resulting in a propensity to get 'stuck' in the details (e.g. Lang *et al.* 2014; Harrison *et al.* 2012; Lopez *et al.* 2008). Benefits of CRT have included greater cognitive and behavioural flexibility, greater readiness to engage in other types of treatment such as cognitive behavioural therapy (CBT), and a positive experience of therapy promoting engagement in treatment (Genders and Tchanturia 2008).

Research

Research into the neurocognitive profiles of adolescent AN populations is still in its infancy and it is yet unclear whether the same difficulties and strengths in set-shifting and central coherence observed in adults with AN are also found in younger populations with AN (see Chapter 1, and Lang *et al.* 2013, 2014). Research examining the neurocognitive profiles of adolescents with AN also relies on knowledge of the normal trajectory of neurocognitive development in healthy young people across the age span from childhood through adolescence into adulthood. Despite these issues, however, there is some evidence to suggest that CRT may be a promising intervention with adolescents with AN (Chapter 8). There have been suggestions that adolescents with AN may have similar set-shifting and global processing difficulties as adults (McAnarney *et al.* 2011, Chapter 1). Clinically, we often observe rigid thinking and behaviours related to food, eating, and body shape and/or weight in the young people we see with AN, as well as significant levels of perfectionism and obsessional behaviours in broader areas of life, for example academic or sporting achievement. This suggests that there may be a group of young people with AN who struggle with similar difficulties in cognitive flexibility as adults with AN. It has also been suggested that adolescents may be more amenable to change as they typically have a less chronic course and a shorter duration of illness than adult populations (Tchanturia and Lock 2011; Nunn *et al.* 2008), and therefore may benefit from a CRT intervention. There has been some preliminary research investigating CRT interventions with adolescent populations on an individual basis (Cwojdzińska *et al.* 2009; Dahlgren *et al.* 2013) and in group settings (Wood *et al.* 2011; Pretorius *et al.* 2012; Zuchova *et al.* 2013) with promising results.

This chapter will describe the development and quantitative and qualitative evaluation of a CRT group for adolescents with AN that we currently run within a day patient programme at the Maudsley Hospital, London. We will also describe how the group has been adapted since its initial development, with examples of novel exercises, followed by clinical reflections and conclusions.

Development of a CRT group for adolescents in the context of a day patient programme for adolescents with AN

We have developed and piloted a CRT group for adolescents with AN, which we currently run as part of a day patient programme (the Intensive Treatment Programme – ITP) within a national and specialist Child and Adolescent Eating Disorders Service. The ITP was initially set up in 2010 for those adolescents with AN who are either not responding to, or require more intensive support than can be provided solely through outpatient care, and to provide an alternative to inpatient admissions. The ITP currently runs from 9.45 until 4pm/6pm (depending on the day) Monday to Friday, and is a structured programme consisting of supervised meals and snacks, education, family meals, family and individual sessions. Adolescents are also offered a variety of different therapy groups based on cognitive behavioural therapy (CBT), dialectical behaviour therapy (DBT), motivational interviewing (MI), and cognitive remediation therapy (CRT) principles, which aim to target maintaining and moderating factors of the illness. The CRT group was named the 'Flexible Thinking' group and was adapted from a CRT group protocol that had been developed initially for adult inpatients with AN at the Maudsley Hospital (Genders and Tchanturia 2010; see Chapter 4 for more details). The group was initially carried out as a 'closed' group and consisted of four weekly sessions of 45 minutes each including a combination of psycho-education, group exercises that practice flexible or bigger picture thinking, group discussions relating different thinking styles to real life situations and contexts, and setting of homework tasks. The group is facilitated by two or three members of staff, a clinical psychologist, assistant psychologist and/or clinical nurse specialist, and is supervised by Dr K. Tchanturia, who developed adult one-to-one and group protocols (Chapter 2, 3, 4). Table 9.1 shows details of the content of each weekly session. Results of the pilot study are reported in Pretorius et al. (2012).

Full details of the original group protocol are described in Chapter 4. Results of the initial and current evaluation of the group will be described in the following sections.

Evaluation of the CRT group for adolescents

The Flexible Thinking group was evaluated in order to determine whether it was associated with an increase in adolescents' cognitive flexibility and if it was acceptable to young people. We also wanted to determine whether it was feasible to run the group in the context of the day programme, and to identify areas that could be developed for future adaptations of the group. In order to achieve these goals, adolescents were asked to complete two questionnaires – once before completing the group and again four weeks later after completion of the group – which were, respectively: 1 – the Cognitive Flexibility Scale (CFS – Martin and Rubin 1995), a self-reported measure of cognitive flexibility;

TABLE 9.1 Session content of the initial 4-session group protocol

Session	Content
1 – Bigger Picture	Introduction to CRT, 'Bigger picture' thinking style, geometric figures task, 'Piccadilly Circus' task, Reflections, Homework (bigger picture/finer detail real life examples)
2 – Switching	Review of previous week's homework, switching tasks (Stroop task in pairs, Illusions task), reflections, Homework (behavioural tasks)
3 – Multi-tasking	Review of previous week's homework, multi-tasking activities (playing 'snap' card game whilst having conversation in pairs, Homework (behavioural tasks)
4 – Summary	Review of previous week's homework, summary of sessions so far, 'occupations' task, mottos

and 2 – a simple Motivational Ruler (MR – Miller and Rollnick 2002) questionnaire consisting of two questions: How important do you think it is to change? and, How much do you feel able to change? where participants were asked to rate their answers on a Likert scale ranging from 1 (not at all) to 10 (extremely). Adolescents were also asked to complete a brief feedback form post-group, consisting of three questions –

1. How much did you enjoy these sessions?
2. How useful were these sessions?
3. Do you feel that you have learnt new skills?

– and two open-ended questions asking what they liked about the group and what they thought could be improved. These outcome measures were chosen in order to be consistent with those used in evaluation of a CRT group intervention with adult inpatients (Genders and Tchanturia 2010), and were considered to be suitable for an adolescent population.

Initial results

Results of an initial evaluation of the group that took place in 2011, and are based on outcome data from N = 24 adolescents, are reported in Pretorius *et al.* (2012). In this pilot study there were no significant differences between pre- and post-treatment scores on the Cognitive Flexibility Scale (CFS) or the Motivational Ruler (MR). Figure 9.1 shows the feedback from adolescents, indicating they thought the group was enjoyable, useful, and that they had learnt new skills. Participants' comments in the open-ended feedback were analysed, and indicated that the group was acceptable to young people and that they found it useful, illustrated by the following quotes:

The groups were fun and interesting and unrelated to eating and anorexia.

It has given me confidence to see the world in a different way.

Flexibility is not scary or intimidating. It can be managed and might give me more freedom in my life.

It was difficult seeing how the way I think has been so irrational and caused some unwanted problems.

Areas of improvement suggested by adolescents included incorporating a wider variety of tasks into the group sessions, and relating the in-session tasks and discussions more to real life examples.

Further development of the group

We have made a number of adaptations to the group since the initial evaluation described above. Firstly, the total number of sessions was increased to eight in order to determine whether a higher 'dose' of sessions is associated with greater improvements in cognitive flexibility. Since the initial evaluation, the ITP has become an 'open' programme where young people can enter the groups at various time points, despite having missed previous sessions. Young people therefore might not complete the same exercises as each other across the eight sessions; however, the same concepts are repeated over the eight sessions regardless of the exercises. The content of the eight sessions consists of the initial four sessions described in the protocol above (Table 9.1), with small adaptations. Remaining group sessions follow the same structure and themes of the first four, with a variety of bigger picture, switching, multi-tasking and summarising tasks, reflections and discussions, and behavioural homework tasks. Group exercises are chosen in order to be appropriate for the particular combination of young people in the group each week (for example, to accommodate those who have already completed several sessions, as well as newcomers). A variety of tasks is aimed for, involving individual exercises, work in pairs or small groups, and whole-group tasks. In addition to increasing the number of sessions, and in response to participants' feedback that they would like a broader variety of tasks, we have also continued to develop and adapt the group tasks to suit adolescent populations and to promote interactivity between group members to foster a fun, light-hearted atmosphere which keeps young people engaged in the group. The group now always begins with an active ice-breaker, which illustrates one or more of the targeted thinking styles (see Table 9.2).

Our eight-session protocol, with examples of skill-specific exercises can be seen in Table 9.3.

An example of an exercise we have developed to practice bigger picture thinking, involves asking young people to convey the main points of an activity in a succinct way. We selected age-appropriate tasks such as downloading a music track, and asked young people to describe how they would go about doing the activity. This task requires prioritising, thinking of the bigger picture (of the desired final

TABLE 9.2 Ice-breaker exercises

Game	Skills
Splat – A 'sheriff' stands in the middle of the circle and points, to (using the word . . .) 'splat' different people. The person who is pointed at crouches down. The two people either side of the person crouching have to point and 'splat' at each other. The slowest person to do this, or anyone who makes a mistake (e.g. crouches when they should 'splat') is eliminated from the game. This continues until there are only two players remaining. At this point, they stand back to back whilst the 'sheriff' says various words of their own choice. When the 'sheriff' says the word 'splat', the first of the two players to turn around and 'splat' the other, is the winner.	Switching
Multi-coloured balls – Requires three different coloured balls (e.g. red, blue, green). Begin with the a certain coloured ball (e.g. red) and assign it a colour that it is not (e.g. blue). The facilitator says 'this is a "blue" ball, what colour is it?' and the young people repeat the colour back. The ball is then passed around in a sequence – each person throwing to the same person in the sequence. As the ball is thrown, it's newly assigned colour is said by the thrower. Once the group has become accustomed to this, a different coloured ball (e.g. blue) is used and assigned a different name (e.g. green) and so on. The aim is to have all three coloured balls, with different names, being thrown around the group at the same time.	Switching, generally being flexible
Acting opposite – Participants are instructed to do the opposite of any instruction given to them. For example, walk anti-clockwise in a circle, stand on your left leg, sit down.	Switching

outcome), deciding on the most salient, important points, and conveying the message to others. We tried to use a game format by asking participants to describe the task by changing the criteria of the instructions from 'use no more words than you would use in a text message' to, 'use no more than ten words' to, 'use only three words'. We also introduced friendly competition by having the young people work in pairs and at the end of the task we asked the pairs to call out their three words to check whether other pairs could guess the activity. We found that young people can often find working in pairs easier before discussing with the wider group.

For our second switching session, we implemented a 'hand tapping' game. Young people and staff sat in a circle on the floor, facing each other. Each person crossed hands with the person on either side of them, so that everyone had one hand from each neighbour in their own hand. A staff member started and chose the direction (e.g. clockwise) for the single tap on the floor, to be 'passed' around the circle. The tap travels in the order of the hands, not necessarily the order of the players. A single tap signals for play to continue to the next hand. Once the group had become accustomed to this and the tap is being passed with speed, a new rule is introduced. Two taps of the same hand indicates a change in direction of play. Again, when this becomes familiar, a third rule is added. Three taps of the same hand indicates missing a hand.

TABLE 9.3 Session content of the revised eight-session group protocol

Session	Content
1 – Bigger picture	Ice-breaker, Introduction to CRT, 'Bigger picture' tasks (geometric figures, 'Piccadilly Circus'), Reflections, Homework (bigger picture/finer detail real life examples)
2 – Switching	Ice-breaker, Review of previous week's homework, switching tasks (Stroop task in pairs, Illusions task), Reflections, Homework (one behavioural task)
3 – Multi-tasking	Ice-breaker, Review of previous week's homework, multi-tasking activities (pat head and rub tummy, playing 'snap' card game whilst having conversation in pairs), Reflections, Homework (notice when you are/could be multi-tasking)
4 – Summary	Ice-breaker, Review of previous week's homework, summary of sessions so far, summarising tasks (adapted 'occupations' task, mottos) Homework (come up with own Flexible-Thinking motto)
5 – Bigger picture	Ice-breaker, Review of previous week's homework, Bigger picture tasks ('How to' texts, London Landmarks game), Reflections, Homework ('difficult meal time' worksheet)
6 – Switching	Ice-breaker, Review of previous week's homework, Switching tasks (Illusions – different to those used in session 2, Name Game, Hand Tapping Game), Reflections, Homework (try as many behavioural tasks as they can)
7 – Multi-tasking	Ice-breaker, Review of previous week's homework, Multi-tasking tasks (Play-Doh and directions, game and current song), Reflections, Homework (practice multi-tasking)
8 – Summary	Ice-breaker, Review of previous week's homework, Summary of sessions so far, Team Bigger-picture vs Team Switch vs Team Multi-task, Mind Maps, Homework (Pros and Cons of Thinking Styles Worksheet)

Another recent development is the use of tablets in the groups; an example follows, of an individual exercise involving multi-tasking which was developed for the group. We asked young people to play the same simple game on portable tablets. At the same time, we played a current pop song notable for its repetitive lyrics. While each young person was trying to get a good score on the game, they were also tasked with counting the number of times a particular word was used in the song. The element of competition in the exercise helped foster good participation. Furthermore, the frustration of multi-tasking led to a light-hearted discussion in the larger group about real examples of needing to develop this skill in the lives of the young people.

For the 'summary' sessions, we have adapted the task of locating the thinking style required in various professions (e.g. accountant, town planner) on an axis on a large board with dimensions of bigger picture/finer detail, and flexible/rigid. We adapted this by asking young people to place figures from the media on the board (e.g. Lord Sugar's apprentice, a boy-band member, X-Factor judge, Olympic athlete). This led to a more lively discussion and allowed humour to be part of the task. We also asked the young people to place their own dream job on to the axis, with the aim of targeting motivation. Importantly, these adaptations helped prompt a discussion of how rigidity or global thinking might manifest in real situations, how detrimental or advantageous these thinking styles might be in different circumstances, and changes the young person may need to consider in order to achieve their goals. In another summary session, a 'mind maps' exercise is used in order to draw together the previous sessions and to think about the skills learnt in the CRT sessions within the context of participants' wider lives and treatment.

One example of a summary task for participants with experience of several group sessions involves splitting the group into three teams (Team Switch, Team Multi-task, and Team Bigger Picture). The teams were tasked with giving two examples of each of bigger picture/finer detail, switching, and multi-tasking from real life situations. For homework, participants were asked to provide one more real example taken from the week, between the sessions, to be fed back in the following session. It was important to provide a reminder of the homework task close to the next session.

Homework exercises are encouraged in order to consolidate the in-session exercises. For example, in a homework exercise where young people were asked to 'try to do something new' from a list of suggested behavioural tasks, one young person tried eating a different type of cereal. There was a discussion around whether she would do this again, how she had found it scary to begin with, and lead to group discussion about trying things they used to do, but had not done since the illness started. The task also enabled two people in the group to acknowledge that they often kept routines in many areas of their life. This was discussed with members the clinical team looking after one of the adolescents, and the possibility of continuing individual sessions of CRT after she left the day programme was also discussed.

We have also designed a 'Difficult Meal Time' worksheet (see Figure 9.1), which is set as a homework task. Young people are asked to think about the thinking styles they notice they use during meal times, what styles might be more helpful and how they can try to implement this change.

Although most of the exercises and discussions do not relate specifically to food, eating, shape, weight, or the illness, sometimes young people will spontaneously offer examples related to these issues. For example, one young person reported how it was helpful to think about how the details of being in the day programme could be seen in the context of the bigger picture of recovery from her illness.

Current results

Despite the challenges an 'open' group presents for evaluation of outcome measures, we have continued to collect quantitative data for each participant pre-group and again after completion of four and eight sessions, in order to continue our evaluation. We hope to compare those young people who completed eight sessions of the

Think about a difficult meal time . . .

What thinking style/s do you notice that you use during difficult meal times? (e.g. Focused or stuck on details? Rigid thinking? Other thinking styles?)

What thinking styles might be more helpful to use at these times? (e.g. Standing back and looking at the bigger picture? Flexible thinking? Other thinking styles?)

What could I do to help me use these helpful thinking styles during difficult meal times?

What might be difficult when trying to use these helpful thinking styles during difficult meal times?

What can I do if this happens?

Now let's give it a go...

Reflections

How was the experiment?

Were you able to notice what thinking style you were using?

Was it a helpful thinking style for this situation? If not, were you able to choose a more helpful thinking style?

What have I learned from this experiment?

FIGURE 9.1 'Think about a difficult meal time' homework sheet

group with those who completed four sessions when we have obtained a large enough sample. To date, we have carried out preliminary analyses with the sample of participants included in the pilot study reported above, combined with those who have completed four sessions since that time, in order to update our results with a larger sample. These results are presented below.

Since our initial pilot study, a further 27 young people have completed four or more group sessions. Of these, six participants did not complete either one or both of the pre/post outcome questionnaires (for unknown reasons) and were not included in the analysis. Analysis was therefore carried out with a combined sample of 45 participants. Results show the mean age was 15.6 years (SD = 1.4 years; range = 12–18 years) and the mean duration of illness was 19.4 months (SD = 18.0 months; range = 0–78 months). Thirty-eight (84.4%) adolescents had a diagnosis of AN and 7 (15.6%) had a diagnosis of Eating Disorder Not Otherwise Specified (EDNOS). The percentage mean Body Mass Index (BMI) was 79.5% (SD = 8.6) pre-group.

Results of the pre- and post treatment scores on the Cognitive Flexibility Scale (CFS) and Motivational Ruler (MR) for this updated sample are shown in Figure 9.1 and Figure 9.2 respectively. Comparison of pre (M = 44.4, SD = 10.2) and post (M = 45.4, SD = 9.4) CFS scores showed no significant differences over time (t = −1.17, df = 44, p = 0.25; d = 0.10). There were also no significant differences (t = 0.23, df = 44, p = 0.82; d = 0.03) between pre (M = 6.9, SD = 2.7) and post (M = 6.8, SD = 2.8) scores on the importance to change MI measure, and a non-significant difference (t = −1.1, df = 43, p = 0.27; d = 0.11) between pre

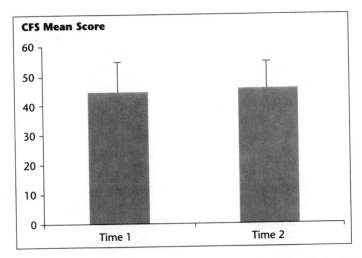

FIGURE 9.2   Mean scores on the Cognitive Flexibility Scale (CFS) pre-group (Time 1) and after session 4 (Time 2)

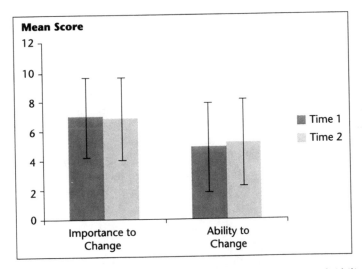

FIGURE 9.3   Mean scores on the Importance to Change and Ability to Change questions of the Motivational Ruler (MR), pre-group (Time 1) and after session 4 (Time 2)

(M = 4.9, SD = 3.0) and post (M = 5.2, SD = 2.9) scores on the ability to change MI measure. The percentage mean BMI was 82.2% (SD = 9.4) post-group.

Clinical reflections and future directions

We have described the development and implementation of a CRT group for adolescents with AN delivered in the context of an intensive day programme within a specialist child and adolescent eating disorders service. Results of an evaluation showed that the group tended to be acceptable to young people and that it was feasible to run in the context of a day patient programme for adolescents with eating disorders. There was however little change in cognitive flexibility over time. The results of the evaluation were consistent with those found with adult inpatients in a group (Genders and Tchanturia 2010; Chapter 4) and individual formats (Tchanturia et al. 2013).

The finding that there were no differences in cognitive flexibility over time may be explained by several factors. First, it may be that the number of sessions (four) was not enough to detect any impact of the group, on changes in cognitive flexibility over time. (See above, reference the eight-session format group, begun in order to assess whether an increased 'dose' of the group is associated with improvements in cognitive flexibility.) Second, it is possible that the self-report outcome measures used in our evaluation were not adequate to detect changes in cognitive flexibility – future studies could include experimental outcome measures administered pre- and post treatment that tap into cognitive flexibility instead of, or alongside self-report questionnaires. Advances in technology might also mean that it becomes more practical to use computerised cognitive assessment tasks to monitor changes in flexibility over time.

As the group has developed, it has become an integrated part of our day patient treatment programme. However, we do take seriously a lack of positive change found in the quantitative outcome measures we have collected so far. As we have reflected on the experience of running the group, we have noticed that its running has become more rewarding as we have adapted and created new tasks. In the early stages of piloting the group with adolescents (using tasks developed for adults), the sessions sometimes seemed slow-paced and interaction could be hard to encourage. These problems seem to have improved along with our confidence, and the sense of fun we have prioritised for new tasks. We have found that giving responsibility to the young people to suggest new exercises that might enable practice of cognitive flexibility can foster a sense of ownership of some of the session content in the groups, and has also improved their engagement and enthusiasm. In addition, staff modelling finding tasks difficult in the group and out of the group, has had a positive effect on the young people's willingness to try something different. These increasingly positive reflections from the clinicians running the group have ensured the group's continuation and the collection of further data. We are also considering whether some of the benefits of group participation may not be captured in the measures we are using. Candidate variables could include improvements in ability to access materials and skills used in other groups, as well as improvements in engagement or therapeutic alliance, reducing the likelihood of premature dropout (Hubert et al. 2013).

That the group took place in a day-patient setting led to various challenges. We found that dynamics outside of the session can cause difficulties in the session itself, especially if not addressed before the group starts. For example, it can be particularly challenging to facilitate the group after a difficult meal. Young people might attend the group feeling upset, stressed and sometimes angry. Skill is also required in balancing dynamics between young people with different levels of motivation, to actively participate in the activities of the programme. This can require careful planning in terms of pair and group work. Communication with the wider team about work being done in the group is another aspect requiring attention, along with managing discussions about how issues directly related to eating and anorexia, relate to the thinking skills being targeted.

There are several strengths and limitations of the analysis of the CRT group for adolescents. First, as the group is one component of an intensive day treatment programme consisting of a variety of interventions, it cannot be concluded that any observed differences are solely attributed to the group. Nevertheless, the group was carried out within the context of a real clinical setting, which indicates it is feasible to carry out the group in a day patient setting. Another limitation is that the group of adolescents included in the results presented here, had completed different combinations of exercises across the four groups, and this made it difficult to evaluate consistently. However, again, this reflected the clinical reality of the day patient service, and as the groups included the same CRT principles, it is expected that all participants were exposed to similar concepts across the group sessions regardless of the actual exercises they carried out.

Future research can continue to explore whether CRT may be useful for young people with AN, for whom it may be most beneficial, and at what point in treatment it is most appropriate. For example, studies of CRT with adults has typically investigated inpatients with a chronic course of illness who are very underweight – might CRT be more beneficial for those adolescents who are lower in weight, have had the illness for longer, or who have traits of cognitive rigidity prior to onset of the illness? Pilot case studies/series examining CRT on an individual basis with young people with AN may be helpful in order to begin to answer these questions. It would also be useful to explore further how CRT may be used most effectively in conjunction with other types of therapy for adolescent ANs, including family therapy and individual therapy. For example, could CRT be used within the Maudsley Model of family therapy and as part of the multi-family therapy treatments we routinely offer young people and their families?

Finally, we are also responding to feedback from young people to increase the variety of CRT tasks, by continuing to develop a new and interesting range of tasks that can engage adolescents of different ages to help practice flexibility and awareness of thinking, challenge rigid thinking styles and behaviours, as well as including tasks that are interactional and make use of the group context in order to promote social connections.

References

Cwojdzińska, A., Markowska-Regulska, K. and Rybakowski, F. (2009). Cognitive remediation therapy in adolescent anorexia nervosa – case report. *Psychiatria Polska*, 43, 115–124.

Dahlgren, C.L., Lask, B., Landrø, N.I. and Rø, Ø. (2013). Neuropsychological functioning in adolescents with anorexia nervosa before and after cognitive remediation therapy: A feasibility trial. *International Journal of Eating Disorders, 46*, 576–581.

Eisler, I., Dare, C., Russell, G.F.M., *et al.* (1997). Family and individual therapy in anorexia nervosa. A 5-year follow-up. *Archives of General Psychiatry, 54*, 1025–1030.

Genders, R. and Tchanturia, K. (2010). Cognitive remediation therapy (CRT) for anorexia in a group format: A pilot study. *Eating and Weight Disorders, 15*: e234–9.

Genders, R., Davies, H., St Louis, L., Kyriacou, O., Hambrook D. and Tchanturia, K. (2008). Long-term benefits of CRT for anorexia. *British Journal of Healthcare Management, 14*, 105–109.

Harrison, A., Tchanturia, K., Naumann, U. and Treasure, J. (2012). Social emotional functioning and cognitive styles in eating disorders. *British Journal of Clinical Psychology, 51*, 261–279.

Hubert, T, Pioggiosi, P., Huas, C., Wallier, J., Maria, A., Apfel, A., Curt, F., Falissard, B. and Godart, N. (2013). Drop-out from adolescent and young adult inpatient treatment for anorexia nervosa. *Psychiatry Research, 209*, 632–637.

Lopez, C., Tchanturia, K., Stahl, D. and Treasure, J. (2008). Central coherence in eating disorders: A systematic review. *Psychological Medicine, 38*, 1393–1404.

Martin, M.M. and Rubin, R.B. (1995). A new measure of cognitive flexibility. *Psychological Reports, 76*, 623–626.

Miller, W.R. and Rollnick, S. (2002). *Motivational Interviewing: Preparing people for change* (2nd edn). New York: Guilford Press.

McAnarney, E., Zarcone, J., Singh, P., Michels, J., Welsh, S., Litteer, T., Wang, H. and Klein, J.D. (2011). Restrictive anorexia nervosa and set-shifting in adolescents: A biobehavioral interface. *Journal of Adolescent Health*, 49, 99–101.

NICE (2004). Eating disorders: Core interventions in the treatment and management of anorexia nervosa, bulimia nervosa and related eating disorders. CG9. London: National Institute for Health and Care Excellence.

Nunn, K.P., Frampton, I., Gordon, I. and Lask, B. (2008). The fault is not in her parents but in her insula – A neurobiological hypothesis of anorexia nervosa. *European Eating Disorders Review, 16* (5), 355–360.

Pretorius, N., Dimmer, M., Power, E., Eisler, I., Simic, M. and Tchanturia, K. (2012). Evaluation of a cognitive remediation therapy group for adolescents with anorexia nervosa: Pilot study. *European Eating Disorder Review, 20*, 321–325. DOI: 10.1002/erv. 2176.

Roberts, M.E., Tchanturia, K., Stahl, D., Southgate, L. and Treasure J. (2007). A systematic review and meta-analysis of set-shifting ability in eating disorders. *Psychological Medicine, 37*, 1075–1084.

Smink, F.R.E., van Hoeken, D. and Hoek, H.W. (2012). Epidemiology of eating disorders: Incidence, prevalence and mortality rates. *Current Psychiatry Reports, 14* (4), 406–414. DOI: 10.1007/s11920-012-0282-y.

Tchanturia, K. and Lock, J. (2010). 'Cognitive remediation therapy (CRT) for eating disorders: Development, refinement and future directions', in R.A.H. Adan and W.H. Kaye (Eds.), *Behavioural Neurobiology of Eating Disorders, Current Topics in Behavioural Neurosciences 6*. Berlin: Springer-Verlag.

Tchanturia, K., Davies, H., Roberts, M., Harrison, A., Nakazato, M., Schmidt, U., Treasure, J. and Morris, R. (2012). Poor cognitive flexibility in eating disorders: Examining the evidence using the Wisconsin Card Sorting Task. *Plos One, 7* (1), e28331.

Tchanturia, K., Harrison, A., Davies, H., Roberts, M., Oldershaw, A., Nakazato, M., Stahl, D., Morris, R., Schmidt, U. and Treasure, J. (2011). Cognitive flexibility and clinical severity in eating disorders. *Plos One, 6* (6), e20462.

Tchanturia, K., Lloyd, S. and Lang, K. (2013). Cognitive remediation in eating disorders. *International Journal of Eating Disorders, Special Issue, 46* (5), 492–496.

Wood, L., Al-Khairulla, H. and Lask, B. (2011). Group cognitive remediation therapy for adolescents with anorexia nervosa. *Clinical Child Psychology and Psychiatry, 16,* 225–231.

Zuchova S., Erler T. and Papezova, H. (2013). Group cognitive remediation therapy for adult anorexia nervosa inpatients: first experiences. *Eating and Weight Disorders, 18,* 269–273. DOI: 10.1007/s40519-013-0041-z.

PART IV

New developments/ ideas worth researching: CRT in the context of family therapy

10

FAMILY COGNITIVE REMEDIATION THERAPY FOR CHILD AND ADOLESCENT ANOREXIA NERVOSA

Suzanne Hutchison, Alice Roberts and Bryan Lask

Introduction

Anorexia nervosa (AN) in childhood and adolescence is a very complex illness with major physical, psychological and socio-cultural correlates (Lask and Bryant-Waugh, 2013). The prognosis is relatively poor with no more than about 50% having made a full and sustained recovery at five year follow-up (Steinhausen, 2002). The cornerstone of treatment is family-focused, with specific attention being paid to assisting the parents to understand and manage the illness (NICE, 2004).

One of the possible contributing factors to the poor prognosis may relate to the underlying cognitive inefficiencies associated with the illness (Chapter 1). These may act as both risk- and maintaining factors, and thus require attention in both assessment and treatment. Additionally there is some evidence of first-degree relatives having similar cognitive styles (Galimberti et al., 2012; Holliday et al., 2005; Roberts et al., 2013; Tenconi et al., 2010). cognitive remediation therapy (CRT) has been designed to target these specific cognitive domains affected by AN. Several recent studies (for a summary, see Tchanturia et al., 2013) have shown evidence of the benefits and effectiveness of CRT in other areas, and more recently for anorexia nervosa (Chapters 4, 5, 6, 7 and 11).

Given the importance of the family focus and the potential benefits of CRT, it seems logical to explore the integration of the two. Thus this chapter explores the development and current use of family approaches for child and adolescent anorexia nervosa and how these may be complimented and enhanced by bringing together CRT with family work as a useful way to aid the treatment of AN. The rationale and application of using family-oriented CRT is described along with some case examples to demonstrate the advantages and benefits of including it in the management for the treatment of anorexia nervosa.

Family oriented work and child/adolescent anorexia nervosa

Family therapy in the treatment for children and adolescents with anorexia nervosa first took centre stage in the 1970's (e.g. Minuchin *et al.*, 1978; Selvini-Palazzoli, 1974) when parents/families were considered to have a significant aetiological role. Minuchin *et al.* (1978) postulated a 'psychosomatic family' model, which proposed that an eating disorder may emerge as a result of specific dysfunctional family dynamics including rigidity, enmeshment, over-involvement and conflict avoidance. Thus the structural family therapy approach developed by Minuchin focused on changing dysfunctional transactional styles and the role the sick child plays in facilitating conflict avoidance Minuchin *et al.* (1978). Similarly in the Milan model, Selvini-Palazzoli and colleagues focused on challenging family belief systems and disruptive 'family games' (Carr, 2006). A change in the family dynamics also became the aim (Fisher *et al.*, 2010). The result of these early ideas was twofold: i) family therapy benefited from further development and recognition (Dare and Eisler, 2008; Eisler, 2005); ii) however, families, or to be more precise, parents, became a source of blame and guilt for the illness. Subsequent research has clearly refuted these ideas and shown that the 'family dynamics' described were more the consequence of the illness rather than the cause of it, as similar patterns were observed in families with other chronic illnesses (Herscovici, 2013). Further, no consistent pattern of family structure or family functioning has been identified, let alone one sufficient to explain the development of AN (Eisler, 2005).

Following Minuchin and Selvini-Palazzoli's influential but ultimately misleading ideas, there have since been several family-oriented approaches to interventions used in this context, including strategic, behavioural, feminist, attachment, solution-focused, narrative, and more recently the Maudsley model/method or family-based therapy (FBT) (Eisler *et al.*, 2010). The latter, which has considerable contemporary influence, outlines three main tasks: i) gaining and maintaining family cooperation; ii) assessing family organization and dynamics, and iii) establishing interventions to create change. Thus there has been a general shift in the family therapy field in the last three decades towards more collaborative approaches, with families being viewed as an important resource for change (Herscovici, 2013).

In summary, interventions in AN now emphasise a shift from 'treatment *of* families [. . .] to treatment *with* families' and sees families as 'the *context* for change rather than the *target* of change' (Eisler *et al.*, 2010, p. 151). Key elements include 'agnosticism as to aetiology, empowering parents (and) seeing the family as the solution rather than the problem' (Eisler, 2013).

Goals of family-oriented work for AN also include the provision of psycho-education to increase the awareness of the serious dangers posed by the illness, whilst containing parental anxiety to enable exploration of concerns (Lask and Bryant-Waugh, 2013). With this comes support for an increased understanding of the illness and young person, whilst relieving the family of blame and guilt, particularly by the use of externalisation of the illness or separating the person/family from the problem. Helping parents to 'take charge' and be in control of eating to regain their child's overall wellbeing is also a crucial part of family oriented support. Work with parents should focus on increasing their collaboration and consistency in challenging the eating disorder. Furthermore, family work should address the impact of the illness on the family in general, as well as exploring what unhelpful patterns the family may have fallen into as a result of being 'high-jacked' by anorexia nervosa, and should include siblings, who are often witness to, and experience the challenges of the struggle with the illness.

Evidence base for family-oriented therapies

Despite the inclusion of family generally being accepted as critical in managing child and adolescent anorexia nervosa, reaching a clear consensus regarding what the 'better' treatment is, remains a challenge. Many varying approaches, individual and family focused, have been and continue to be used to treat anorexia nervosa however, overall, there is a lack of rigorous and consistent evaluation of interventions to determine what works best to treat the illness (Fisher et al., 2010).

Family therapy (of various types) is the most-widely studied treatment for child/ adolescent anorexia nervosa (Eisler et al., 2010; Downs and Blow, 2013), and is recommended as an important component of the treatment for this population (NICE, 2004). Studies indicate that a family-oriented approach for those patients below age eighteen, with a relatively short illness (less than a year) and whose BMI is not far below 17.5, will lead to improvement in nutritional status in 50–60% at between one- and five-year follow-up. Some but not all studies also show some improvement in eating disorder psychopathology. However, the studies used as a base for this claim are overall relatively small, with very many methodological limitations (e.g. Fairburn, 2005; Strober, 2014), and nor has there has been sufficient research comparing family therapy to other treatments (Eisler, 2005). Nevertheless, there is a general acceptance, for now, of family oriented approaches as being the primary intervention for adolescent anorexia nervosa, in the context of a lack of better evidence for other approaches.

Rationale for integrating CRT and family therapy

There is strong neuropsychological evidence (Lopez et al., 2008; Tchanturia et al., 2012; Chapter 1) indicating that people with AN have particular cognitive inefficiencies in areas such as central coherence, set-shifting and visuo-spatial processing (see Chapter 1 and Rose et al., 2012; Stedal, Frampton et al., 2012; Stedal, Rose et al., 2012). It has been postulated that these may function as risk factors for the development and/or maintenance of anorexia nervosa. In addition, cognitive styles identified in patients with AN have also been observed in their first degree relatives, in both set-shifting (e.g. Roberts et al., 2010) and central coherence (Lopez et al., 2009). These findings lend evidence to the view of such styles as representing an endophenotype of AN (see Chapter 1 for more details).

As described in the literature (Tchanturia *et al.*, 2013), cognitive remediation therapy (CRT) aims to remedy these underlying cognitive styles. It has been used successfully both individually and in groups with adolescents (Chapters 8, 9), found to enhance motivation and engagement in other therapies, and to be associated with improvements in both psychopathology and neuropsychological functioning (Tchanturia *et al.*, 2013; Wood *et al.*, 2011). Introducing CRT within the family context appears to be a logical development, integrating the necessity and value of working with the family and tackling underlying cognitive difficulties (Lask and Roberts, 2014).

Although family-oriented CRT has not been implemented in any of the other disorders in which CRT is often used, family-oriented interventions consisting of similar principles to CRT, for schizophrenia (Friedman-Yakoobian *et al.*, 2009) and acquired brain injury (Braga *et al.*, 2004; Wade *et al.*, 2006) have been reported to be efficacious in combating cognitive deficits associated with these disorders.

Additionally, it has been identified that patients suffering from schizophrenia, and their first degree relatives, are unaware of the cognitive deficits associated with the disorder, yet for cognitive remediation interventions to be effective, awareness of such is likely to be crucial (Poletti *et al.*, 2012). It is probable that patients suffering from AN and their family members are similarly unaware of the cognitive weaknesses associated with the disorder. Acknowledging such in the child and perhaps also within family members is likely to yield considerable benefits for treatment.

Furthermore, CRT compliments family work on other levels, by supporting some of its goals which in practice often prove challenging to achieve. For example, Whitney and Murray (2005) discuss how parents are often perplexed by the underlying mechanisms of AN despite their attempts to educate themselves. Understanding the cognitive styles may help further psycho-education as well as relieving families of blame and guilt, which often paralyses them. Eisler (2005) has also described how in the presence of anorexia nervosa, often the family (and everything it does!) become organised around the illness with everyone feeling 'frozen' and rigid around a routine. Family CRT invites families to practice flexibility (set-shifting) and regain view of the 'bigger picture' (central-coherence) together. Additionally, families in the grip of AN struggle to tolerate uncertainty and to take any risks, with roles in the family often becoming fixed (Eisler *et al.*, 2010). CRT allows families to explore different possibilities and perspectives in a less 'risky' environment and usually in a non-confrontational or challenging way.

Finally, an important area where CRT and family oriented work are very well suited is in the essential task of engagement. Adolescents with anorexia nervosa are by nature of the illness, usually reluctant to engage in any treatment that aims to eradicate it. More often than not, engaging and empowering parents, as is encouraged in family work, may also make the adolescent feel excluded and opposed to the therapy (or therapist!), let alone to her parents. By using CRT as a fun, collaborative and non-intrusive language to think about thinking, families are allowed to engage in new conversations more easily, and may initiate talking about difficulties from different perspectives, usually leading to increased empathy amongst family members.

CASE 1

Anna, aged 16, had been treated for AN for the previous two years without success. At the time of referral to us she was unable to think and talk of anything but weight, shape and calories, manifesting extreme distress, sensitivity and preoccupation with her appearance and dread of fat. She had previously been treated with CBT with which she was completely unable to engage, and her parents had received occasional updates but no real advice and support.

BL initiated family-oriented therapy, combining sessions with Anna alone, some with her parents and some with all three together. Over six weeks this had little impact, as Anna's morbid preoccupation completely dominated content. BL suggested to Anna we try a different approach and introduced the concept and practicalities of CRT. She accepted with interest and we started with geometric figures, an exercise that involves one person – commonly the patient – describing various figures which are unseen to another, who has to try and draw such figures from the description provided. No questions may be asked and neither the 'describer' nor the 'drawer' may see each other's figures. This task is a useful exercise in both central coherence and visuo-spatial processing.

Anna initially found this difficult but enjoyed the challenge. Her tendency was to focus on the fine detail of the figure at the cost of the big picture, making it hard for the 'drawer' to understand the essence of the diagram. With discussion after each exercise, by the end of the session she was able to acknowledge her over-focus on fine detail at the cost of the big picture and commented that her mother had the same problem. She asked if her mother could join us for the next meeting, which proved enlightening in that her mother did indeed manifest very similar difficulties. Anna enjoyed her one-up position and mocked her mother's ineptitude but the atmosphere was light-hearted. In the third session both parents attended, and more central coherence tasks were undertaken with enthusiasm and teasing banter.

What was most striking about these three sessions and thereafter, was a complete absence on Anna's part of any discussion of weight, shape and calories. Indeed she was able to fully engage in meaningful discussion of more deep-rooted issues – not least of which, an intense but previously concealed marital conflict in which Anna was caught up. Over the next few months Anna moved into recovery and has remained well for several years subsequently.

Therapist's reflection: It was striking how rapidly Anna moved from her morbid preoccupation with weight, shape and calories to discussion of more significant issues. Whilst it is difficult to be certain, it is possible that this rapid change occurred as a result of the meta-cognitive discussion of Anna's fine detail approach. This was perhaps assisted by the marital conflict becoming openly discussed for the first time, allowing Anna to move out of her 'triangulated' position.

CASE 2

Sian, aged 13, had had AN for at least two years, and presented at assessment as angry, withdrawn, miserable, and antagonistic to all attempts at help. She refused to talk, with bowed head and stooped shoulders, her face hidden by her long hair. She was accompanied by both her parents who worked hard to engage her without success. Discussion of how to manage her at home led to enraged screaming, threats to leave the room, never to speak to them, and even suicide.

BL suggested CRT to which Sian responded with extreme sarcasm, and criticism of his having the temerity to be paid so much just to play games! The parents in contrast were eager to try anything that might help. In the absence of Sian's involvement we simply did some geometric figures between the parents. Perhaps predictably, Sian surreptitiously watched what was happening and eventually could not contain her sarcasm at her parents' efforts. Her mother invited her to teach her how to do it, which Sian did with initial grudgingness, but soon entered into with gusto.

In the next session we used *Rush-Hour* (copyright 1996, 2003 ThinkFun Inc. US Pat. No. D 395,468), a 'sliding-block' type game in which the aim is to navigate various gridlock scenarios, in order to clear a path for a particular vehicle to reach an exit. This task allowed some focus on big picture thinking, flexibility, planning and visual memory. This led to an animated, but friendly discussion of how these issues permeated family life, with a tendency for father to be an obsessional planner much to the irritation of others. He acknowledged his contribution and the family agreed a strategy of each person behaving differently in relation to planning and big picture thinking. This involved each family member 'secretly' doing something different in these areas each day and other family members had to see if they could detect the difference.

Subsequent sessions revealed enthusiastic participation in the tasks, with Sian becoming more engaged in family life and in motivational enhancement therapy. Over the next six months Sian's AN gradually remitted and at follow up four years later she remains well.

Therapist's reflection: Sian's shift from angry dismissal of everyone and everything around her to acceptance of the therapeutic endeavour is most likely to be a result of both the playful nature of the CRT and the chance for her to take the one-up position and in fact demonstrate her expertise. These simple manoeuvres appeared to affect a change in Sian's ability to relate more constructively with others, and thus a more open discussion of both her internal and family issues than had previously been possible.

CASE 3

Lina, aged 18, had been hospitalised six times over five years for AN, with considerable comorbid OCD and extreme compulsive exercising. She was a sweet girl, in contemplation, who understandably conveyed a sense of despair for her future. Numerous therapies had been implemented previously including FBT and CBT but with no substantial impact. Neuropsychological assessment demonstrated significant problems with abstract thinking and some components of working memory. Lina's parents were warm and supportive but also feeling hopeless about her future. Her elder siblings were angry with her for her seeming refusal to get better and for the adverse effect on family life. We implemented family CRT, involving initially all family members but logistics led to varying attendance over the subsequent five sessions. However, one parent was always present.

As usual we started with geometric figures as this allows for animated interaction between family members, as well as focusing on the common problem of over-focus on fine detail. Lina proved to be the most competent at this, much to her pleasure and the chagrin of her angry older brother. *Rush Hour* proved far more difficult but this was shared by all family members and proved a unifying activity. The 'Silhouette illusion' (retrieved from creator Nobuyuki Kayahara's website: www.procreo.jp/labo/labo13) depicts the silhouette of a female dancer pirouetting, who can be perceived as spinning either clockwise or anticlockwise. It is extremely difficult to switch between these two perceptions at will, and requires considerable cognitive flexibility. This proved particularly challenging for all concerned but allowed for detailed discussion of flexibility and how the lack of this within the family was a source of irritation for all. In particular, Lina's brother was critical of her for her rigidity but other family members jokingly pointed out his own rigid behaviours. The whole family were keen to pursue some of the games and activities at home which they subsequently reported had proved helpful to them all. This applied especially to Lina who, with parental help, started developing strategies for her most problematic areas – anything that involved abstract thinking and absence of concrete and tangible cues.

Over subsequent months, though not without considerable struggle, Lina made significant progress, specifically in relation to her ability to manage eating and compulsive exercising, and most heart-warmingly, her relationship with her siblings improved considerably.

Therapist's reflection: Lina's self-esteem was enhanced by her proving to be better at some of the exercises than her brother who had been so critical of her. Additionally, progress seemed to have occurred as a result of the family joining in a number of games, leading to playful, and then constructive discussion of every-day irritations and specifically the whole family's tendency to rigidity. The shared understanding enhanced family warmth, closeness and cooperation.

Discussion

These three examples comprised part of a feasibility study of family CRT, with a focus on the recruitment process, the materials used, the delivery of the intervention and clinical experiences. The *ad hoc* sample, recruited between 2010–2013 from specialized in-patient and out-patient services, consisted of 19 families, all with a daughter with AN, and aged between 11 and 18. The inclusion criteria were one or more of: a) the patient was unable to engage in treatment, b) we had failed to help the patient, and c) evidence of neurocognitive weaknesses in the patient. For all the families, BL was the therapist but with a co-therapist in three cases. Frequency varied from weekly to monthly and the number of sessions varied from two to six.

The materials used for CRT with children and adolescents with eating disorders have been described in detail elsewhere (www.rasp.no) and consist of games, puzzles and riddles, child- and adolescent friendly, but which also engage adults. (A full resource pack is available at: www.rasp.no).

The findings suggest that overall, family CRT seems feasible with regard to:

- Recruitment – all the invited families participated and remained in treatment;
- CRT materials – these were adapted to suit all ages and found to be suitable and very acceptable;
- Delivery – this was individually tailored to suit each patient and family, and delivered *ad hoc*;
- Clinical experiences –
  - All the families completed treatment, were very enthusiastic about it, and recognised the relevance of the treatment, both for their daughters and themselves. Several requested more therapy and some became engaged with it, after previous resistance to other therapeutic approaches. There was unusually friendly and animated discussion of family dynamics, an ability to adopt new strategies and apply these to daily life, and clinical improvements not evident prior to family CRT.
  - All the families grasped the concepts of the intervention, subsequently developing the ability to recognize cognitive styles within themselves and other family members, and developing alternative methods of problem solving to overcome them. Additionally, all involved, demonstrated the ability to generalize such problem solving methods to real life examples, and specifically to symptoms associated with AN.
  - It appeared that approaching problems associated with the eating disorder in such a manner was far less threatening to patients, who were thus more willing to engage in conversation surrounding these. Some patients and family members even expressed their appreciation of the sessions as 'fun', and it seemed that engagement and motivation within the entire treatment process of previously largely resistant patients was a core theme.
  - Throughout, improved communication and cooperation between family members was noted. It seemed that approaching emotionally charged

topics concerning problems associated with symptoms of the disorder in this way seemed less threatening to patients, who thus became engaged with them more easily.

o Another possible reason behind the acceptability of CRT for patients is that the focus of therapy diverts from being solely on themselves and symptoms of the disorder, as all family members are encouraged to contribute towards the session equally.

o Often similar thinking styles were observed between patients and their first-degree relatives, which further facilitated communication and cooperation through understanding of one another's difficulties and working together to overcome such cognitive styles together.

Observations

As with the development of any therapeutic intervention, it is likely that numerous challenges will be encountered along the way:

One caution regarding family CRT is that it is not a sole treatment for AN, but has the potential to enhance the effect of more traditional therapies, through increasing engagement and motivation in the whole treatment process. Where time and financial constraints exist, it may be possible to incorporate aspects of family CRT into family therapy as a means of broaching emotionally charged topics. However, it is hoped that the establishment of a strong evidence base for family CRT through continued investigation of its effectiveness will encourage its use as a significant component of therapy for child and adolescent AN.

It is possible that some families will find the concept of CRT initially hard to grasp, and perhaps be sceptical of its value. For example, it may be hard to deviate parents from talk of symptoms of the disorder and weight gain, and thus they may be unwilling to engage in these seemingly 'irrelevant' games and tasks. However, it is often the case that parents who attempt to focus solely on the immediate symptoms of their child's disorder are faced with hostility from the child, and progress is often compromised as the child becomes so resistant to any intervention as a result. When the purpose of CRT was explained fully to the parents and re-feeding was not neglected, parents were often willing to engage, particularly when current (i.e. TAU – treatment as usual) progress was slow. It was in these cases that the family found CRT most beneficial, and the initial reluctance of the parents to engage in CRT may actually demonstrate deficits in central coherence and set-shifting, manifesting as a difficulty in deviating from particular symptoms associated with the disorder.

Potential complications specific to family CRT are not yet known. However, we have not encountered any as yet and believe them to be unlikely due to its unthreatening and playful nature, where emotional topics are actively avoided. Nonetheless, it is important for therapists to keep in mind potential challenges whilst implementing family CRT, so that its application may be refined as it develops.

As is the case with all therapies, family CRT will not be suitable for all patients, and more knowledge is required. Possible exclusion criteria may include the inability to get the entire family together for a session. Logistically this is often a problem but in our experience this has not appeared to be a handicap to the usefulness of the treatment, as it has appeared to be beneficial even when only one parent and no siblings attended the sessions.

The flexibility of CRT to be tailored to individual patients and their families is both a significant benefit and a possible challenge.

Tailoring CRT to the neurocognitive profiles of the patient and their family members means that aspects irrelevant for that patient need not be used. However, this presents challenges for teaching and evaluating of this intervention, as it does not seem logically possible to manualise family CRT. As a result, effective guidelines and training along with an attempt to standardise the intervention are potentially problematic, especially when constructing a Randomized Controlled Trial. In the meantime, we encourage therapists to be flexible in selecting the correct content for sessions.

In our team we conduct the Ravello Profile as a standard part of the initial assessment of all new patients – allowing us a baseline for later comparison, as well as an opportunity to identify and describe the cognitive styles. It is perhaps not necessary to subject family members to neurocognitive testing (indeed this would be very time consuming), as a skilled therapist should be able to identify cognitive deficits easily through family members' performance on the tasks involved in CRT.

Flexibility on behalf of the therapist is also required in creating boundaries between family CRT and other forms of therapy (see Chapters 2 and 3). Within CRT, focus around emotionally charged topics associated with symptoms of AN is usually avoided, but in our experience this can prove very difficult. In fact it has seemed useful to 'go with the flow', given that the atmosphere is so often lightened by the playful nature of CRT.

Conclusions

Our experiences as outlined above suggest that family CRT has the potential to be a valuable addition to treatment of child and adolescent AN, particularly in family work. Not only does it appear to engage and motivate previously treatment-resistant individuals, but it also facilitates improved communication and cooperation between family members, which may have been compromised since the development of the illness. Furthermore, following family CRT, patients appear to generally make great steps towards recovery, which appear significant considering that previously many had made little or no progress.

However, there continues to be much to be learned concerning the utilisation of family CRT for child and adolescent AN. At present we do not have the necessary knowledge to determine specific indications and contraindications, nor to provide answers to issues such as at what point during treatment should it be introduced, how best to integrate it with more traditional therapies, or the optimal number of sessions.

In order to help resolve such issues, future investigation should attempt to define the 'active ingredients' of family CRT (Medical Research Council, 2000), through the implementation of a phase-two exploratory trial. Following this, it is hoped that it may be possible to attempt to establish a more robust structure and guidelines for delivery and assessment of family CRT, in order for a Randomized Controlled Trial to be implemented to determine the effectiveness and feasibility of family CRT for AN.

In light of the need to continue to develop new interventions and improve current ones in the treatment of anorexia nervosa, targeted and evidenced approaches are warmly welcomed and warranted (Bulik *et al.*, 2012) and we hope that family CRT will receive the attention we believe it deserves.

References

Braga, L. W., Da Paz Junior, A. C. and Ylvisaker, M. (2004). Direct clinician-delivered versus indirect family-supported rehabilitation of children with traumatic brain injury: A Randomized controlled trial. *Brain Injury, 19*, 819–831.

Bulik, C., Brownley, J., Shapiro, J. and Berkman, N. (2012). 'Anorexia nervosa', in P. Sturmey and M. Hersen (Eds.), *Handbook of evidence-based practice in clinical psychology*, Chapter 25. New Jersey: John Wiley and Sons, Inc.

Carr, A. (2006). *Family therapy: Concepts, process and practice* (2nd edn). New Jersey: John Wiley and Sons, Inc.

Dare, C. and Eisler, I. (2008). Family interventions in adolescent anorexia nervosa. *Child and Adolescent Psychiatric Clinics of North America, 18*, 159–173.

Downs, K. and Blow, A. (2013). A substantive and methodological review of family-based treatment for eating disorders: the last 25 years of research. *Journal of Family Therapy, 35*, 3–28.

Eisler, I. (2005). The empirical and theoretical base of family therapy and multiple family day therapy for adolescent anorexia nervosa. *Journal of Family Therapy, 27*, 104–131.

Eisler, I. (2013). Family therapy for adolescent eating disorders: a special form of therapy or family therapy with a special focus? *Journal of Family Therapy, 35*, 1–2.

Eisler, I., Lock, J. and LeGrange, D. (2010). 'Family-based treatments for adolescents with anorexia nervosa: single-family and multifamily approaches', in C. Grilo, and J. Mitchell (Eds.) *The treatment of eating disorders: A clinical handbook*. New York, London: The Guilford Press.

Fairburn, C. (2005). Evidence-based treatment of anorexia nervosa. *International Journal of Eating Disorders, 37*, S26–S30.

Fisher, C., Hetrick, S. and Rushford, N. (2010). Family therapy for anorexia nervosa (Review). *The Cochrane Collaboration*. New Jersey: John Wiley and Sons, Inc.

Friedman-Yakoobian, M. S., Mueser, K. T., Giuliano, A., Goff, D. C. and Seidman, L. J. (2009). Family-directed cognitive adaptation for schizophrenia. *Journal of Clinical Psychology: In Session, 65*, 854–867.

Galimberti, E., Fadda, E., Cavallini, M. C., Martoni, R. M., Erzegovesi, S. and Bellodi, L. (2012). Executive functioning in anorexia nervosa patients and their unaffected relatives. *Psychiatry Research, 208*, 238–244.

Harisson, A., Tchanturia, K. and Treasure, J. (2011). Measuring state trait properties of detail processing and global integration ability in eating disorders. *The World Journal of Biological Psychiatry, 12* (6), 462–472.

Herscovici, C. R. (2013). 'Family approaches', in B. Lask and R. Bryant-Waugh (Eds.) *Eating disorders in childhood and adolescence* (4th edn.), Chapter 13, London: Routledge.

Holliday, J., Tchanturia, K., Landau, S., Collier, D. and Treasure, M. D. (2005). Is impaired set-shifting an endophenotype of anorexia nervosa? *The American Journal of Psychiatry, 162,* 2269–2275.

Lask, B. and Bryant-Waugh, R. (2013). 'Overview of management', in B. Lask, and R. Bryant-Waugh (Eds.) *Eating disorders in childhood and adolescence* (4th edn), Chapter 10. London: Routledge.

Lask, B. and Roberts, A. (2014). Family-based cognitive remediation therapy for anorexia nervosa. *Clinical Child Psychology and Psychiatry* (in press).

Lopez, C., Tchanturia, K., Stahl, D. and Treasure, J. (2008). Central coherence in eating disorders: a systematic review. *Psychological Medicine, 38* (10), 1393–1404.

Lopez, C., Tchanturia, K., Stahl, D. and Treasure, J. (2009). Weak central coherence in eating disorders: A step towards looking for an endophenotype of eating disorders. *Journal of Clinical and Experimental Neuropsychology, 31,* 117–125.

Medical Research Council (2000). *A framework for development and evaluation of RCTs for complicated interventions to improve health.* Medical Research Council. Retrieved from www. mrc.ac.uk/Utilities/Documentrecord/index.htm?d=MRC003372

Minuchin, S., Rosman, B. and Baker, L. (1978). *Psychosomatic families: anorexia nervosa in context.* Cambridge, MA: Harvard University Press.

NICE (2004). *Eating disorders: core interventions in the treatment and management of anorexia nervosa and related eating disorders.* CG9. London: National Institute for Health and Clinical Excellence.

Poletti, S., Anselmetti, S., Riccaboni, R., Bosia, M., Buonocore, M., Smeraldi, E. and Cavallaro, R. (2012). Self-awareness of cognitive functioning in schizophrenia: Patients and their relatives. *Psychiatry Research, 198,* 207–211.

Roberts, M. E., Tchanturia, K. and Treasure, J. L. (2010). Exploring the neurocognitive signature of poor set-shifting in anorexia and bulimia nervosa. *Journal of Psychiatric Research, 44,* 964–970.

Roberts, M. E., Tchanturia, K. and Treasure, J. L. (2013). Is attention to detail a similarly strong candidate endophenotype for anorexia and bulimia nervosa? *World Journal of Biological Psychiatry, 14* (6), 452–463. DOI:10.3109/15622975.2011.639804

Rose, M., Frampton, I. and Lask, B. (2012). A case series investigating distinct neuropsychological profiles in children and adolescents with anorexia nervosa. *European Eating Disorders Review, 20,* 32–38.

Selvini-Palazzoli, M. (1974). *Self-starvation: From the intrapsychic to the Transpersonal Approach to anorexia nervosa.* London: Chaucer.

Stedal, K., Frampton, I., Landrø, N. and Lask, B. (2012). An examination of the Ravello profile – a neuropsychological test battery for anorexia nervosa. *European Eating Disorders Review, 20* (3), 175–181.

Stedal, K., Rose, M., Frampton, I., Landro, N. I. and Lask, B. (2012). The neuropsychological profile of children, adolescents, and young adults with anorexia nervosa. *Archives of Clinical Neuropsychology, 27* (3), 329–337.

Steinhausen, H. C. (2002). The outcome of anorexia nervosa in the 20th century. *American Journal of Psychiatry, 159* (8), 1284–1293.

Strober, M. (2014). Family-based therapy is over-valued. *Advances in Eating Disorders – Theory, Research and Practice.* DOI: 10.1080/21662630.2014.898395.

Tchanturia, K., Davies, H., Harrison, A., Roberts, M., Nakazato, M., Schmidt, U., Treasure, J. and Morris, R. (2012). Poor cognitive flexibility in eating disorders: Examining the evidence using the Wisconcin Card Sorting Task. *Plos One, 7* (1), e28331.

Tchanturia, K., Lloyd, S. and Lang, K. (2013). Cognitive Remediation in eating disorders. *International Journal of Eating Disorders Special Issue, 46* (5), 492–496.

Tenconi, E., Santonastaso, P., Degortes, D., Bosello, R., Mapelli, D. and Favaro, A. (2010). Set-shifting abilities, central coherence, and handedness in anorexia nervosa patients, their unaffected siblings and healthy controls: Exploring putative endophenotypes. *The World Journal of Biological Psychiatry, 11,* 813–823.

Wade, S. L., Michaud, L. and Brown, T. M. (2006). Putting the pieces together: Preliminary efficacy of a family problem-solving intervention for children with traumatic brain injury. *Journal of Head Trauma Rehabilitation, 21,* 57–67.

Whitney, J., Murray, J., Gavan, K., Todd, G., Whitaker, W. and Treasure, J. (2005). Experience of caring for someone with anorexia nervosa: qualitative study. *The British Journal of Psychiatry, 187,* 444–449.

Wood, L., Al-Kairulla, H. and Lask, B. (2011). Group cognitive remediation therapy for adolescents with anorexia nervosa. *Clinical Child Psychology and Psychiatry, 16,* 225–231.

11

EXPLORING BRAIN STRUCTURE AND THE NEUROCOGNITIVE PROFILE OF ANOREXIA NERVOSA USING MAGNETIC RESONANCE IMAGING

Leon Fonville, Nick P. Lao-Kaim and Kate Tchanturia

Neuroimaging techniques have allowed researchers to explore revealing global and regional changes in brain structure as well as brain function, including neurotransmitter systems, glucose metabolism, cerebral blood flow and connectivity of neural networks. Magnetic resonance imaging (MRI) is one of the most widely used techniques to examine the brain *in vivo* and has become a mainstay in psychiatric research. Using MRI, researchers have been able to improve upon our knowledge of the size and shape of the brain in anorexia nervosa (AN) as well as identify which regions present aberrant activity as compared to the general population. In comparison to many other psychiatric conditions, neuroimaging research of AN is still in its infancy and important questions remain that may help us better understand this complex disorder. For instance, are these structural and functional changes a consequence of malnutrition, or do they play a causal role in the pathological behaviour present in AN? To what extent do they contribute to its maintenance? If we move beyond the core body and weigh-related symptoms, how are these related to the variety of cognitive processing inefficiencies often reported in neuropsychological studies of AN? In this chapter we will discuss some of the findings in neuroimaging literature and provide an overview with regard to novel research by our group on the neurocognitive profile of AN.

Brain volume in anorexia nervosa

(For more details and complete reference list: Fonville, L., Giampietro, V., Williams, S. C., Simmons, A. and Tchanturia, K. [2013]. Alterations in brain structure in adults with anorexia nervosa and the impact of illness duration. *Psychological Medicine, 42,* 1–11.)

Perhaps one of the earliest findings in anorexia nervosa using neuroimaging has been the enlargement of cortical sulci, which indicates shrinkage or atrophy of the brain. Originally found using computerised tomography (CT), brain atrophy in ill patients has remained a consistent finding, replicated using more suitable and modern techniques such as magnetic resonance imaging. It is now believed that atrophy of grey matter, which comprises the neuronal cell bodies, underlies this reduction in brain volume. Whilst the overall volume of grey matter (GMV) differs extensively between individuals, the density of neuronal cell bodies in a specific region of the brain is associated with the ability or skill of the function associated with that brain region. A clear example of this can be found in a study by Castro-Fornieles *et al.* (2009) on adolescents with AN where a reduction of GMV in temporal and parietal areas of the brain was correlated with poorer performance on the Rey Complex Figure Test – a measure of visual memory and visuo-spatial ability (discussed previously in Chapters 1 and 6).

Although it is clear that there are changes in GMV and that a decrease in density is likely to affect cognitive abilities, further elucidation of whether these changes are region-specific or merely a result of a non-specific global decrease is essential. The former would imply that specific functions are affected and this might manifest as an impairment or inefficiency. A meta-analysis of several studies assessing regional changes in AN reported reductions in the left hypothalamus, left inferior parietal lobule, right lentiform nucleus and right caudate nucleus (Titova *et al.* 2013). This led the authors to conclude that alterations in AN are specific to regions associated with appetite and somatosensory processing. However, this reasoning was drawn from studies that report region-specific changes as well as a global decrease in GMV without taking necessary steps to ensure these findings are clearly separable. If we assume that both are present at the same time, then region-specific changes should be *additive* to a global decrease in volume.

In total, three out of eight studies of currently ill patients have taken global changes into account when assessing regional changes; two reported a global decrease in GMV (Gaudio *et al.* 2011; Fonville *et al.* 2013a) and two found region-specific changes (Brooks *et al.* 2011; Gaudio *et al.* 2011) but we do not observe an overlap in their findings.

Finally, some studies have explored associations between brain volume and clinical characteristics observed in anorexia patients. Body mass index became a prominent candidate early on, through positive correlations with total GMV and negative correlations with total cerebrospinal fluid (CSF) (Katzman *et al.* 1996), but attempts at replication have led to mixed results (Joos *et al.* 2010; Brooks *et al.* 2011; Boghi *et al.* 2011; Fonville *et al.* 2013a). Continuing from preliminary findings of Boghi *et al.* (2011), which related greater volume loss to more chronic cases in the cerebellum, a recent study from our group further illustrated this by finding a negative correlation between illness duration and GMV in the cerebellum, illustrating greater atrophy of grey matter in more chronic cases (Fonville *et al.* 2013a). The cerebellum is a well-connected structure that has been implicated in many functions; within the current context it is of particular interest that animal studies of AN have found that reductions in cerebellar volume play a role in the ability to maintain low weight (Zhu and Wang 2008). The same relationship was also found in two parts of the midbrain, namely the ventral tegmental area and the substantia nigra. These regions have been implicated in motivation and anticipation of food reward and intake, as well as over-exercising via dopaminergic projections to higher order cortico-limbic regions of the brain that regulate affect and cognition (Naranayan *et al.* 2010; Verhagen *et al.* 2011; van Zessen *et al.* 2012). Taken together, this would imply that some of the core symptoms of AN, such as low BMI and altered reward value of food and exercise, might become easier to maintain in chronic cases (long duration of illness) due to changes in brain structure.

Whilst there are clear GMV changes during the ill state, studies looking at weight-recovered patients report either full recovery of GMV loss (Wagner *et al.* 2006; McCormick *et al.* 2008; Favaro *et al.* 2012) or an intermediate profile between the general population and underweight patients (Lambe *et al.* 1997; Swayze *et al.* 2003; Roberto *et al.* 2010; Mühlau *et al.* 2007; Joos *et al.* 2010; Friederich *et al.* 2012). These findings could suggest that brain volume improves with weight recovery and supports the idea that AN is not the result of reduced GMV, but rather that brain atrophy is a consequence of chronic malnutrition.

Efficiency of cognitive functions and a potential role for CRT

Working memory in AN

(For more details and complete reference list: Lao-Kaim N.P., Giampietro, V., Williams, S.C.R., Simmons, A. and Tchanturia, K. [2013]. Functional MRI investigation of verbal working memory in adults with anorexia nervosa. *European Psychiatry*, DOI: 10.1016/j.eurpsy.2013.05.2003.)

Working memory is defined as a limited capacity store where information is held, maintained and manipulated in order to plan and carry out behaviour as well as to facilitate other cognitive processes such as learning and reasoning (Miller *et al.* 1960). In AN, the neuropsychological literature on working memory has been inconsistent, with reports of either inferior or no difference in performance, and some researchers even alluding to superior performance in comparison to healthy control groups. In addition, while preparing for an fMRI investigation of verbal working memory (vWM), we found that some of these studies used neuropsychological tasks that may not have been probing the intended cognitive process (Lao-Kaim *et al.* 2013). The term 'working' implies the involvement of both short-term memory (STM) and processing mechanisms that make use of items stored in STM (Cowan 2008).

It is useful to conceptualise this difference with the example of mental arithmetic: short-term memory allows one to first retain an original mathematical problem and keep it active in memory, whereas working-memory processes involve mentally juggling the numbers held in the short-term store to help calculate an answer. Re-classifying the existing literature based on this understanding led to the realisation that only four studies had assessed vWM in AN; two reported superior performance in AN (Brooks *et al.* 2012; Dickson *et al.* 2008), one reported inferior performance (Seed *et al.* 2002) and one reported no difference (Nikendei *et al.* 2011).

In terms of neuroimaging, we were able to identify only one article using fMRI to assess vWM in adolescents with AN (Castro-Fornieles *et al.* 2010). The paradigm however, was more suitable for measuring vigilance and did not capture all the components of verbal working memory (Smith *et al.* 1998). We decided to explore the neurocorrelates associated with vWM in AN using a task in which the difficulty increased as a result of increasing the number of items participants committed to memory (Lao-Kaim *et al.* 2013). The letter version of the *n*-back task (Braver *et al.* 1997) required participants to press a button when the letter presented on-screen during fMRI acquisition was identical to the one they saw *n* trials before, where *n* was 1, 2 or 3. In terms of performance, both AN and healthy controls became slower at responding and made more errors on the task as the number of items committed to vWM increased. There were no significant performance differences between the two groups at any task difficulty. We also were not able to find any differences in brain function between the groups, both when cognitive load conditions were considered separately and when they were treated as a systematic increase in difficulty. Given our group size (the largest study in the eating disorder literature, with a total of 62 participants), these results are difficult to dispute. In fact, because of the sheer number of tests that are conducted, null findings are probably amongst the most reliable within neuroimaging research. In essence, this can be likened to the probability of rolling a certain number on a die; the chances of landing a six only increase the more you roll.

Detailed assessment of previous vWM studies shows that both reports of superior performance involved subliminal/supraliminal presentation of neutral, aversive and food images in conjunction with the *n*-back task (Brooks *et al.* 2012; Dickson *et al.* 2008). These results may therefore enlighten on the differential effects of provocation and distracting stimuli on cognitive processing; however, they cannot make firm conclusions regarding vWM itself, particularly because the images and their content may have affected performance of the healthy control group as well as the AN group. This is perhaps the reason for very different results when vWM is tested in near isolation.

Seed *et al.* (2002) found that AN were significantly slower than healthy controls at a memory scanning task in which participants had to respond when one of five pre-specified numbers appeared on-screen. In combination with the most recent report of no performance or neural differences, it would appear that verbal working memory is as efficient in AN as it is in healthy comparison group and that there is no indication of the utilisation of different cognitive strategies. Importantly, it raises the point that there is no need for therapies to pursue remediation of verbal working memory in AN and moreover, suggests that it may be worth considering the use of vWM assessment scores as an active control condition in future large-scale studies on the efficacy of CRT.

Enhanced attention to local detail

(Detailed references and figures can be found in our article in open access journal freely downloadable from the website: Fonville, L., Lao-Kaim, N.P., Giampietro, V., Van den Eynde, F., Davies, H., Lounes, N., Andrew, C., Dalton, J., Baron-Cohen, S., Simmons, A., Williams, S.C.R. and Tchanturia, K. [2013b]. Evaluation of Enhanced Attention to Local Detail in anorexia nervosa using the Embedded Figures Test. *Plos One, 2013*; 8.)

Central coherence is broadly defined as the ability to capture the general meaning of information rather than focusing on specific details within the 'bigger picture'. It has been suggested that in those with Autism Spectrum Disorder (ASD), this cognitive function – often referred to as weak central coherence – is lacking (Happé and Frith 2006). Comparisons between the neurocognitive profiles of AN and ASD have revealed behavioural similarities on emotional theory of mind, set-shifting as well as this detail-focused processing (Oldershaw *et al.* 2011). A systematic review of the prevalence of ASD in EDs found higher rates compared to healthy controls (Huke *et al.* 2013) and clinical observations of social impairments and obsessive-compulsive traits point to links between AN and ASD. Women with AN also display a greater number of self-reported autistic traits compared to healthy controls, especially on items related to global thinking ('bigger picture'), and inflexibility of thinking (Tchanturia *et al.* 2013; Chapter 13). With regard to research into central coherence, people with AN do not seem to have superior local processing as in ASD, but they do seem to experience difficulties with central coherence (Lang *et al.* 2004; Lopez *et al.* 2008). This neuropsychological finding has been found quite consistently, but there is no research into the underlying brain function in AN.

To further complicate the matter, many of the behavioural findings from ASD studies, using tasks such as the Embedded Figures Test (EFT – Witkin *et al.* 1971), have not been replicated in fMRI studies, that *do* find changes in neural activation (Fonville *et al.* 2013b). One of the limitations to these studies is small sample sizes and heterogeneity in methodologies, making the comparisons within ASD literature difficult. Studies that have employed a low level baseline, such as a fixation cross, found greater activation in occipital and parietal regions in ASD compared to healthy controls and less activation in frontal regions (Ring *et al.* 1999; Damarla *et al.* 2010). Other studies that used a baseline similar to the EFT itself, such as a matching figures task, in an attempt to isolate the visuo-spatial searching component of the task, found either no difference at all (Manjaly *et al.* 2007) or less activation in ASD in occipital regions, with greater activation in temporal regions (Spencer *et al.* 2012a). Using a different methodological approach, the latter group also found greater task-related deactivation of the default mode network in parietal regions and the posterior cingulate cortex in ASD than in healthy controls, as well as in unaffected siblings of those with ASD (Spencer *et al.* 2012b).

Taken together, it becomes challenging to link both behavioural findings with brain function, and to further link AN and ASD on a neural level. Our own research utilized a modified version of the EFT, altered to an fMRI context, to explore the neural substrates of a local processing bias in AN compared to healthy controls in light of fMRI findings in ASD (Fonville *et al.* 2013b). The original version of the EFT requires participants to find a target geometrical shape in an embedded figure, and contour the found shape in this figure once found. The embedded figures could either be simple (SEF) or complex (CEF) to add a level of difficulty to the task. The modified version differs in that participants had to indicate if one of two figures contained a target geometrical shape using a joystick (left or right).

While no difference in reaction time was found, the healthy controls made *fewer* errors on the task overall. This finding is not in line with overall AN or ASD literature, but it is important to note that the changes made to the paradigm could have changed the task in such a manner that a different cognitive strategy is required to optimally perform the task. Indeed, fMRI studies in ASD have failed to replicate the previous behavioural studies and often find no difference in reaction time between ASD and healthy controls (Ring *et al.* 1999; Damarla *et al.* 2010; Manjaly *et al.* 2010; Spencer *et al.* 2012a). The finding that healthy controls perform better at distinguishing which of two figures contains a simple shape is not in disagreement with AN literature, as the change from a yes/no response to a single stimulus, to a left/right choice between two stimuli requires a different approach and the argument could be made that a more global search strategy would be beneficial vs. attention to detail. This is further supported by a clear ceiling effect of 100% accuracy in healthy controls on the Simple Embedded Figures (SEF).

With regard to imaging findings, the AN group showed greater task-related activation in the fusiform gyrus, with a trend for greater activation in the superior parietal lobule, and greater task-related deactivation in the posterior cingulate cortex. The increase in the fusiform gyrus and superior parietal lobule, associated with visuo-spatial searching and object perception (Grill-Spector *et al.* 2003; James *et al.* 2010), are consistent with some ASD findings (Ring *et al.* 1999; Damarla *et al.* 2010), but not others (Baron-Cohen *et al.* 2006; Spencer *et al.* 2012a,b). The differences made to the paradigm and the differences across studies with regard to the paradigm and samples, make any comparison problematic.

In summary, those with AN make more errors on the task, whilst demonstrating showing greater neural effort during the task. These findings suggest that central coherence remains an important aspect in the neurocognitive profile of AN and might even suggest a potential overlap with ASD in terms of the neural networks that are involved.

Cognitive flexibility

Cognitive flexibility encompasses the ability to switch between thinking about several different concepts in order to advantageously modify one's behaviour in response to changes in the environment (Scott 1962). A meta-analysis of studies using a variety of neuropsychological tests to assess cognitive flexibility indicated that people with AN exhibit problems in this executive domain (described in greater detail in Chapter 1). Specifically, they tend to perseverate, that is to say, they consistently respond to stimuli using a strategy that may have yielded positive outcomes previously but has since begun to yield negative outcomes (Tchanturia et al. 2012). More recently, the discovery of inefficient cognitive flexibility within unaffected sisters (Tenconi et al. 2010) and children who have mothers with AN (Kothari et al. 2013), as well its presence following recovery (Tchanturia et al. 2012; Tenconi et al. 2010), has fuelled speculation that cognitive flexibility may possibly be an endophenotype of the disorder. Although there has been some disagreement as to whether it constitutes a genetic risk factor, or whether merely living closely with someone who has AN nurtures inflexible thinking styles (Galimberti et al. 2013), the fact remains that inefficient cognitive flexibility results in obsessive-compulsive- and perfectionistic traits (Tchanturia et al. 2012) that not only facilitate control over appetite but also make therapy incredibly challenging (Tchanturia et al. 2011).

Given the importance as both a risk- and maintaining factor, surprisingly few neuroimaging studies have looked at cognitive flexibility in AN. This could be due to difficulties in both defining what cognitive flexibility means – whether it encompasses task switching, attention, learning or a combination – and isolating such behaviour in the scanning environment. It is perhaps because of these reasons that Zastrow et al. (2007) used a visual discrimination task during fMRI instead of a more complex neuropsychological paradigm to assess brain function during both behavioural and cognitive flexibility in AN. Interestingly, it was during behavioural flexibility that AN exhibited significantly lower activity in motivation-related fronto-striatal network (putamen, thalamus and anterior cingulate cortex), with no further group differences during cognitive flexibility. In addition, dominant activation was recorded in the temporoparietal junction and middle frontal gyrus, which would suggest a greater level of cognitive supervisory control over task-performance.

According to this experiment, behavioural flexibility – which involves switching between different response options regardless of whether a shift to a different task rule occurs or not – could be the source of cognitive flexibility inefficiencies observed in previous neuropsychological studies. However, Sato et al. (2013) were able to indicate the presence of further functional alterations during flexible thinking. A more holistic approach was used, in which discrete events pertaining to efficient cognitive shifting and efficient maintenance of abstract rules during the Wisconsin Card Sorting Task (WCST; described in the Chapter 1) were compared. The authors found alterations of brain activity in the inferior frontal gyrus and para-hippocampal gyrus during cognitive flexibility.

The lack of overlap between studies effectively evaluating the same phenomena is not uncommon within the field of neuroimaging. In this case, it may stem from sample sizes (15 in both studies) deemed inadequate by modern standards, or more likely, the different experimental tasks used. For instance, it could be argued that the visual discrimination task lacked sensitivity to detect alterations related to cognitive flexibility whereas the WCST is well documented to show cognitive flexibility problems in AN. Although results are inconsistent, recent work from our research group has taken the first steps to linking these seemingly unique findings. Lao-Kaim *et al.* (2014) used a similar method to Sato *et al.* (2013) in identifying discrete events during performance of the WCST to, first, evaluate cognitive flexibility and second, to evaluate instrumental learning, in a group of 32 AN patients as compared to 32 non eating-disorder participants. We were also able to subtract activity – related to strings of correct choices – by using a high-level fMRI baseline as opposed to mere fixation or rest, meaning that our signal should theoretically be independent of behavioural flexibility processes. It is noteworthy that previous to this, there were no neuroimaging reports on learning in AN; however, we reasoned that to be cognitively flexible, one must be able to form associations between actions and their outcomes.

Perhaps not surprisingly, we found lower activity in the caudate body, precuneus and cerebellum but higher activity in the posterior cingulate cortex when AN participants were *learning* a new rule. The caudate is a part of the dorsal striatum and frontostriatal network – involved in both the formation and reversal of action-outcome contingencies. Whilst there was no evidence to say that this difference in caudate activity resulted in poor action-outcome formation, it is possible that it may affect the way in which previously learned associations are unlearned, which in turn may lead to perseverative behaviour.

We also found a greater fluctuation of activity in areas of the frontoparietal control network (middle frontal gyrus and precuneus) when looking at cognitive flexibility, in which AN had higher activity during cognitive shifts and lower activity when they were sticking to the same rule – as compared to healthy controls (Lao-Kaim *et al.* 2014). This network, also found in Zastrow *et al.* (2007), acts as a master switch that redirects cognitive resources towards either internal (default-mode network) or external goal-directed cognition (Spreng *et al.* 2010, 2013). The presence of a strong interaction in the posterior cingulate cortex in the previous learning comparison only adds to this possibility, since this region is a central hub of the default-mode network which, amongst other processes including day-dreaming and future/past projection, has shown heightened functional connectivity with the frontoparietal control network during internal cognitive tasks such as autobiographical planning (Spreng *et al.* 2010). Interestingly, the posterior cingulate cortex shares reciprocal connections with the medial temporal lobe memory system via the para-hippocampal gyrus (Lavenex *et al.* 2002; Parvizi *et al.* 2006), an area previously identified by Sato *et al.* (2013) during their assessment of cognitive flexibility in AN. Taken together, it may be that people with AN are unable to remain engaged with external stimuli, such as the cards shown during the WCST, and instead gravitate towards an internally focussed form of goal-directed cognition.

In summary, people with AN display widespread functional abnormalities during the performance of tasks requiring cognitive flexibility. Aberrant activity in the frontoparietal control network may indicate a difficulty in maintaining attention towards external stimuli that are necessary for an informed change of behaviour, and instead adopt an internal strategy. Fronto-striatal alterations, particularly within the caudate body may additionally indicate an inefficiency of learning and/or reverse learning, which could potentially result in a tendency to stick with the same behaviour even if it is detrimental. Perseverative tendencies could therefore be a substrate of changes in multiple high-order processes and may contribute to the maintenance of AN.

Does CRT have any effect on cognition?

Pilot study exploring attention to detail (central coherence) in AN after CRT

While studies looking at the effects of CRT in schizophrenia have reported improvements in domains such as attention, reasoning and working memory, along with changes in brain activation (Wexler et al. 2000; Wykes et al. 2002; Bor et al. 2011; Penades et al. 2013), the effects of CRT in AN have not been assessed using fMRI. In this section we will briefly review the findings of the first longitudinal study on the effects of CRT on central coherence, as measured by a variant of the Embedded Figures Test (EFT).

As previously mentioned, in our cross-sectional investigation, we found greater accuracy on this task in non eating-disorder participants, with less neural effort when compared to AN (Fonville et al. 2013b). This research was extended with a subset of this sample, comprised of ten patients with AN who had received ten sessions of CRT, and fourteen healthy controls who had not received any therapy. This subset of patients and controls was reanalysed to assess difference in performance and brain function at baseline before any treatment was administered in the patient group (T1). After an equivalent interval of time (T2), both were scanned again while performing the exact same task (EFT) as before (see section on Central Coherence, Chapter 1. We hypothesized that CRT would have a positive effect on both performance and brain function, translated into faster reaction times with fewer errors and a decrease in oxygen consumption in task-related regions that were previously found to indicate greater neural effort.

Due to a clear ceiling effect in both groups for the simple embedded figures (SEF), analysis focused only on the complex embedded figures (CEF). Both groups showed an improvement on the task in terms of reaction time, and accuracy over time. However, there was no difference in the amount of improvement between the two groups, which would have been indicative of a CRT-specific effect. Neuroimaging data revealed a *group* x *time* interaction for CEF in the medial frontal gyrus, fusiform gyrus and middle occipital gyrus. Further exploration of these findings revealed that task-related activation in the fusiform gyrus and middle occipital gyrus decreased to a greater extent from T1 to T2 in the AN group, and although a decrease was observed in the healthy control group, this was not as pronounced. Additionally, less task-related deactivation was also found at T2 in AN in the medial frontal gyrus.

Since the improvements on performance did not differ between the two groups, this could be regarded as a practice effect. Accordingly, the fMRI results revealed less task-related activation in visual areas (Grill-Spector et al. 2003; James et al. 2010), but because this decrease was stronger in AN, it could be indicative of a change due to CRT, on top of a practice effect. Because task-related deactivation negatively correlates with task-related activation (Uddin et al. 2009; Pfefferbaum et al. 2011), a decrease in task-related activation along with a decrease in task-related deactivation would provide further support for an increase in neural effort. This is precisely what is found, as the right medial frontal gyrus – which has been implicated in the default mode network (Laird et al. 2009; Zhang and Li 2012) – shows exactly this type of relation in regard to the task-related activation in visual regions.

It is important to note that this variant of the EFT requires participants to switch their attention between two stimuli during visuo-spatial searching and as such, necessitates a more global approach during performance. The previous cross-sectional investigation revealed greater neural effort along with poorer performance and so, such greater efficiency of brain function could be a sign of successfully adopting a more global strategy during the task. In addition, this study did not include a 'treatment as usual' patient group, and therefore we are unable to rule out differences in practice effects between AN and healthy controls. It is also possible that with a larger sample size, differences in improvement over time may surface, as this study might have lacked power to accurately capture what is occurring.

One final caveat of this study is that these findings may be limited to this sample. Unlike the cross-sectional investigation, the subsample for the longitudinal study did not show differences between the two groups at baseline assessment. While this does mean that any changes found afterwards are purely due to time and CRT, it also means that this group is different from the larger sample of AN. Indeed, the current subsample consists mostly of daycare patients instead of a more balanced group containing patients with severer symptoms. It is possible that severe cases could show greater improvement, but the current sample is limited in any predictions. Further studies with larger samples are required to evaluate the effects of CRT on cognitive inefficiencies using fMRI.

Summary

In this chapter, we have outlined a snapshot of the current MRI literature on AN and cognition, as well as a small pilot study targeting cognitive performance/functioning instead of the core symptoms. Throughout our own research on brain volume, it became clear that the apparent consensus might have been presumptuous, and more research is needed to assess region-specific changes. Similarly, a detailed exploration of working memory in AN revealed that there is actually no real difference compared to the general population. Our findings on central coherence matched the behavioural literature and were consistent with detail-oriented processing. When assessing cognitive flexibility, we found that those with AN seem to show changes in neural circuitry relating to learning and are inclined towards an internally-focused form of goal-directed cognition, unable to remain engaged in external tasks. Finally, a small pilot study on CRT revealed some changes in neural response that could be indicative of an effect due to CRT.

Aside from this overall 'first look' into the neural substrates of cognitive characteristics seen in AN, our findings also provide some support for previous investigations implicating the chemical messenger dopamine in AN pathology (Kaye, Fudge and Paulus 2009; Kaye et al. 2013). Region-specific loss of GMV in the midbrain – an area associated with dopamine synthesis – that worsens with chronicity, could lead to alterations in neural circuits that are dependent on dopamine to function properly. Indeed, the caudate body as well as the posterior cingulate cortex in part rely on effective dopaminergic signalling, thus it follows that the functional differences observed in these regions during our investigation of cognitive flexibility further the suggestion of a dysregulated dopamine system. Current observations regarding the exact changes of dopamine function are complex and as such are beyond the focus of this chapter; however, it suffices to say that its role in the maintenance of AN has rightfully attracted great interest over recent years.

Despite its novelty, we believe our work has clarified that alterations are present without the use of symptom provoking stimuli, and could be part of a larger neurocognitive profile. This novelty also means that replication studies are of utmost importance in order to move forward, and the continuing rise in the number of studies in AN using fMRI is promising. Additionally, the ever increasing complexity and variety in methodology will allow for a deeper understanding of the alterations that are present. As of yet, little research has been done into how different parts of the brain communicate in AN and whether there are any changes in its connectivity, be it functional or structural.

Finally, anorexia nervosa is one of very few psychiatric disorders with serious physiological consequences, and through longitudinal investigations, assessment of the trajectory of recovery is vital for research that aims for translation to clinical practice.

Acknowledgments

This work would not have been possible without the contributions made by our entire team. We would like to thank Professor Steven Williams, Dr Vincent Giampietro, Dr Andy Simmons, Dr Simon Surguladze, Dr Helen Davies, Naima Lounes, Dr Frederique Van den Eynde and Christopher Andrew for all of their contributions to: 'The BRCACE project: Exploring brain structure and the neurocognitive profile of anorexia nervosa using magnetic resonance imaging.'

This work was supported by the Swiss Anorexia Nervosa Foundation, the Psychiatry Research Trust, the NIHR Biomedical Research Centre for Mental Health at South London and Maudsley NHS Foundation Trust, and the Institute of Psychiatry, King's College London.

References

Main references of this chapter can be found in our peer reviewed papers

Fonville, L., Giampietro, V., Williams, S., Simmons, A. and Tchanturia, K. (2013). Alterations in brain structure in adults with anorexia nervosa and the impact of illness duration. *Psychological Medicine, 44,* (9), 1965–1975.

Fonville, L., Lao-Kaim, N.P., Giampietro, V., Van den Eynde, F., Davies, H., Lounes, N., Andrew, C., Dalton, J., Baron-Cohen, S., Simmons, A., Williams, S.C.R. and Tchanturia, K. (2013). Evaluation of enhanced attention to local detail in anorexia nervosa using the Embedded Figures Test. *Plos One 8* (5): eb3964.

Lao-Kaim, N.P., Giampietro, V., Williams, S.C.R., Simmons, A. and Tchanturia, K. (2013). Functional MRI investigation of verbal working memory in adults with anorexia nervosa. *European Psychiatry,* DOI: 10.1016/j.eurpsy.2013.05.2003.

Additional references for the chapter

Baron-Cohen, S., Ring, H., Chitnis, X., Wheelwright, S., Gregory, L. *et al.* (2006). fMRI of parents of children with Asperger Syndrome: a pilot study. *Brain and Cognition, 61,* 122–130.

Boghi, A., Sterpone, S., Sales, S., D'Agata, F., Bradac, G.B., Zullo, G. and Munno, D. (2011). In vivo evidence of global and focal brain alterations in anorexia nervosa. *Psychiatry Research – Neuroimaging, 192,* 154–159.

Bor, J., Brunelin, J., D'Amato, T., Costes, N., Suaud-Chagny, M.F., Saoud, M. and Poulet, E. (2011). How can cognitive remediation therapy modulate brain activations in schizophrenia? An fMRI study. *Psychiatry Research, 192,* 160–166.

Braver, T.S., Cohen, J.D., Nystrom, L.E., Jonides, J., Smith, E.E. and Noll, D.C. (1997). A parametric study of prefrontal cortex involvement in human working memory. *NeuroImage, 5,* 49–62.

Brooks, S., Barker, G.J., O'Daly, O.G., Brammer, M., Williams, S.C.R., Benedict, C., Schiöth, H.B., Treasure, J. and Campbell, I.C. (2011a). Restraint of appetite and reduced regional brain volumes in anorexia nervosa: a voxel-based morphometric study. *BMC Psychiatry, 11,* 179.

Brooks, S.J., O'Daly, O.G., Uher, R., Schioth, H.B., Treasure, J. and Campbell, I.C. (2012). Subliminal food images compromise superior working memory performance in women with restricting anorexia nervosa. *Consciousness and Cognition, 21,* 751–763.

Castro-Fornieles, J., Bargalló, N., Lázaro, L., Andrés, S., Falcon, C., Plana, MT. and Junqué, C. (2009). A cross-sectional and follow-up voxel-based morphometric MRI study in adolescent anorexia nervosa. *Journal of Psychiatric Research, 43,* 331–340.

Castro-Fornieles, J., Caldu, X., Andres-Perpina, S., Lazaro, L., Bargallo, N., *et al.* (2010). A cross-sectional and follow-up functional MRI study with a working memory task in adolescent anorexia nervosa. *Neuropsychologia, 48,* 4111–4116.

Cowan, N. (2008). What are the differences between long-term, short-term, and working memory? *Progress in Brain Research, 169,* 323–338.

Damarla, S.R., Keller, T.A., Kana, R.K., Cherkassky, V.L., Williams, D.L. *et al.* (2010). Cortical underconnectivity coupled with preserved visuospatial cognition in autism: Evidence from an fMRI study of an embedded figures task. *Autism Research, 3,* 273–279.

Dickson, H., Brooks, S., Uher, R., Tchanturia, K., Treasure, J. and Campbell, I.C. (2008). The inability to ignore: distractibility in women with restricting anorexia nervosa. *Psychological Medicine, 38,* 1741–1748.

Favaro, A., Santonastaso, P., Manara, R., Bosello, R., Bommarito, G., Tenconi, E. and Di Salle, F. (2012). Disruption of visuospatial and somatosensory functional connectivity in anorexia nervosa. *Biological Psychiatry*, 72, 864–870.

Fonville, L., Lao-Kaim, N.P., Giampietro, V., Van den Eynde, F., Davies, H., Lounes, N., Andrew, C., Dalton, J., Baron-Cohen, S., Simmons, A., Williams, S.C.R. and Tchanturia, K. (2013b). Evaluation of enhanced attention to local detail in anorexia nervosa using the Embedded Figures Test. *Plos One 8* (5): eb3964.

Friederich, H.C., Walther, S., Bendszus, M., Biller, A., Thomann, P., Zeigermann, S., Katus, T., Brunner, R., Zastrow, A. and Herzog, W. (2012). Grey matter abnormalities within cortico-limbic-striatal circuits in acute and weight-restored anorexia nervosa patients. *NeuroImage*, 59, 1106–1113.

Galimberti, E., Fadda, E., Cavallini, M.C., Martoni, R.M., Erzegovesi, S. and Bellodi, L. (2013). Executive functioning in anorexia nervosa patients and their unaffected relatives. *Psychiatry Research*, 208, 238–244.

Gaudio, S., Nocchi, F., Franchin, T., Genovese, E., Cannatà, V., Longo, D. and Fariello, G. (2011). Gray matter decrease distribution in the early stages of anorexia nervosa restrictive type in adolescents. *Psychiatry Research: Neuroimaging 191*, 24–30.

Grill-Spector, K. (2003). The neural basis of object perception. *Current Opinion in Neurobiology*, 13, 159–166.

Happé, F. and Frith, U. (2006). The weak coherence account: Detail-focused cognitive style in autism spectrum disorders. *Journal of Autism and Developmental Disorders*, 36 (1), 5–25.

Ho, D.E., Imai, K., King, G. and Stuart, E.A. (2007). Matching as nonparametric preprocessing for reducing model dependence in parametric causal inference. *Political Analysis*, 15, 199–236.

Huke, V., Turk, J., Saeideh, S., Kent, A. and Morgan, J.F. (2013). Autism spectrum disorders in eating disorder populations: a systematic review. *European Eating Disorder Review*, 21 (5), 345–351.

James, T.W., Huh, E. and Kim, S. (2010). Temporal and spatial integration of face, object, and scene features in occipito-temporal cortex. *Brain and Cognition*, 74, 112–122.

Joos, A., Klöppel, S., Hartmann, A., Glauche, V., Tüscher, O., Perlov, E., Saum, B., Freyer, T., Zeeck, A. and van Elst, L.T. (2010). Voxel-based morphometry in eating disorders: correlation of psychopathology with grey matter volume. *Psychiatry Research – Neuroimaging*, 182, 146–151.

Katzman, D.K., Lambe, E.K., Mikulis, D.J., Ridgley, J.N., Goldbloom, D.S. and Zipursky, R.B. (1996). Cerebral gray matter and white matter volume deficits in adolescent girls with anorexia nervosa. *Journal of Pediatrics*, 129, 794–803.

Kaye, W. H., Fudge, J. L. and Paulus, M. (2009). New insights into symptoms and neurocircuit function of anorexia nervosa. *Nature Reviews Neuroscience*, 10 (8), 573–584.

Kaye, W.H., Wierenga, C.E., Bailer, U.F., Simmons, A.N. and Bischoff-Grethe, A. (2013). Nothing tastes as good as skinny feels: the neurobiology of anorexia nervosa. *Trends in Neurosciences*, 36 (2), 110–120.

Kothari, R., Solmi, F., Treasure, J. and Micali, N. (2013). The neuropsychological profile of children at high risk of developing an eating disorder. *Psychological Medicine*, 43, 1543–1554.

Laird, A.R., Eickhoff, S.B., Li, K., Robin, D.A., Glahn, D.C. et al. (2009). Investigating the functional heterogeneity of the default mode network using coordinate-based meta-analytic modeling. *Journal of Neuroscience*, 29, 14496–1505.

Lambe, E.K., Katzman, D.K., Mikulis, D.J., Kennedy, S.H. and Zipursky, R.B. (1997). Cerebral gray matter volume deficits after weight recovery from anorexia nervosa. *Archives of General Psychiatry*, 54, 537–542.

Lao-Kaim, N.P., Fonville, L., Giampietro, V.P., Williams, S.C.R., Simmons, A. and Tchanturia, K. (under review). Aberrant function of brain networks associated with learning and cognitive control underlies inefficient cognitive flexibility in anorexia nervosa.

Lavenex, P., Suzuki, W.A. and Amaral, D.G. (2002). Perirhinal and parahippocampal cortices of the macaque monkey: projections to the neocortex. *Journal of Comparative Neurology, 447*, 394–420.

Lopez, C., Tchanturia, K., Stahl, D. and Treasure, J. (2008). Central coherence in eating disorders: a systematic review. *Psychological Medicine, 38* (10), 1393–1404.

Manjaly, Z.M., Bruning, N., Neufang, S., Stephan, K.E., Brieber, S. *et al.* (2007). Neurophysiological correlates of relatively enhanced local visual search in autistic adolescents. *NeuroImage, 35*, 283–291.

McCormick, L. M., Keel, P. K., Brumm, M. C., Bowers, W., Swayze, V., Andersen, A. and Andreasen, N. (2008). Implications of starvation-induced change in right dorsal anterior cingulate volume in anorexia nervosa. *International Journal of Eating Disorders, 41*, 602–610.

Miller, G.A., Galanter, E. and Pribram, K. (1960). *Plans and the Structure of Behaviour*. New York: Holt.

Mühlau, M., Gaser, C., Ilg, R., Conrad, B., Leibl, C., Cebulla, M.H., Backmund, H., Gerlinghoff, M., Lommer, P., Schnebel, A., Wohlschläger, A.M., Zimmer, C. and Nunnemann, S. (2007). Gray matter decrease of the anterior cingulate cortex in anorexia nervosa. *American Journal of Psychiatry, 164*, 1850–1857.

Narayanan, N.S., Guarnieri, D.J. and DiLeone, R.J (2010). Metabolic hormones, dopamine circuits, and feeding. *Frontiers in Neuroendocrinology, 31*, 104–112.

Nikendei, C., Funiok, C., Pfuller, U., Zastrow, A., Aschenbrenner, S., *et al.* (2011). Memory performance in acute and weight-restored anorexia nervosa patients. *Psychological Medicine, 41*, 829–838.

Oldershaw, A., Treasure, J., Hambrook, D., Tchanturia, K. and Schmidt, U. (2011). Is anorexia nervosa a version of autism spectrum disorders? *European Eating Disorder Review, 19* (6), 462–474.

Parvizi, J., Van Hoesen, G.W., Buckwalter, J. and Damasio, A. (2006). Neural connections of the posteromedial cortex in the macaque. *Proceedings of the National Academy of Sciences of the United States of America, 103*, 1563–1568.

Penades, R., Pujol, N., Catalan, R., Massana, G., Rametti, G. *et al.* (2013). Brain effects of cognitive remediation therapy in schizophrenia: a structural and functional neuroimaging study. *Biological Psychiatry, 73*, 1015–1023.

Pfefferbaum, A., Chanraud, S., Pitel, A.L., Muller-Oehring, E., Shankaranarayanan A. *et al.* (2011). Cerebral blood flow in posterior cortical nodes of the default mode network decreases with task engagement but remains higher than in most brain regions. *Cerebral Cortex, 21*, 233–244.

Ring, H.A., Baron-Cohen, S., Wheelwright, S., Williams, S.C., Brammer, M. *et al.* (1999). Cerebral correlates of preserved cognitive skills in autism: a functional MRI study of embedded figures task performance. *Brain, 122* (7), 1305–1315.

Roberto, C.A., Mayer, L.E.S., Brickman, A.M., Barnes, A., Muraskin, J., Yeung, L.K., Steffener, J., Sy, M., Hirsch, J., Stern, Y. and Walsh, B.T (2011). Brain tissue volume changes following weight gain in adults with anorexia nervosa. *International Journal of Eating Disorders, 44*, 406–411.

Sato Y., Saito N., Utsumi A., Aizawa, E., Shoji, T., *et al.* (2013). Neural basis of impaired cognitive flexibility in patients with anorexia nervosa. *Plos One, 8* (5).

Scott, W.A. (1962). Cognitive complexity and cognitive flexibility. *American Sociological Association, 25*, 405–414.

Seed, J.A., McCue, P.M., Wesnes, K.A., Dahabra, S. and Young, A.H. (2002). Basal activity of the HPA axis and cognitive function in anorexia nervosa. *International Journal of Neuropsychopharmacology, 5*, 17–25.

Smith, E.E., Jonides, J., Marshuetz, C. and Koeppe, R.A. (1998). Components of verbal working memory: evidence from neuroimaging. *Proceedings of the National Academy of Sciences of the United States of America, 95*, 876–882.

Spencer, M.D., Holt, R.J., Chura, L.R., Calder, A.J., Suckling, J. *et al.* (2012a). Atypical activation during the Embedded Figures Task as a functional magnetic resonance imaging endophenotype of autism. *Brain, 135,* 3469–3480.

Spencer, M.D., Chura, L.R., Holt, R.J., Suckling, J., Calder, A.J. *et al.* (2012b). Failure to deactivate the default mode network indicates a possible endophenotype of autism. *Molecular Autism, 3,* 15.

Spreng, R.N., Stevens, W.D., Chamberlain, J.P., Gilmore, A.W. and Schacter, D.L. (2010). Default network activity, coupled with the frontoparietal control network, supports goal-directed cognition. *NeuroImage, 53* (1), 303–317.

Spreng, R.N., Sepulcre, J., Turner, G.R., Stevens, W.D. and Schacter, D.L. (2013). Intrinsic architecture underlying the relations among the default, dorsal attention, and frontoparietal control networks of the human brain. *Journal of Cognitive Neuroscience, 25* (1), 74–86.

Swayze, V.W., Andersen, A.E., Andreasen, N.C., Arndt, S., Sato, Y. and Ziebell, S. (2003). Brain tissue volume segmentation in patients with anorexia nervosa before and after weight normalization. *International Journal of Eating Disorders, 33,* 33–44.

Tchanturia, K., Harrison, A., Davies, H., Roberts, M., Oldershaw, A., Nakazato, M., Morris, R., Schmidt, U. and Treasure, J. (2011). Cognitive flexibility and clinical severity in eating disorders. *Plos One, 6* (6), e20462. DOI:10.1371/journal.pone.0020462.

Tchanturia, K., Davies, H., Harrison, A., Roberts, M., Nakazato, M., Schmidt, U., Treasure, J. and Morris, R. (2012). Poor cognitive flexibility in eating disorders: Examining the evidence using the Wisconsin Cart Sorting Task. *Plos One, 7* (1), e28331.

Tchanturia, K., Smith, E., Weineck, F., Fidanboylu, E., Kern, N., Treasure, J. and Baron-Cohen, S. (2013). Autistic traits in anorexia: a clinical study. *Molecular Autism, 4* (1), 44.

Tenconi, E., Santonastaso, P., Degortes, D., Bosello, R., Titton, F., *et al.* (2010). Set-shifting abilities, central coherence, and handedness in anorexia nervosa patients, their unaffected siblings and healthy controls: exploring putative endophenotypes. *World Journal of Biological Psychiatry, 11,* 813–823.

Titova, O.E., Hjorth, O.C., Schioth, H.B. and Brooks, S.J. (2013). Anorexia nervosa is linked to reduced brain structure in reward and somatosensory regions: a meta-analysis of VBM studies. *BMC Psychiatry, 13,* 110.

Uddin, L. Q., Clare Kelly, A. M., Biswal, B. B., Xavier Castellanos, F., and Milham, M. P. (2009). Functional connectivity of default mode network components: correlation, anti-correlation, and causality. *Human Brain Mapping, 30* (2), 625–637.

van Zessen, R., van der Plasse, G. and Adan, R.A. (2012). 'Contribution of the mesolimbic dopamine system in mediating the effects of leptin and ghrelin on feeding.' *Proceedings of the Nutrition Society 71,* 435–445.

Verhagen, L.A., Luijendijk, M.C. and Adan, R.A. (2011). Leptin reduces hyperactivity in an animal model for anorexia nervosa via the ventral tegmental area. *European Neuropsychopharmacology, 21,* 274–281.

Wagner, A., Greer, P., Bailer, U.F., Frank, G.K., Henry, S.E., Putnam, K., Meltzer, C.C., Ziolko, S.K., Hoge, J., McConaha, C. and Kaye, W.H. (2006). Normal brain tissue volumes after long-term recovery in anorexia and bulimia nervosa. *Biological Psychiatry, 59,* 291–293.

Wexler, B.E., Anderson, M., Fulbright, R.K. and Gore, J.C (2000). Preliminary evidence of improved verbal working memory performance and normalization of task-related frontal lobe activation in schizophrenia following cognitive exercises. *The American Journal of Psychiatry, 157,* 1694–1697.

Witkin, H., Oltman, P.K., Raskin, E. and Karp, S.A. (1971). *A manual for the Embedded Figure Test.* California: Consulting Psychologists Press.

Wykes, T., Brammer, M., Mellers, J., Bray, P., Reeder, C., *et al.* (2002). Effects on the brain of a psychological treatment: cognitive remediation therapy. Functional magnetic resonance imaging in schizophrenia. *The British Journal of Psychiatry, 181,* 144–152.

Zastrow, A., Kaiser, S., Stippich, C., Walther, S., Herzog, W., Tchanturia, K., Belger A., Weisbrod, M., Treasure, J. and Friederich, H. (2009). Neural correlates of impaired cognitive-behavioral flexibility in anorexia nervosa. *American Journal of Psychiatry, 166* (5), 608–616.

Zhang, S. and Li, C.S.R. (2012). Functional connectivity mapping of the human precuneus by resting state fMRI. *NeuroImage, 59,* 3548–3562.

Zhu, J.N. and Wang, J.J. (2008). The cerebellum in feeding control: possible function and mechanism. *Cellular and Molecular Neurobiology, 28,* 469–478.

12

COGNITIVE REMEDIATION THERAPY FOR OBESITY

Evelyn Smith, Phillipa Hay and Jayanthi Raman

Worldwide approximately 1 billion adults are currently overweight (Body mass index (BMI) 25–29.9 Kg/m^2), and a further 475 million are obese (BMI >30 Kg/m^2) (Bray *et al.* 1998). In 2004, increased BMI alone was estimated to account for 2.8 million deaths, while the combined total with physical inactivity was 6 million (WHO: www.who.int/whr/2004/en/2004). The World Health Organization has stated, 'obesity is one of the greatest public health challenges of the 21st century' (WHO, op. cit.). Although the world is in the middle of an obesity epidemic, our treatments for this condition are poor.

Current treatments for obesity usually comprise nutritional counselling, meal and exercise planning, with or without 'diet sheets' of meal plans. The most stringent treatment is the behavioural weight loss (BWL) program. The BWL program targets diet and exercise through behavioural modification techniques. Participants receive comprehensive education about nutrition, and problem-solving techniques are taught to help participants deal with difficult situations that threaten their weight control efforts. Occasionally, cognitive techniques, such as identifying and changing dysfunctional thinking, behaviour, and emotional responses, are applied to complement this treatment. Motivation enhancement and relapse prevention strategies are also taught, to enable individuals to maintain their weight loss.

Research has found that BWL programs work in the short- but not the long-term. Indeed, around 50% of people regain weight at one-year follow up. By 3–5 years post-treatment, about 85% of the patients have regained weight or even exceeded their pre-treatment weight (Wadden and Osei 2002). Recommendations for obese individuals include losing and maintaining a loss of 5–10% of body weight in order to reduce the risk of developing chronic medical conditions (Klein *et al.* 2004). Although a 5–10% weight loss may not return an obese to a non-obese state, the positive health benefits of a 5–10% weight loss are well documented (National Heart, Lung, and Blood Institute 1998). Although such degrees of weight loss are associated with clear health benefits, the prevention of weight regain has remained a challenge. Even with the help of professionals and extended behavioural treatments, weight regain typically occurs when professional contact ends (Perri and Corsica 2002). One aspect that may be contributing to the weight regain in obese individuals is an impairment in their executive function. Numerous studies have found that obesity is associated with deficiencies in executive function, in children, adolescents and adults (Smith *et al*. 2011; Fitzpatrick *et al*. 2013; Reinert *et al*. 2013). Executive function encompasses a diverse range of cognitive processes and behavioural competencies facilitating initiation, planning, regulation, sequencing and achievement of complex goal-oriented behaviour and thought, which may impact on eating behaviour (Stuss and Benson 1996). Thus, executive function has a direct impact on self-regulation (Hofmann *et al*. 2012). This, however, does not mean an overall impairment of intelligence, as people can learn to compensate for these deficiencies. Research suggests that increased adiposity affects executive function independently of medical conditions such as diabetes, hypertension and cancer, which are themselves associated with adverse cognitive effects (Battersby *et al*. 1993; Anderson-Hanley *et al*. 2003; Biessels 2008). Importantly, the results were also independent of socioeconomic status (SES) in the studies that controlled for SES, including one that divided SES into six levels and compared normal weight and obese within each SES and found the same effect at each level. The results in the elderly, however, are not as straightforward, due in part to changes in body composition as we age (Smith *et al*. 2011).

In three separate studies, obese participants showed impaired performance in the Iowa Gambling Task (IGT), a neuropsychological task of executive function designed to simulate real-life decision making and learning in terms of reward and punishment (Davis *et al*. 2004). Obese participants in this task did not learn from their mistakes. Interestingly, obese individuals perform similarly on the IGT compared to those with anorexia nervosa (Tchanturia 2007), similarly to patients with orbitofrontal dysfunction (Bechara *et al*. 1994), and worse than those who are substance dependent (Bechara and Damasio 2002). A recent study showed that the executive function deficits are similar in anorexia nervosa and obesity; however, obese showed lower performance in the inhibition response measured by the Stroop test when compared to individuals with anorexia nervosa and to healthy controls (Fagundo 2012).

Furthermore, one longitudinal study found that poor executive function at age 4 yrs predicted a high BMI at age six (Guxens *et al*. 2009). Thus the relationship between obesity and executive function seems to be bidirectional. Cognitive deficiencies may contribute to increased adiposity by exacerbating weight gain or regain after weight loss, and targeting these deficits in the obese has the potential of improving participants' response to therapy. Based on the limited success of current behavioural weight loss programs, and coupled with the data on their executive function deficiencies in obesity, it appears likely that improving the individual's executive function has the potential to enhance treatment outcomes for obesity.

Cognitive remediation therapy and executive function training

Manualised cognitive remediation therapy (CRT) has been shown to be effective at addressing cognitive inefficiencies in anorexia nervosa, and in turn addressing cognitive styles, such as inflexible thinking and extreme attention to detail, helping patients with AN to stay in the treatment (lower drop-out rates as shown in Chapters 6, 7 and 8) and improving their cognitive style and quality of life (Chapter 8). Cognitive remediation therapy, as described in previous chapters, aims at promoting reflection on thinking styles, developing metacognition, and helping explore and apply new thinking strategies in everyday life.

Individuals with anorexia nervosa are cognitively inflexible, have extreme impulse control and develop cognitive inefficiencies that have been hypothesized to maintain the disorder (Verbeken et al. 2013; Houben and Jansen 2011). Similarly, but to the other extreme, we propose that obese individuals are *too* flexible, have limited capacity to organize their eating habits well long-term, and have problems controlling their impulses (all aspects of executive function). A meta-analysis on the relationship between obesity and executive function (Bondal and Smith, in preparation) shows that the effect sizes of the executive deficiency are medium to large (e.g. for Wisconsin Sorting Test r = 0.34, 95% CI 0.233–0.446, heterogeneity and inconsistency non-significant, n = 460), and larger than those found in anorexia nervosa for the Wisconsin Sorting Test (r = 0.24, n = 286) (Tchanturia et al. 2012).

The cognitive remediation therapy approach has been used in addiction and has been shown to change individuals' need for immediate reward, delay punishment, and improving decision-making (Vocci 2008). In obesity, computerized executive function training was recently used in 44 obese children aged 8 to 14 years who were undergoing inpatient treatment for their obesity (Verbeken et al. 2013). Specifically, participants were randomized into a 6-week computerized executive function training program or to a 6-week 'care as usual' program. In this trial, the executive function training consisted of twenty-five 40-minute computerized-training sessions over six weeks, in inhibition and working memory. It was found that children in the executive function training condition showed better performance on the working memory task and were more likely to have maintained the weight loss at 8 weeks post-training, compared to the children in the care as usual. Experimental studies have also shown that practicing inhibitory control – an aspect of executive function – reduces consumption of high calorie foods (Houben and Jansen 2011; Veling 2011). Specifically, these studies showed that improving inhibition of behaviour towards high calorie items, via a computerized go/no-go task, reduced the amount of consumption of palatable foods across a one-day period.

Although weight loss alone improves measures of executive function (Siervo, et al. 2011), the effect-size after weight loss via dieting, in measures of executive function is small in magnitude (r = 0.14, 95% CI = 0.01–0.27), whereas the effect size of the executive deficiency is medium to large (r = 0.34, 95% CI = 0.233–0.446).

Thus further help in this area could improve outcomes. The effectiveness of cognitive remediation therapy on obese adults needs to be established within a Randomized controlled trial (RCT).

We have modified CRT for anorexia (Tchanturia *et al*. 2010) for people who are obese. Although weight-related issues are not discussed in the CRT sessions with AN patients, with obese individuals, where the opportunity occurred or when participants brought it up, it was openly discussed with the therapist in the context of CRT. Connections were made between the skills that were learnt in therapy and how they could be applied to their weight management in real life. Table 12.1

TABLE 12.1 Outlining changes to the Manual on Cognitive Remediation Therapy

Attention to detail

Task	Aim
Patterns	Participants are asked to connect the dots and replicate a geometric figure on a grid.
A very short story	Participants have to read a given short story (half a page to one page) and recount it with all the little details in it.
Spot it	Participants are presented with two cards, between which there is only one matching symbol.
Brain box	Participants study a card for ten seconds, then flip it over and answer questions to recall details.
Estimation tasks	Participants are asked to estimate the number of items in a bag, or number of blocks in a picture.
Complex figure draw	Retained from the original CRT-AN manual.
Embedded words and word searches	Retained from the original CRT-AN manual.
Pansoft square	By stretching a freehand square on a tablet, participants are asked to accurately gauge a perfect square.

Problem solving, planning and organization skills

Task	Aim
On the dot	A card representing a combination of several coloured dots is presented to the participant, along with four transparent plastic cards, also with coloured dots in different positions. By rotating and flipping the cards and trying them in different orders, the participant has to superimpose them to obtain the same combination as the card on the table.
Path Word Search	Participants are asked to place translucent puzzle pieces to cover all the letters so that a complete word is revealed under each piece.
IQ link	The aim is to fit all puzzle pieces on the game board. There are 36 puzzle parts but only 24 free places on the game board. Open rings and balls of different puzzle pieces can occupy the same place when linked the right way.

(Continued)

TABLE 12.1 *(Continued)*

'How to'	Retained from the original CRT-AN manual.
Symbolic reasoning	Number and letter sequences are completed by the participant.
Mind Map	Participants are asked to draw a mind map, starting at the centre of a blank page, with the keyword 'obesity'. The first set of obesity-associated words may generate their own constellation of other words which then form the mind map. The lines between the words need to be connected, starting from the central keyword. By seeing new creative pathways in the map, problem solving skills are encouraged during CRT.

Set-shifting

Task	Aim
Scattergories	Participants are asked to name objects within a set of categories, given an initial letter, within a time limit.
Multi-skilling (originally Dual task)	Participants are asked to say a letter or number sequence in a loop while tapping on the desk with their non-dominant hand and crossing out a said shape with their dominant hand.
Illusions; Stroop; Up and Down; Search and Count, and Switching Attention	Retained from the original CRT-AN manual.

Creative thinking

Tasks	Aim
Random generation	Participants are asked to generate numbers/letters in random order with no two items appearing in sequence.
To do two new things between two sessions	Participants are asked to engage in two novel behaviours that they have never tried before.

Reflection and Consolidation

Task	Aim
Letter to the therapist	Retained from the original CRT-AN manual.

Behavioural Homework – examples

Original	Modified
Leave house untidy and clean later in the evening	Leave house tidy.
Add an item to the shopping list	Delete two items from the shopping list.
	Exposure and response prevention homework exercises are added from session 4 onwards to facilitate set-shifting skills.

outlines some important modifications to adapt CRT to obesity. In brief, we replaced tasks that encouraged abstract, global thinking with tasks that facilitated attention to detail. We also added tasks that looked at problem-solving skills. In the other tasks that we retained from the CRT-AN manual, reflective thinking techniques were redirected to enhance organization, planning, and problem solving in a focused fashion.

We are undertaking a randomized controlled trial (RCT) to investigate the efficacy of our modified CRT for obesity. Out of a target sample of 90, 85 adults with obesity have been recruited from the community. Participants have BMI > 30, aged 18–55 years, and have completed 10 years of education in English. The RCT does not include people with morbid obesity (>180 kg) due to logistical reasons, including the need for reinforced chairs and scales that measure very high weights. Participants were screened for significant psychiatric (including alcohol and substance use disorders), medical and neurological comorbidities. However, participants with depression, binge eating disorder, hypertension (medicated or not medicated), type 2 diabetes, and/or high cholesterol were included.

After establishing eligibility criteria via a phone interview, a clinical assessment was conducted to assess for comorbidities and to collect baseline measures. We collected a standardized measure of height and weight from which to derive body mass index (BMI), and measurements of hip and waist circumference to derive waist to hip ratio. The assessment battery will collect data on their demographics, mood, quality of life, health literacy, habitual cluster behaviours, disordered eating and included neuropsychological measures. The trial was registered in the Australian and New Zealand Clinical Trials Register (ACTRN12613000537752) and a description of all the measures can be found there.

All participants complete three 90 minute weekly sessions of a group Behavioural Weight Loss (BWL) program. At the end of the BWL program, half the participants were randomized to a CRT individual program conducted twice weekly for four weeks and the other half do not receive further treatment. A control condition is not implemented in this preliminary trial as we wished to only examine the efficacy of CRT both short term and long term. However, changes in executive function are expected to predict changes in weight.

Participants complete all assessments at baseline, at post-treatment (or at similar times for the waitlisted participants), at three month follow up, and at one year follow up. Anthropometric measures were taken at each interval, including post BWL. Outcomes are conducted by a blinded assessor for all participants at the one year follow up. The RCT is expected to be completed by April 2015.

Case studies

Case studies of two women who completed the CRT program are presented below, including selected data at baseline, post-treatment and three-month follow-up. The one-year follow-up data is not included.

LORRIE

Lorrie is a 27 year-old young mother of two children from an affluent suburb of a large Australian city. At the start of treatment she had a BMI of 30.1, with her height measuring 168 centimetres and her weight at 85 kilograms. She has been binge eating since her parents separated when she was 14 years old. Back then she was fit and involved in various sporting activities in her school and university years, which helped her maintain a healthy BMI range. She completed a professional degree and works part-time at a local firm. She has a supportive husband and enjoys a good network of friends and extended family.

Since the birth of her first child four years ago, Lorrie started to gain weight and put on even more weight after her second child was born 18 months ago. Despite knowing her BMI, she never thought of herself as obese. It was only when her General Practitioner mentioned that she was obese, she realized that she needed to address her weight management seriously.

Although on entry to CRT she was apprehensive about how helpful CRT would be in her weight management, she was a motivated and an involved participant. She was punctual to the sessions, remained consistently interested and involved in the program and always diligent in her behavioural homework tasks. The CRT tasks focused on improving set-shifting, attention to detail over global-processing, novel ways of thinking, planning and problem solving. Three behavioural homework tasks were given after each session that involved changing routines at home, and other lifestyle changes.

During the therapy sessions, motivational interviewing-style questions were asked as to what she had learned from the tasks, how helpful or unhelpful were the strategies she used to solve them and how the tasks related to her real life. It was emphasized that what was important in the CRT program was reflective learning and not performance. After the first two sessions, in a collaborative manner, it was discovered that if Lorrie could improve more on her attention to detail that would also benefit her planning and organizational skills in a practical way. In the following sessions, Lorrie's insight and awareness increased significantly. For example, during the fourth session, she became an expert in vocally identifying her thinking style as she went through the tasks and correcting them as she went along.

By session six, there were noticeable improvements in Lorrie's performance in tasks that demanded problem solving, planning and attention to detail. She was also able to connect the in-session CRT tasks to her behavioural homework tasks. For example, she said that the in-session set-shifting tasks had greatly helped her to think of new ways of behaving. She had changed her daily routine to having breakfast in the morning, using smaller bowls and plates and having dinner at the table with her husband in lieu of TV dinners. She had started reading food product labels before purchase and was able to plan meals for her family a few days in advance.

At the end of session 7, the idea of writing a letter to the therapist was discussed as an exercise of consolidation and reflection. In the last session, Lorrie was confident but also realistic in being able maintain her gains post the CRT program. She had developed an overarching goal for the following three months. She had also made a week by week plan for the following month with regard to her physical activities, meal plans, social outings and budgeting. She said that she wanted to continue with the behavioural tasks that were prescribed by the CRT. Her reflective thinking and her ability to work through any new challenges without guidance had improved significantly by session 8.

Outcomes

Lorrie's anthropometric data, including BMI, waist circumference and waist to hip ratio are presented for baseline, post-treatment and three-month follow up in Table 12.2. Although Lorrie completed a comprehensive neuropsychological assessment, only raw data from the Wisconsin Sorting Task, the Behaviour Rating Inventory of Executive Function – Adults (BRIEF-A), and the Trail Making Test B (TMTB) are presented in Table 12.2, together with the results of the Depression, Anxiety Stress Scale (DASS-42) and the Eating Disorder Examination Questionnaire (EDE-Q). Her NART score was 61.

Lorrie lost 7% of her body weight after treatment and this loss was maintained at follow-up. Her waist circumference reduced by 25 centimetres from baseline to follow-up and her hip circumference reduced by 11 centimetres. This loss is equivalent to what individuals lost on average after a 20 week, 15-session, behavioural weight loss program (Klem *et al.* 1997), or 40 week low calorie diet (Wadden *et al.* 2004).

Her performance on the Wisconsin Sorting Task improved considerably as outlined in Table 12.2. For example, her total errors went from 32 at baseline (3rd percentile) to 7 at follow-up (90th percentile). Her self-report score on the BRIEF-A also improved, from 57% to 32% of dysfunction, lower scores signifying higher executive function. Her depression, anxiety and stress scores were normal and were maintained. However, her weight and shape concern, as measured by the EDE-Q, decreased, perhaps because she had lost a significant amount of weight.

From the brief clinical interview, and supported by the EDE-Q, Lorrie engaged in binge eating around three times a week and was classified with Binge Eating Disorder (BED) at baseline; however, she no longer met criteria for BED at post-treatment, engaging in only one binge eating episode in four weeks; or follow-up, engaging in no binge eating.

TABLE 12.2 Lorrie's measures at baseline, post-treatment and three-month follow-up

Lorrie (58)	Baseline	Post-treatment (4–6 weeks after baseline)	Three-month follow-up
Anthropometric measures			
Weight (kg)	85	79	79
Body Mass Index	30	27.9	27.9
Waist circumference (cms)	112	98	87
Hip circumference (cms)	116	107	105
Waist to hip ratio	.97	.92	.83
Wisconsin sorting test – 64 Card version computerized★			
Total correct	32	49	57
Total errors	32 (3%)	15 (42%)	7 (90%)
Perserverative errors	27 (<1%)	8 (32%)	6 (53%)
Perserverative responses	23 (<1%)	7 (37%)	6 (50%)
Non-perserverative errors	9 (23%)	8 (30%)	1 (99%)
Conceptual Level responses	23 (2%)	45 (30%)	57 (81%)
Categories completed	2	4	5
Trials to complete 1st category	21	12	10
BRIEF – Adults★			
Behavioural Regulation Index	37 (27%)	34 (17%)	32 (12%)
Meta-cognition Index	75 (79%)	62 (55%)	57 (44%)
Global Executive Composite	112 (57%)	96 (40%)	89 (32%)
Trail Making Test – B (TMT-B)			
TMT-B (in seconds)	51.6	24.6	24.8
EDE-Q			
Dietary Restrain	1.6	3.6	1.6
Eating Concern	3	0.6	0.4
Weight Concern	3.4	2.8	1.4
Shape Concern	4.4	3.9	1.6
DASS – 42			
Depression	8 (Normal)	4 (Normal)	6 (Normal)
Anxiety	0 (Normal)	0 (Normal)	0 (Normal)
Stress	20 (Moderate)	10 (Normal)	10 (Normal)

★ Higher raw scores and percentiles represent higher executive dysfunction
EDE-Q: Eating disorder examination questionnaire; DASS-42: Depression Anxiety Stress Scale;
BRIEF – Adults: Behavioural Rating Inventory of Executive Function

Letter excerpts from Lorrie to the therapist

To be honest, my mindset was that this would never change, that I would always be overweight for life. I couldn't see how brain puzzles and attention to detail could impact on my weight struggles.

In time, doing the brain exercises reinforced for me that my brain can learn and change. If it can learn to think differently it can also learn to break bad eating habits and develop positive new thoughts about food and exercise. It was fun to watch my brain improve through exercises like word searching and recall of fine details.

I had always thought of myself as a 'big picture person' and I had left the fine details to others. I realize now it's just that the fine details part of my brain wasn't getting a good work out to build up its muscles.

For me, the big picture goals don't help much with weight loss. I would have a big picture goal (say lose 20kg), try to diet, over-control everything in an unsustainable way, fail and despair. Then of course I would comfort my despair by eating. It felt like an unbreakable lifelong cycle since my teens.

I've learnt that weight loss is in the fine details – that's why this study matters. It's packing a healthy lunchbox for the day so I don't get stuck with the temptation of a takeout lunch. It's meal planning for this week and cooking healthy food for my freezer when I'm too tired to cook and would otherwise order take away food.

I'm losing weight, small sustainable losses without feeling like I'm depriving myself at all. I don't feel like I'm on a diet I can fail at, instead I've re-engaged my brain into the process of eating, telling me when I'm hungry or not and learning new behaviours of doing the things I CAN do to help myself, like having healthy foods ready to enjoy.

I'm thinking differently, in fact, just thinking about food this way is a new habit. Don't get me wrong, I'm still going to need to battle bad habits. I still have an inner binger who needs reminding that there are other, better, options to deal with my feelings.

I feel privileged to have been part of this learning process and hope others can benefit from the skills and findings that you make. This is a much needed area for change and I have every confidence that many lives will be transformed through this. Others will be able to live life without the burden of an unhealthy relationship with food, even those who didn't know they bore that burden, like me.

CATHY

Cathy is a 49-year-old young grandmother of one who migrated to Australia from a Pacific island during her teenage years. She is single and did not complete High School. She works as a cleaner in the hospitality industry close to her home. Her adult daughter, who is single, and her three young children live with Cathy and are financially dependent on her.

She came from a disadvantaged background but one that was a community (in her words 'social race') of people who had frequent food gatherings. She had a pattern of overeating from childhood and an established pattern of grazing even when not hungry.

On entry into CRT, Cathy was obese, weighing 94 kilograms with a height of 157 centimetres and a BMI of 38. In her first CRT session she said that she is not a 'thinking kind of a person' and doubted whether she is wasting her time with CRT. Her first positive comment came after the second CRT session when she said she did not know 'learning could be so much fun.' Her insight and involvement increased multi-fold after this. She initiated several lifestyle changes on her own, performed more homework tasks in a creative manner than was asked of her, and transported her CRT skills to various other aspects of her life including financial management. She particularly enjoyed the tasks that made her think creatively, plan and problem solve. On completion, she weighed 89 kilograms with a BMI of 36 – a two-point drop in four weeks. Cathy was however anxious that she may lose the skills that she has learned in CRT over a period of time. In the last CRT session, while she was reading her letter to me, this concern was addressed and strategies discussed as to how she can devise and continue with her brain training games without guidance.

Outcomes

Cathy's anthropometric data, including BMI, waist circumference and waist to hip ratio are presented for baseline, post-treatment and three-month follow up in Table 12.3. Although Cathy completed a comprehensive neuropsychological assessment, only raw data from the Wisconsin Sorting task, the Behaviour Rating Inventory of Executive Function – Adults (BRIEF-A) and the Trail Making Test B (TMTB) are presented in Table 12.3, together the results of the Depression, Anxiety Stress Scale (DASS-42) and the Eating Disorder Examination Questionnaire (EDE-Q). Her NART score was 45.

Similarly to Lorrie, Cathy's weight reduced during treatment by 5% and this loss was maintained at follow-up. Her waist circumference reduced by 14 centimetres from baseline to follow-up and her hip circumference reduced by 11 centimetres.

TABLE 12.3 Cathy's measures at baseline, post-treatment and three-month follow-up

Cathy (61)	Baseline	Post-treatment (4–6 weeks after baseline)	Three-month follow-up
Anthropometric measures			
Weight (kg)	94	89	89
Body Mass Index	38	36	36
Waist circumference (cms)	118	113	104
Hip circumference (cms)	135	128	124
Waist to hip ratio	.87	.88	.84
Wisconsin sorting task (computerized)			
Total correct	44	48	55
Total errors	20 (25%)	16 (39%)	9 (75%)
Perserverative responses	13 (27%)	8 (47%)	4 (68%)
Perserverative errors	12 (23%)	8 (42%)	4 (70%)
Non-perserverative errors	8 (34%)	8 (34%)	5 (55%)
Conceptual Level responses	40 (30%)	45 (45%)	51 (66%)
Categories completed	3	4	5
Trials to complete 1st category	27	22	11
BRIEF – Adults			
Behavioural Regulation Index	64 (93%)	49 (76%)	51 (87%)
Meta-cognition Index	80 (91%)	80 (91%)	69 (81%)
Global Executive Composite	144 (92%)	129 (87%)	120 (83%)
Trail Making Test – B			
TMT-B (seconds)	44	34.3	27.2
EDE-Q			
Dietary Restrain	3	3.6	2
Eating Concern	2.2	0.5	2.4
Weight Concern	4	3	4.2
Shape Concern	4.5	3.5	4.3
DASS-42			
Depression	38 (Extr. severe)	4 (Normal)	8 (Normal)
Anxiety	16 (Severe)	6 (Normal)	10 (Moderate)
Stress	28 (Severe)	18 (Mild)	20 (Moderate)

Cathy's performance on the Wisconsin sorting task improved considerably as outlined in Table 12.3. For example, total her errors went from 20 at baseline (25th percentile) to 9 at follow-up (75th percentile). Her self-report score on the BRIEF-A also improved, from 92% to 82% of dysfunction, lower scores signifying higher executive function. Her depression scores went from extremely severe at baseline to normal at follow up, and both her anxiety and stress scores went from severe at baseline to moderate at follow-up. Her eating disorder symptoms – as measured by the EDE-Q – decreased, but did not change much from baseline to follow-up.

From the brief clinical interview, and supported by the EDE-Q, Cathy engaged in binge eating once a week and was classified with Binge Eating Disorder at baseline; however, she no longer met criteria for BED at post-treatment, as she no longer binged. However this was not maintained at follow-up and she once again started binge eating, but this did not impact her weight.

Letter from Cathy to the therapist

I would like to take this opportunity to thank you for the most interesting and life changing experience I have had participating in your obesity research.

As a child I was used to not eating what was put in front of me or binge eating when I loved the food.

We are a very social race of people, so we have lots of group gatherings. We usually sit around talking and eating instead of playing games or doing physical activities. We eat for the sake of eating and not because we are hungry.

I am not the type of person that analyses situations or my thought processes, never thinking about the consequences of my actions. It just felt unnatural and time consuming for me to have to think things through. Sometimes it seems too much work to get started I just won't bother.

You have given me new insights regarding the way I think and shown me new ways to look at life and the ways I think not only about food but of the things in general that I would normally take for granted or rush through without thought.

I did not know learning could be so much fun … all of this new found information will help me with my journey.

After 7 weeks of extreme brain training, I am starting to see subtle changes. Last week I sat down at the kitchen table and drew up a financial budget.

It is interesting to work through this letter. I am actually thinking about and analysing each session starting from our first session. There is so much you have taught me to help with my journey. I look forward to sharing my progress with you in the very near future.

Once again, thank you very much for giving me this opportunity and teaching me new ways to approach not only weight management, but most aspects of my life including financial budgeting and socializing without overeating and drinking.

Reflection from the therapist, Jayanthi Raman

The majority of the 85 obese individuals we have assessed for our study have been through several weight management programs, albeit with limited success in maintaining their weight loss. Most of our study participants reported that they felt 'stuck' in their condition. Although they knew what to do in their eating and exercise behaviours, they said their brain did not 'co-operate' with their best intentions.

Having read the literature on patient non-compliance with therapy in AN, I was apprehensive about how our obese participants would respond to CRT. In this trial, the participant response has been very positive and heartening. Just about all our participants attended their CRT on time, were compliant with their homework and have shown a high level of involvement in the therapeutic process. After the first three sessions, many participants described CRT using positive words such as 'awakening', 'mind became alive', 'I did not know my mind could think this way until now', and 'CRT gave me new ways of looking at life.' Even the most sceptical of them were able to see the 'method behind the mad tasks' after the first two sessions.

Many have actively volunteered and reminded me about our follow up testing even before I brought up the topic, keen to show me their progress in three months. Some participants have expressed their concern that an eight-week program is too brief and that they may lose the skillsets that they have gained in CRT. These concerns typically came up in the last session, while they were reading their letter to me. They were then educated on the ongoing importance of brain exercises and how it can be made into a lifestyle choice. Several examples were provided such as playing brain games with family and flatmates after dinner each day instead of watching television, making a routine of doing puzzles at a certain time each day, carrying their games with them when they travel for work and repeating many of the CRT tasks where appropriate as a booster when the need arises. It was emphasized that all of the above need to be done within a framework of 'reflective learning' – a skillset that they have learned in the program.

The heat off the performance, the emphasis on reflective learning and collaborative exploration of the thinking process made the sessions very enjoyable to me, as the therapist. Despite its scientific backbone, CRT, by its very nature is non-confrontational, motivational, hands-on and light-hearted in its approach.

Having been a clinical psychologist for over 15 years and practicing CBT with patients, it was an interesting shift for me to move away from the thought content to the thought processes. Although some behavioural homework practices (such as the exposure and response prevention) mimicked a behavioural experiment that would be employed in a CBT program, the focus was on the participants' thinking *style*, not *what* they thought. Overall, it has been a very gratifying experience to blend my skills as a cognitive behavioural therapist with my CRT skills. Having had hands-on experience with 40 participants, my clinical intuition tells me CRT has significant potential in the treatment of obesity, whether as a precursor to other treatments, as an adjunct to a mainstream therapy or even as a standalone therapy. Future research has the potential to investigate all of these promising possibilities.

Future directions

There is still much to learn, about the benefits of CRT. However, the majority of participants found CRT beneficial, and many seem to be losing weight. Taking into account that weight loss usually stops after therapeutic contact ends, long-term follow-up data is very important. Our experience and the results of the RCT will inform further developments of CRT including its use as an adjunctive therapy to a longer behavioural weight-loss program.

References

Anderson-Hanley, C.S.M., Riggs, R., Agocha, V.V. and Compas, B.E. (2003). Neuropsychological effects of treatments for adults with cancer: a meta-analysis and review of the literature. *Journal of The International Neuropsychological Society, 9*, 967–982.

Bechara, A., Damasio, A.R., Damasio, H. and Anderson, S.W. (1994). Insensitivity to future consequences following damage to human prefrontal cortex. *Cognition, 50*, 7-15.

Bechara, A. and Damasio, H. (2002). Decision-making and addiction: Impaired activation of somatic states in substance dependent individuals when pondering decisions with negative future consequences. *Neuropsychologia, 40*, 1675–1689.

Biessels, G.J. (2008). Cognition and diabetes: a lifespan perspective. *Lancet Neurology, 7*, 184–190.

Battersby, C.H.K., Fletcher, A.E., Markowe, H.J.L., Brown, R.G. and Styles, W. (1993). Cognitive function in hypertension: A community based study. *Journal of Human Hypertension, 7*, 117–123.

Bray, G.A., Bouchard, C. and James, W.P.T. (1998). *Handbook of Obesity*. New York: Marcel Dekker.

Davis, C.L.R., Muglia, P., Bewell, C. and Kennedy, J. (2004). Decision-making deficits and overeating: A risk model for obesity. *Obesity Research, 12*, 929–935.

Fagundo, A.B. (2012). Executive functions profile in extreme eating/weight conditions: From anorexia nervosa to obesity. *PLOS ONE, 7*, e43382.

Fitzpatrick, S., Gilbert, S. and Serpell, L. (2013). Systematic review: Are overweight and obese individuals impaired on behavioural tasks of executive functioning? *Neuropsychology Review, 23*, 138–156.

Guxens, M., Julvez, J., Plana, E., Forns, J., Basagana, X., Torrent, M. and Sunyer, J. (2009). Cognitive function and overweight in preschool children. *American Journal of Epidemiology, 170*, 438–446.

Hofmann, W., Schmeichel, B.J. and Baddeley, A.D. (2012). Executive functions and self-regulation. *Trends in Cognitive Sciences, 16*, 174–180.

Houben, K. and Jansen, A. (2011). Training inhibitory control: recipe for resisting sweet temptations. *Appetite, 56*, 345–349.

Klein, S., Burke, L.E., Bray, G.A., *et al.* (2004). Clinical implications of obesity with specific focus on cardiovascular disease: a statement for professionals from the American Heart Association Council on Nutrition, Physical Activity, and Metabolism. *Circulation, 110*, 2952–2967.

Klem, M.L., Wing, R., Simkin-Silverman, L. and Kuller, L.H. (1997). The psychological consequences of weight gain prevention in healthy, premenopausal women. *International Journal of Eating Disorders, 21*, 167–174.

National Heart, Lung and Blood Institute. (1998). Obesity Education Initiative Expert Panel on the Identification, Evaluation, and Treatment of Obesity in Adults. *Obesity Research, 6*, 51S-210S.

Perri, M.G. and Corsica, J.A. (2002). 'Improving the maintenance of weight lost in behavioral treatment of obesity', in T.A. Wadden and A.J. Stunkard (Eds.), *Handbook of Obesity Treatment*, 357–359. New York: Guilford Press.

Reinert, K.R., Po'e, E.K. and Barkin, S.L. (2013). The relationship between executive function and obesity in children and adolescents: a systematic literature review. *Journal of Obesity*, 820956.

Smith, E., Hay, P., Campbell, L. and Trollor, J. (2011). A review of the relationship between obesity and cognition across the lifespan: implications for novel approaches to prevention and treatment. *Obesity Reviews*, *12*, 740–755.

Stuss, D.T. and Benson, D. (1996). *The Frontal Lobes*. New York: Raven Press.

Tchanturia, K. (2007). An investigation of decision making in anorexia nervosa using the Iowa Gambling Task and skin conductance measurements. *Journal of The International Neuropsychological Society*, *13*, 635–641.

Tchanturia, K., Davies, H., Reeder, C., Wykes, T. (2010). www.national.slam.nhs.uk/wp-content/uploads/2014/04/Cognitive-remediation-therapy-for-Anorexia-Nervosa-Kate-Tchanturia.pdf

Tchanturia, K., Davies, H., Roberts, M., Harrison, A., Nakazato, M., Schmidt, U., Treasure, J. and Morris, R. (2012). Poor cognitive flexibility in eating disorders: Examining the evidence using the Wisconsin Card Sorting Task. *PLOS ONE*, *7*, e28331.

Verbeken, S., Braet, C., Goossens, L. and van der Oord, S. (2013). Executive function training with game elements for obese children: A novel treatment to enhance selfregulatory abilities for weight-control. *Behaviour Research and Therapy*, *51*, 290–299.

Veling, H. (2011). Using stop signals to inhibit chronic dieters' responses toward palatable foods. *Behaviour Research and Therapy*, *49*, 771–780.

Vocci, F. J. (2008). Cognitive remediation in the treatment of stimulant abuse disorders: a research agenda. *Experimental and Clinical Psychopharmacology*, *16*, 484–497.

Wadden, T.A. and Osei, S. (2002). 'The treatment of obesity: an overview', in T.A. Wadden and A. J. Stunkard (Eds.) *Handbook of Obesity Treatment*. New York: Guilford Press.

Wadden, T.A., Foster, G.D., Sarwer, D.B., *et al.* (2004). Dieting and the development of eating disorders in obese women: results of a randomized controlled trial. *The American Journal of Clinical Nutrition*, *80*, 560–568.

WHO. www.who.int/whr/2004/en/2004.

13

COGNITIVE REMEDIATION THERAPY FOR ANOREXIA NERVOSA: HOW DO WE KNOW IT WORKS?

Kate Tchanturia, Heather Westwood and Helen Davies

Throughout this book we have highlighted the reasons why CRT for eating disorders (EDs) was developed, including a lack of treatment choices, poor patient engagement in existing psychological therapies and cognitive inefficiencies (Chapters 1, 6 and 7). We have also shown how CRT is used in the field of EDs in both individual (Chapters 2, 3, 5, 6, 7 and 8) and group formats (4, 9). We have described CRT for different age groups (Chapters 7, 8 and 9 focus on young people whilst the remaining chapters address CRT with adults), and we have discussed ways to report outcomes across the chapters. Overall, this book has aimed to present the latest research in this area. This final chapter aims to appraise the evidence available to date.

CRT is a well established treatment in several psychiatric conditions. The most researched area is psychosis, where CRT varies in terms of the focus and approach of the treatment – some promoting 'drill and practice', some motivational learning, and others computerised treatments. In anorexia there can be comorbid conditions such as obsessive compulsive disorder (OCD) and autism spectrum disorder (ASD). For example, our recent audit and research study on an inpatient ward (Tchanturia *et al.* 2013) clearly showed that a high proportion of patients with anorexia had high scores on an autism screening questionnaire developed by Simon Baron-Cohen and his group (for more details see Tchanturia *et al.* 2013 and Figures 13.1–13.3). Therefore, the question is raised as to how best tailor CRT for patients with these disorders where certain approaches used in CRT for psychosis could be paradoxical for best outcomes in anorexia.

The first pie chart shows current audit data from our inpatient national eating disorder service; 33% of the patients scored highly on the self-report ASD questionnaire. The second pie chart shows audit data from our day hospital programme for AN; 24% of patients scored highly on the self-report ASD

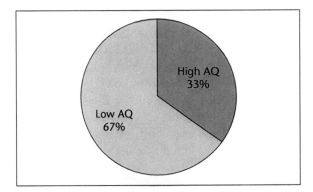

FIGURE 13.1A   Audit data from our inpatient national eating disorder service

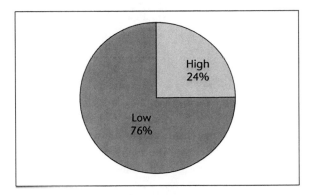

FIGURE 13.1B   Audit data from our day hospital programme for AN

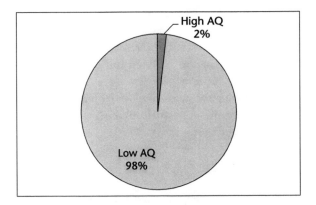

FIGURE 13.1C   Healthy control group self-report data

questionnaire. In the third pie chart, the well matched healthy control group self-report data is presented. High scorers are people who reported above the cut-off score of 6 out of 10. More details in the Tchanturia *et al.* (2013) paper.

From our literature appraisal it is clear that in OCD, cognitive training is related to improving the organisation of visuo-spatial information. Two studies to date (Buhlmann *et al.* 2006; Park *et al.* 2006) show improvements in visual organisational strategies and visual memory following the training, which aims to provide strategies in breaking down complex figures into meaningful structures.

The targets of Cognitive Rehabilitation in ASD are both social and non-social information processing, where group activities and computer-based training focusing on repetitive practice, strategy training and homework are employed. To our knowledge only one pilot study is available on cognitive enhancement therapy. In ASD there is a wide use of technology in interventions. Wass and Porayska-Pomsta (2013) reviewed technology-enhanced interventions using concepts such as 'point and click' and virtual reality to target three main domains, namely emotion and face recognition, language and literacy, and social skills. The authors raise the question about generisability of computer-based interventions to everyday life, which is an important issue in all CRT approaches.

As we have highlighted, CRT for anorexia was mainly tailored to the neuropsychological traits of flexibility and bigger picture thinking, and gradually expanded to address perfectionism and social difficulties which are problematic and exacerbated with starvation. The style of delivery is motivational, with strong engagement of the therapist who is able to model inefficiencies and imperfect performance such as highlighting errors within a safe and contained environment. As was highlighted above, this would be a different approach to the task compared to working with a patient with psychosis, where the emphasis would be on amending mistakes in a 'practice makes perfect' approach.

CRT for anorexia in a one-to-one format is a brief intervention which provides a good introduction to further psychological treatment. It encourages patients to discover the ways in which they think, and to decide what they would like to change about their thinking style, and how. CRT also encourages the use of inter-session experimentation with different ways of thinking and behaving, which can then be reflected upon during the next session.

CRT can be delivered by therapists with multidisciplinary backgrounds (psychology, nursing, occupational therapy, social work); training and supervision are essential, as in any other psychological form of treatment.

Data

Initially, seven case studies from both inpatient and outpatient settings served as a background and evidence base to develop a CRT manual tailored for patients with anorexia nervosa (AN) (see Table 13.1). From these case studies, a wealth of useful information and experience was deduced. For example, instead of using timed set-shifting tasks and praising patients for improvements in time efficiency, we decided

TABLE 13.1 Summary of published studies reporting CRT in AN

Publication	Description of patients and study design	Main findings
Davies, H. and Tchanturia, K. (2005). Cognitive remediation therapy as an intervention for acute anorexia nervosa; a case report. *European Eating Disorders Review*, 13 (5), 311–316.	Case study; inpatient adults; x̄ age = 21 yrs, x̄ Illness duration = 8 years	Marked improvement in neuropsychological set-shifting tasks.
Tchanturia, K., Whitney, J. and Treasure, J. (2006). Can cognitive exercises help treat anorexia nervosa? *Eating and Weight Disorders – Studies on Anorexia, Bulimia and Obesity*, 11 (4), e112–e116.	Case study	Improvements in neuropsychological set-shifting tasks.
Tchanturia, K., Davies, H. and Campbell, I.C. (2007). Cognitive remediation for patients with anorexia nervosa: preliminary findings. *Annals of General Psychiatry*, 6 (14), DOI:10.1186/1744-859X-6-14.	N = 4; Inpatient adults; Age range = 21–42; Illness duration range = 7–24 years.	Improvements in neuropsychological task performance (set-shifting measured in different domains) post treatment (medium to large effect sizes).
Pretorius, N. and Tchanturia, K. (2007). Anorexia nervosa: how people think and how we address it in psychological treatment. *Therapy*, 4 (4), 423–433.	Case study; Inpatient adult (31 years); Illness duration = 1 year	Patient's clinical improvements and feedback on tasks reported.
Tchanturia, K., Davies, H., Lopez, C., Schmidt, U., Treasure, J. and Wykes, T. (2008). Neuropsychological task performance before and after cognitive remediation in anorexia nervosa: A pilot case series. *Psychological Medicine*, 38 (9), 1371–1373.	N = 23; Inpatient Adults; x̄ age = 28.8 (9.6); Illness duration x̄ = 13.1 (9.6)	Medium to large effect size improvements in set-shifting and global processing cognitive style. Low drop-out rate (4/27).
Cwojdzińska, A., Markowska-Regulska, K. and Rybakowski, F. (2009). Cognitive remediation therapy in adolescent anorexia nervosa – case report. *Psychiatria Polska*, 43 (1), 115–124. [Article in Polish].	Case study, adolescent	The paper is in Polish; The abstract reports general improvements in clinical symptoms and set-shifting.
Genders, R. and Tchanturia, K. (2010). Cognitive remediation therapy (CRT) for anorexia in group format: a pilot study. *Eating and Weight Disorders*, 15 (4), e234–239.	N = 18; Inpatients, group format	Short group format found to be acceptable for patients. Statistically significant changes on the 'ability to change' scale. No significant changes in self-reported cognitive flexibility.

(Continued)

TABLE 13.1 *(Continued)*

Publication	Description of patients and study design	Main findings
Pitt, S., Lewis, R., Morgan, S. and Woodward, D. (2010). Cognitive remediation therapy in an outpatient setting: a case series. *Eating and Weight Disorders*, 15 (4), e281–286.	N = 7; Outpatient Adults; age = 29; Illness duration range = 3–22 years.	Improvements in self-reported flexibility of thinking after individual CRT. Mixed results for self-reported perfectionism.
Wood, L., Al-Khairulla, H. and Lask, B. (2011). Group cognitive remediation therapy for adolescents with anorexia nervosa. *Clinical Child Psychology and Psychiatry*, 16 (2), 225–231.	N = 9; Inpatient adolescents; Age range = 9–13.	Positive observations from group members and clinicians were reported.
Abbate-Daga, G., Buzzichelli, S., Marzola, E., Amianto, F and Fassino, S. (2012). Effectiveness of cognitive remediation therapy (CRT) in anorexia nervosa: a case series. *Journal of Clinical and Experimental Neuropsychology*, 34 (10), 1009–1015.	N = 20; Outpatient; adults; x̄ age = 22.5 (SD = 3.9); Illness duration x̄ = 5.8 years.	Medium to large effect sizes reported on most neuropsychological tasks, e.g. TMT, WCST (Cohen's d = 0.6) and positive improvement in clinical characteristics.
Pretorius, N., Dimmer, M., Power, E., Eisler, I., Simic, M. and Tchanturia K. (2012). Evaluation of a cognitive remediation therapy group for adolescents with anorexia nervosa: pilot study. *European Eating Disorders Review*, 20 (4), 321–325.	N = 30 (7 groups); Daypatient adolescents; x̄ age = 15.6 (SD 1.4); Illness duration x̄ = 2 years.	Small effect size for self-reported cognitive flexibility post-group. Adolescents found the group interesting and useful; however, some wanted more support with application to real life.
Dahlgren, C., Lask, B., Landrø, N. and Rø, Ø. (2013). Three publications in 2013 from the same group with the same sample.	Child adolescent inpatient and outpatient; N = 20; x̄ age = 15.9.	Improvement in cognitive profile; clinical measures. Feasibility of The CRT Resource Pack for Children and Adolescents. (Owen, Lindvall and Lask, 2011).
Zuchova, S., Erler, T. and Papezova, H. (2013). Group cognitive remediation therapy for adult anorexia nervosa inpatients: first experiences. *Eating and Weight Disorders*, 18 (3), 269–273.	2 groups of adult AN inpatients; N = 14 and 20; received ten 45-min CRT sessions; x̄ ages = 26.8 (SD 6.12) and 25.47 (SD 5.11) respectively; Illness duration x̄ = 8.2 (SD 6.7) and 7.3 (SD 5.8) respectively.	Group CRT was well received by severely malnourished and chronically ill patients who did not have access to other psychological treatments. The implementation of CRT was found to be feasible. Further neuropsychological testing was needed to evaluate the effect of group CRT.

Reference	Design	Findings
Lock, J., Agras, W.S., Fitzpatrick, K.K., Bryson, S.W., Jo, B, and Tchanturia, K. (2013). Is outpatient cognitive remediation therapy feasible to use in randomized clinical trials for anorexia nervosa? *International Journal of Eating Disorders, 46*, 567–575. DOI: 10.1002/eat.22134.	46 outpatients randomisation to 8 sessions of CRT or Cognitive Behavioural Therapy (CBT) over 2 months, followed by 16 sessions of CBT for 4 months.	Lower drop-out rate in the CRT group (13%) compared to the CBT group (33%). Also improvements in cognitive efficiencies in the CRT group compared to the CBT group at the end of the trial. Suggestion that CRT may be an acceptable and feasible treatment for use in an RCT for AN treatment.
Brockmeyer, T., Ingenerf, K., Walther, S., Wild, B., Hartmann, M., Herzog, W. and Friederich, H.-C. (2014). Training cognitive flexibility in patients with anorexia nervosa: a pilot randomized controlled trial of cognitive remediation therapy. *International Journal of Eating Disorders, 47* (1), 24–31. DOI: 10.1002/eat.22206.	40 inpatients; N = 40; Randomized to CRT (only set-shifting) or non-specific neurocognitive therapy (NNT) which focused on attention, memory and deductive reasoning.	CRT participants significantly out-performed the NNT group in set-shifting. Patient feedback was also more positive for CRT compared to NNT.
Dingemans, A.E., Danner, U.N., Donker, J.M., Aardoom, J.J., van Meer, F., Tobias, K., van Elburg, A.A. and van Furth, E.F. (2014). The effectiveness of cognitive remediation therapy in patients with a severe or enduring eating disorder: A randomized controlled trial. *Psychotherapy and Psychosomatics, 83*, 29–36. DOI: 10.1159/000355240.	82 inpatients; CRT versus treatment as usual	Adapted and intense, computer-assisted form of CRT (30 intensive sessions: 21 computer-assisted and 9 face-to-face); could be an addition to treatment as usual. CRT associated with significant improvements in quality of life at the end of treatment and significant improvements in ED psychopathology at follow-up. CRT was not associated with any additional changes in neuropsychological performance in set-shifting or central coherence tasks: performance on the tasks improved significantly in both groups; could be due to practice effects of non-specific ingredients of treatment.
Steinglass, J.E., Albano, A.M., Simpson, H.B., Wang, Y., Zou, J., Attia, E. and Walsh, B.T. (2014). Confronting fear using exposure and response prevention for anorexia nervosa: A randomized controlled pilot study. *International Journal of Eating Disorders, 47*, 174–180. DOI: 10.1002/eat.22214.	32 Inpatients (weight restored); comparison of CRT to Exposure and Response Prevention for AN (AN-EXRP)	Higher caloric intake at a test meal in the AN-EXRP group; this improvement was significantly associated with eating-related anxiety.

x̄: mean; SD: standard deviation. Cohen's d effect sizes: negligible effect (≥ −0.15 to <0.15); small effect (≥ 0.15 to < 0.40); medium effect (≥ 0.40 to < 0.75); large effect (≥ 0.75 to <1.10); very large effect (≥1.10 to <1.45).

to keep exercises simple; not to time tasks but rather to highlight the importance of doing and reflecting on the tasks. This transformed the therapeutic environment from one of doing 'tests' and emphasizing achievement, to one of trying tasks and reflecting on thinking styles. We also added more 'bigger picture tasks', with some of them created in discussions during the sessions and through supervision and revised versions of the manual. For example, patients were asked to give an instruction, such as a journey to the shops, but with less detail, or were asked to summarise and bullet point a clinical letter. Development of the manual is described in the following papers: Tchanturia and Hambrook (2009); Tchanturia, Davies and Lopez (2011) and in the in-house clinical manual (Tchanturia *et al.* 2010).

Following the development of the work from our group (King's College London and South London and Maudsley NHS Foundation Trust), the development of this intervention in the context of EDs advanced, through addressing its feasibility in a case series and study from our own group (Tchanturia *et al.* 2008), as well as from other eating disorder clinical groups (Pitt *et al.* 2010; Abbate-Daga *et al.* 2012; Dahlgren *et al.* 2013). Most of the practitioners involved in the advancement of this work participated in the London Workshop of CRT for Eating Disorders and received the manual from these workshops (for more details, see www.katetchanturia. com). At present, we have delivered training to 700 professionals through annual training sessions at King's College London and internationally (e.g. Italy, Spain, Norway, Switzerland, Austria, USA, Chile, Argentina, New Zealand, Hong Kong and Japan).

Most of the studies and publications therefore use different versions of the King's College London manual (Tchanturia *et al.* 2007, 2010), though there are a couple of exceptions from the current literature (e.g. Dahlgren *et al.* 2013 – two publications with an overlapping sample). These authors used a resource pack which again follows the exact principles and protocol outlined in our original clinical manual (Tchanturia *et al.* 2010), whilst adding creative developments to tools and referring to games available online. It also expands on the original toolbox developed for CRT for AN. Training and supervision for this resource pack was to our knowledge delivered by the senior author who was trained in CRT during London courses in 2007 and 2008.

Studies

The evidence based on CRT case studies and case series, as well as theoretical papers, was summarised in a special issue of *The International Journal of Eating Disorders* (Tchanturia *et al.* 2013), with the conclusion that CRT is an acceptable treatment for both patients and therapists and produces improvements in cognitive performance in two domains – flexibility and bigger picture thinking.

Recent developments have seen four RCTs conducted to build on the evidence-base for CRT. Firstly, an RCT in the context of severe and enduring AN (Dingemans *et al.* 2014) investigated CRT versus treatment as usual (TAU) by randomly assigning

TABLE 13.2 Updated evaluation of the case series (n = 60) presented: cognitive task performance before and after CRT in individual format

	Before CRT (SD)	After CRT (SD)	Significance (p-value)	Effect size (Cohen's d)
Brixton (set-shifting task): Total (n = 60)	13.2 (6.2)	9.2 (5.7)	< .001	0.66
RCFT Style index (n = 59): Central coherence task	1.14 (0.4)	1.26 (0.5)	.09	0.16
Cognitive Flexibility Scale CFS (n = 50): Self-report measure	43.05 (10.1)	46.19 (10.0)	.03	0.32

82 patients to CRT plus TAU (N = 41) or TAU only (N = 41). Assessments were conducted at baseline, after 6 weeks and after 6 months. CRT was associated with significant improvements in quality of life at the end of treatment and significant improvements in ED psychopathology at follow-up. CRT in this RCT was not associated with any additional changes in neuropsychological performance in either set-shifting or central coherence tasks; in fact, performance on the tasks improved significantly in both groups; the authors concluded that this could be due to practice effects of non-specific components of treatment.

A second RCT (Brockmeyer et al. 2014) then assessed the feasibility and efficacy, as assessed via effect size, of tailored CRT compared to a non-specific cognitive training. AN inpatients (N = 40) were Randomized to CRT (N = 20) or non-specific neurocognitive therapy (NNT; N = 20) and patients were offered a more intensive 30 sessions of CRT (with each session lasting 45 minutes) over 3 weeks for both conditions. The sessions comprised 21 computer-assisted and 9 face-to-face sessions; overall a total of 25 participants completed treatment. The NNT focused only on attention, memory and deductive reasoning. Both conditions featured computer-assisted homework. The manual-based CRT was tailored and focused solely on set-shifting; the authors omitted the central coherence which, they argue, was to remove any potentially confounding factors with regard to the control condition. The primary outcome, assessed pre- and post-intervention, was performed on a computer-based task-switching paradigm. Overall, CRT participants significantly out-performed the NNT group in set-shifting. Patient feedback was also more positive for CRT compared to NNT, for example, with regard to whether the training matched their problems and whether they felt more flexible afterwards. The authors concluded that specific tailored neurocognitive training for AN is more effective than NNT (medium effect size), confirming the feasibility of CRT for AN. They also suggested that this adapted and more intense, computer-assisted form of CRT could be an addition to treatment as usual. It is to be noted however that, due to the omission of the central coherence component, the findings of this study are not entirely comparable to other studies.

Trials

An RCT in an outpatient setting also assessed the feasibility of using CRT, with the focus on reducing drop-out rates in AN RCTs (Lock *et al.* 2013). The authors Randomized 46 outpatients to 8 sessions of CRT or Cognitive Behavioural Therapy (CBT) over 2 months, followed by 16 sessions of CBT for 4 months. The authors found a lower drop-out rate in the CRT group (13%) compared to the CBT group (33%); this study found improvements in cognitive efficiencies in the CRT group compared to the CBT group at the end of the trial. The conclusion from this study was that CRT may reduce drop-out rates in the short term and that CRT also appears to be an acceptable and feasible treatment for use in an RCT for AN treatment.

Furthermore, a recent RCT (Steinglass *et al.* 2014) compared CRT to Exposure and Response Prevention for AN (AN-EXRP) – which is a new approach that targets maladaptive eating behaviour by addressing eating-related anxiety. Inpatients who had weight restored (BMI over 18.5) were offered 12 sessions of AN-EXRP or CRT. The main outcome measure was caloric intake at a test meal, which the authors found was higher in the AN-EXRP group; this improvement was also significantly associated with eating-related anxiety. The inpatients in this study were weight restored, therefore differing significantly from participants in all the other CRT studies. This was a very small RCT, not reporting cognitive outcomes and using CRT as a non-specific control condition. In the first three RCTs described, the therapists received training at King's College London from the first author of this chapter; however, the last RCT was conducted without any input from our clinical and research group, which makes it difficult to comment on what kind of CRT was used and how.

Summary and future directions

In summary, a number of case series and RCTs show promising evidence for CRT for AN. Studies reporting findings from neuropsychological task performance, self-report measures and clinical measures all show that CRT appears to be associated with improvements in set-shifting abilities and in central coherence. It is also consistently reported that CRT seems to be an acceptable treatment from the patients' perspectives, who also report improvements in perceived perfectionism and the ability to think more flexibly, and overall drop-out rates are low (10–15%; Tchanturia, Lloyd, and Lang 2013). Although not as well researched as individual CRT, feasibility and pilot studies have begun to examine the effectiveness of CRT for group format with both adults and adolescents with AN (Chapters 4 and 9 respectively). Despite some promising findings in this area, further research is needed, to establish the effectiveness of group CRT using pre- and post-intervention neuropsychological measures.

There are a number of promising avenues for future research. These include:

1. Directly comparing the effectiveness of CRT to that of other therapies, to determine whether the benefits of cognitive efficiency and quality of life

improvements are specific to CRT or represent broader changes, for example, as a result of re-feeding.

2. Exploring how cognitive improvements may influence AN symptomatology and broader outcomes, such as work and social functioning.

3. Examining the dosage of CRT, to clarify which patients benefit from short and long formats of the intervention. Further research is also needed regarding whether individual or group formats of CRT are most beneficial for patients with AN.

4. Research has also highlighted the importance of involving family members and carers in the treatment of AN. Future research aims to focus on the development of a 'user-friendly' module of CRT which could be delivered by carers. Further work is needed to evaluate the effectiveness and acceptability of CRT delivered in this way.

5. Further work is needed to explore the brain mechanisms implicated in cognitive inefficiencies in AN (e.g. more neuroimaging studies), in order to understand this better; this would also enable investigation of the cognitive and functional brain changes associated with clinical improvements following CRT.

A further, more ambitious direction for future research is to investigate how socio-emotional focused interventions can be integrated with this line of treatment. There is support for such an approach based upon the strong evidence for socio-emotional impairments in AN, as well as evidence for the superior effectiveness of interventions which focus upon associations between cognitions, emotions and behaviours in treating eating disorders. Initial research in this area has already started (Money et al. 2011; Davies et al. 2012; Tchanturia et al. 2014). Cognitive Remediation and Emotion Skills Training (CREST) is a brief social cognition intervention (10 sessions) which incorporates some exercises from CRT, focusing on the concepts of set-shifting and central coherence and, similarly to CRT, is not related to core ED symptomatology and is a preparatory, low-intensity manualised treatment protocol. It addresses two of the maintaining features of the aforementioned maintenance model (Schmidt and Treasure 2006), namely cognitive inflexibility and emotional processing difficulties. It aims to target thinking styles, emotion recognition and the expression and regulation of emotion by using psychoeducation and skills-based strategies which allow for the reflection and development of emotion-processing skills.

A pilot CREST case study (Money, Davies and Tchanturia 2011) provided preliminary support for the acceptability and effectiveness of the intervention, and a qualitative study (Money et al. 2011) which analysed patient end of therapy reflection forms (N = 28 inpatients) confirmed the intervention's acceptability and feasibility. A third study on CREST (Davies et al. 2012) compared to it TAU and found that the intervention was acceptable, with some improvements with performance-based outcomes. A recent evaluation of CREST for AN in group format (Tchanturia, Doris and Fleming 2014) showed that social anhedonia decreased significantly following treatment with a small effect size. Motivation to

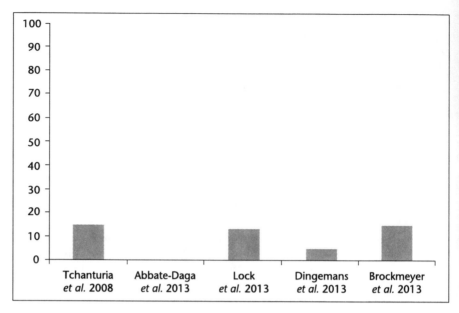

FIGURE 13.2 Shows reported percentage drop out rates from the available studies

Notes: i) The first two studies are case series (Tchanturia, and Abbate-Daga), the last three studies are RCTs; ii) NICE guidelines in 2004 reported 35–60% drop out rates from available RCTs in 2004; iii) From three RCTs shown in this figure, attrition rates in the comparison treatment groups were significantly higher than in the CRT groups.

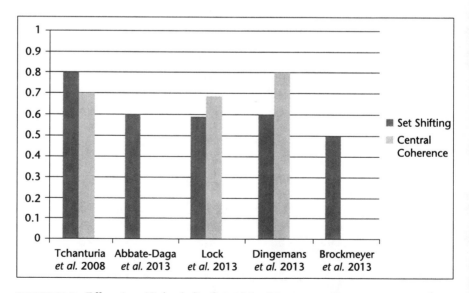

FIGURE 13.3 Effect sizes (Cohen's d) of cognitive improvements

Notes: 0.5 is regarded as a medium size effect, 0.7 and above are large size improvements. Two studies (one case series) by Abbate-Daga *et al.* (2012) and Brockmeyer *et al.* (2014) have not reported Central Coherence.

change also increased with a small effect size, though this was not found to be statistically significant. Overall, CREST received positive feedback by both patients and therapists. Further large-scale research on CREST is needed to consolidate these findings.

With growing evidence and popularity of CRT it is inevitable that variations in protocol, training and expertise occur. This book hopefully will help both researchers and clinicians to have access to the most up-to-date information in order to plan the use of CRT in the best informed fashion. When novel interventions for the ED field are developing we think it is highly important to document outcomes when possible. As we can see from the available literature, neurocognitive self-report and clinical outcomes are all helpful to inform us of what changes we can expect after delivering CRT. Having said that, we are mindful of big individual differences and of the importance of tailoring CRT to the individual needs of each patient.

References

Abbate-Daga, G., Buzzichelli, S., Marzola, E., Amianto, F. and Fassino, S. (2012). Effectiveness of cognitive remediation therapy (CRT) in anorexia nervosa: a case series. *Journal of Clinical and Experimental Neuropsychology*, *34* (10), 1009–1015.

Brockmeyer, T., Ingenerf, K., Walther, S., Wild, B., Hartmann, M., Herzog, W. and Friederich, H. C. (2014). Training cognitive flexibility in patients with anorexia nervosa: a pilot randomized controlled trial of cognitive remediation therapy. *International Journal of Eating Disorders*, *47* (1), 24–31. DOI: 10.1002/eat.22206.

Buhlmann, U., Deckersbach, T., Engelhard, I., Cook, L. M., Rauch, S. L., Kathmann, N., Wilhelm, S. and Savage, C. R. (2006). Cognitive retraining for organizational impairment in obsessive–compulsive disorder. *Psychiatry Research*, *144*, 109–116. DOI: 10.1016/j.psychres.2005.10.012.

Cwojdzińska, A., Markowska-Regulska, K. and Rybakowski, F. (2009) Cognitive remediation therapy in adolescent anorexia nervosa – case report. *Psychiatria Polska*, *43* (1), 115–124 [in Polish].

Dahlgren, C., Lask, B., Landrø, N. and Rø, Ø. (2013). Neuropsychological functioning in adolescents with anorexia nervosa before and after cognitive remediation therapy: A feasibility trial. *International Journal of Eating Disorders*, *46* (6), 576–581.

Davies, H. Fox, J., Naumann, U., Treasure, J., Schmidt, U. and Tchanturia, K. (2012). Cognitive remediation and emotion skills training for anorexia nervosa: An observational study using neuropsychological outcomes. *European Eating Disorders Review*, *20* (3), 211–217. DOI: 10.1002/erv.2170.

Davies, H. and Tchanturia, K. (2005). Cognitive remediation therapy as an intervention for acute anorexia nervosa: A case report. *European Eating Disorders Review*, *13* (5), 311–316. DOI: 10.1002/erv.655.

Dingemans, A.E., Danner, U.N., Donker, J.M., Aardoom, J.J., van Meer, F., Tobias, K., van Elburg, A.A. and van Furth, E.F. (2014). The effectiveness of cognitive remediation therapy in patients with a severe or enduring eating disorder: A randomized controlled trial. *Psychotherapy and Psychosomatics*, 2014; *83*, 29–36. DOI: 10.1159/000355240.

Eack, S. M., Bahorik, A. L., Hogarty, S. S., Greenwald, D. P., Litschge, M. Y., Mazefsky, C. A. and Minshew, N. J. (2013). Brief report: Is cognitive rehabilitation needed in verbal adults with autism? Insights from initial enrolment in a trial of cognitive enhancement therapy. *Journal of Autism and Developmental Disorders*, 43, 2233–2237. DOI: 10.1007/s10803-013-1774-2.

Eack, S. M., Bahorik, A. L., McKnight, S. A. F., Hogarty, S. S., Greenwald, D. P., Newhill, C. E., Phillips, M. L., Keshavan, M. S. and Minshew, N. J. (2013). Commonalities in social and non-social cognitive impairments in adults with autism spectrum disorder and schizophrenia. *Schizophrenia Research*, 148, 24–28. DOI: 10.1016/j.schres.2013.05.013.

Eack, S. M., Greenwald, D. P., Hogarty, S. S., Bahorik, A. L., Litschge, M. Y., Mazefsky, C. A. and Minshew, N. J. (2013). Cognitive enhancement therapy for adults with autism spectrum disorder: results of an 18-month feasibility study. *Journal of Autism and Developmental Disorders*, DOI: 10.1007/s10803-013-1834-7.

Genders, R. and Tchanturia, K. (2010). Cognitive remediation therapy (CRT) for anorexia in group format: a pilot study. *Eating and Weight Disorders – Studies on Anorexia, Bulimia and Obesity*, 15 (4), e234–239.

Huke, V., Turk, J., Saeidi, S., Kent, A. and Morgan, J. F. (2013). Autism spectrum disorders in eating disorder populations: A systematic review. *European Eating Disorders Review*, 21, 345–351. DOI: 10.1002/erv.2244.

Lock, J., Agras, W.S., Fitzpatrick, K.K., Bryson, S.W., Jo, B. and Tchanturia, K. (2013). Is outpatient cognitive remediation therapy feasible to use in randomized clinical trials for anorexia nervosa? *International Journal of Eating Disorders*, 46 (6), 567–575. DOI: 10.1002/eat.22134.

Lopez, C., Davies, H. and Tchanturia, K. (2012). 'Neuropsychological inefficiencies in anorexia nervosa targeted in clinical practice: The development of a module of cognitive remediation therapy', in *Eating and Its Disorders* (1st edn). John R.E. Fox and Ken P. Goss (Eds.). Chichester: John Wiley and Sons, Ltd.

Money, C., Davies, H. and Tchanturia, K. (2011). A case study introducing cognitive remediation and emotion skills training for anorexia nervosa inpatient care. *Clinical Case Studies*, 10 (2), 110–121. DOI: 10.1177/1534650110396545.

Money, C., Genders, R., Treasure, J., Schmidt, U. and Tchanturia, K. (2011). A brief emotion-focused intervention for inpatients with anorexia nervosa: A qualitative study. *Journal of Health Psychology*, 16 (6), 947–958. DOI: 10.1177/1359105310396395.

Park, H. S., Shin, Y.-W., Ha, T. H., Shin, M. S., Kim, Y. Y., Lee, Y. H. and Kwon, J. S. (2006). Effect of cognitive training focusing on organizational strategies in patients with obsessive-compulsive disorder. *Psychiatry and Clinical Neurosciences*, 60, 718–726. DOI:10.1111/j.1440-1819.2006.01587.x.

Pitt S., Lewis, R., Morgan, S. and Woodward, D. (2010). Cognitive remediation therapy in an outpatient setting: A case series. *Eating and Weight Disorders*, 15, e281–e286.

Pretorius, N., Dimmer, M., Power, E., Eisler, I., Simic, M. and Tchanturia, K. (2012). Evaluation of a cognitive remediation therapy group for adolescents with anorexia nervosa: Pilot study. *European Eating Disorders Review*, 20 (4), 321–325. DOI:10.1002/erv.2176.

Pretorius, N. and Tchanturia, K. (2007). Cognitive remediation therapy in an outpatient setting: A case series. *Therapy*, 4 (4), 423–431. DOI: 10.1586/14750708.4.4.423.

Savage, C. R., Baer, L., Keuthen, N. J., Brown, H. D., Rauch, S. L. and Jenike, M. A. (1999). Organizational strategies mediate nonverbal memory impairment in obsessive-compulsive disorder. *Biological Psychiatry*, 45, 905–916. DOI: 10.1016/S0006-3223(98)00278-9.

Schmidt, U. and Treasure, J. (2006). Anorexia nervosa: Valued and visible. A cognitive-interpersonal maintenance model and its implications for research and practice. *British Journal of Clinical Psychology*, 45, 343–366. DOI: 10.1348/014466505X53902.

Segalàs, C., Alonso, P., Labad, J., Jaurrieta, N., Real, E., Jiménez, S., Menchón, J. M. and Vallejo, J. (2008). Verbal and nonverbal memory processing in patients with obsessive-compulsive disorder: Its relationship to clinical variables. *Neuropsychology*, 22 (2), 262–272. DOI: 10.1037/0894-4105.22.2.262.

Shin, N. Y., Lee, T. Y., Kim, E. and Kwon, J. S. (2013). Cognitive functioning in obsessive-compulsive disorder: A meta-analysis. *Psychological Medicine*, *44* (6). DOI: 10.1017/S0033291713001803.

Siegle, G. J., Ghinassi, F. and Thase, M. E. (2007). Neurobehavioral therapies in the 21st century: Summary of an emerging field and an extended example of cognitive control training for depression. *Cognitive Therapy Research*, *31*, 235–262. DOI: 10.1007/s10608-006-9118-6.

Steinglass, J.E., Albano, A.M., Simpson, H.B., Wang, Y., Zou, J., Attia, E. and Walsh, B.T. (2014). Confronting fear using exposure and response prevention for anorexia nervosa: A randomized controlled pilot study. *International Journal of Eating Disorders*, *47*, 174–180. DOI: 10.1002/eat.22214.

Steinhausen, H.-C. (2002). The outcome of anorexia nervosa in the 20th century. *American Journal of Psychiatry*, *159* (8), 1284–1293. DOI:10.1176/appi.ajp.159.8.1284.

Svetlana, Z., Erler, T. and Pepezova, H. (2013). Group cognitive remediation therapy for adult anorexia inpatients: first experiences. *Eating and Weight Disorders – Studies on Anorexia, Bulimia and Obesity*, *18* (3), 269–273.

Tchanturia, K., Whitney, J. and Campbell, I. C. (2006). Can cognitive exercises help treat anorexia nervosa? *Eating and Weight Disorders – Studies on Anorexia, Bulimia and Obesity*, *11* (4), e112–e116.

Tchanturia, K., Davies, H. and Campbell, I.C. (2007). Cognitive remediation therapy for patients with anorexia nervosa: Preliminary findings. *Annals of General Psychiatry*, *6* (14). DOI:10.1186/1744-859X-6-14.

Tchanturia, K., Davies, H., Lopez, C., Schmidt, U., Treasure, J. and Wykes, T. (2008). Correspondence. *Psychological Medicine*, *38* (9), 1371–1373. DOI: 10.1017/S0033291708003796.

Tchanturia, T., Davies, H., Roberts, M., Harrison, A., Nakazato, M., Schmidt, U., Treasure, J. and Morris, R. (2012). Poor cognitive flexibility in eating disorders: Examining the evidence using the Wisconsin Card Sorting Task. *Plos One*, *7* (1), e28331. DOI: 10.1371/journal.pone.0028331.

Tchanturia, K., Davies, H., Reeder, C. and Wykes, T. (2010). *Cognitive remediation therapy for anorexia nervosa*. London: King's College London, University of London.

Tchanturia, K., Happé, F., Godley, J., Treasure, J., Bara-Carril, N. and Schmidt, U. (2004). 'Theory of mind' in anorexia nervosa. *European Eating Disorders Review*, *12*, 361–366. DOI: 10.1002/erv.608.

Tchanturia, K., Harrison, A., Davies, H., Roberts, M., Oldershaw, A., Nakazato, M., Stahl, D., Morris, R., Schmidt, U. and Treasure, J. (2011). Cognitive flexibility and clinical severity in eating disorders. *Plos One*, *6* (6), e20462. DOI:10.1371/journal/pone.0020462.

Tchanturia, K., Lloyd, S. and Lang, K. (2013). Cognitive remediation therapy for anorexia nervosa: current evidence and future research directions. *International Journal of Eating Disorders*, *46* (5), 492–495. DOI: 10.1002/ eat.22106.

Tchanturia, K., Smith, E., Weineck, F., Fidanboylu, E., Kern, N., Treasure, J. and Baron-Cohen, S. (2013). Exploring autistic traits in anorexia: A clinical study. *Molecular Autism*, *4* (44), DOI: 10.1186/2040-2392-4-44.

Tchanturia, K., Doris, E. and Fleming, C. (2014). Effectiveness of Cognitive Remediation and Emotion Skills Training (CREST) for anorexia nervosa in group format: A naturalistic pilot study. *European Eating Disorders Review*, *22* (3), 200–205. DOI: 10.1002/erv.2287.

Turner-Brown, L., Perry, T., Dichter, G. S., Bodfish, J. W. and Penn, D. L. (2008). Brief report: Feasibility of social cognition and interaction training for adults with high functioning autism. *Journal of Autism and Developmental Disorders*, *38* (9), 1777–1784. DOI:10.1007/s10803-008-0545-y.

Wass, S. V. and Porayska-Pomsta, K. (2013). The uses of cognitive training technologies in the treatment of autism spectrum disorders. *Autism*. DOI: 10.1177/1362361313499827.

Whitney, J., Easter, A. and Tchanturia, K. (2008). Service users' feedback on cognitive training in the treatment of anorexia nervosa: A qualitative study. *International Journal of Eating Disorders*, *41* (6), 542–550. DOI: 10.1002/eat.20536.

Wood, L., Al-Khairulla, H. and Lask, B. (2011). Group cognitive remediation therapy for adolescents with anorexia nervosa. *Clinical Child Psychology and Psychiatry*, *16* (2), 225–231. DOI: 10.1177/1359104511404750.

Wykes, T., Reeder, C., Landau, S., Everitt, B., Knapp, M., Patel, A. and Romeo, R. (2007). Cognitive remediation therapy in schizophrenia: Randomized controlled trial. *British Journal of Psychiatry*, *190*, 421–427. DOI: 10.1192/bjp.bp.106.026575.

Wykes, T. and Spaulding, W. D. (2011). Thinking about the future cognitive remediation therapy – What works and could we do better? *Schizophrenia Bulletin*, *37* (2), S80–90. DOI:10.1093/schbul/sbr064.

14

DEVELOPING COGNITIVE REMEDIATION THERAPY – LESSONS FROM THE FIELD OF SCHIZOPHRENIA

Clare Reeder and Til Wykes

Cognitive remediation therapy (CRT) first emerged as a means to improve cognitive functioning in people who had sustained a traumatic brain injury. By 'cognitive functioning' we refer to cognitive processes which have typically been assessed by neuropsychological assessments. Since then, this form of rehabilitation has been adapted for use in a number of conditions in which cognitive impairment is a predominant endophenotype. In particular, it has been used to improve cognitive functioning associated with a variety of mental health problems, which are very frequently associated with cognitive deficits, most notably in executive functions.

A concentration of efforts on cognition, particularly in individuals with a diagnosis of schizophrenia, has been due to the noted associations between cognition and future functioning (Wykes *et al.* 1994), and because poorer cognition limited these same recovery outcomes even when every effort was made with state of the art rehabilitation programmes (e.g. Wykes *et al.* 1994; Bell *et al.* 2004; Velligan *et al.* 1999).

CRT is now an established form of psychological therapy for a schizophrenia diagnosis. It is recommended within some governmental guidelines (e.g. SIGN 2012) and is increasingly becoming accepted as part of routine clinical practice. We have been conducting research into CRT for people with a diagnosis of schizophrenia for more than twenty years, and running international training courses for researchers and clinicians for almost as long. Consequently, we had have had the opportunity to contribute to the development of the field, and to witness some of the successes and pitfalls that have occurred along the way, some of which continue to impact the rate and route of development for the therapy.

With the exciting emergence of CRT for anorexia nervosa, pioneered by Kate Tchanturia and colleagues at the Institute of Psychiatry, and show-cased in this book, we take this opportunity to share some of our thoughts, with hindsight, about the way in which CRT for schizophrenia has been developed over the last few decades, in the hope that this may raise some issues for consideration in shaping the future development of CRT for anorexia nervosa.

The route to implementation

Although some early studies of cognitive remediation (CR), investigating behavioural strategies such as verbalisation of action instructions (e.g. Meichenbaum 1969) appeared to be effective in improving certain cognitive skills in schizophrenia, it wasn't until cognitive deficits began to be revisited as a core feature of schizophrenia, that cognition came to be considered a potentially worthy treatment target in schizophrenia. At this stage, the mood was pessimistic and somewhat antagonistic, with a number of field leaders recommending that CR was an enterprise doomed to failure (e.g. Bellack 1992). This stance posed something of a challenge to the research field, which then began to abound with experimental studies whose aim it was to improve performance on specific neuropsychological tasks – particularly the Wisconsin Card Sorting Test – for people with a schizophrenia diagnosis.

Gradually, it became apparent that cognition was not the 'immutable' impairment that had been feared (e.g. Goldberg et al. 1987), and with this, studies of both experimental techniques to improve neuropsychological test performance and more holistic attempts to rehabilitate cognitive function in general, burgeoned. These studies provided a bedrock of evidence to show which techniques were the most effective in improving specific cognitive skills in schizophrenia, and in particular that they were clearly generalised from trained tasks to cognitive tests.

In 2003, Krabbendam and Aleman published the first meta-analysis of CR for schizophrenia, which included twelve controlled studies, and which reported a mean effect for cognition of 0.45, which easily matched the effect sizes for other more established psychological therapies for schizophrenia, such as Cognitive Behavioural Therapy for psychosis (Pilling et al. 2002). Krabbendam and Aleman concluded that whilst benefits for cognitive task performance were apparent, even for those which had not been practiced during the training procedure, 'Future studies should include more real-world outcomes and perform longitudinal evaluations'.

This reflects the emerging consensus at the time, that not only should cognitive effects of CR be durable, but that they were an insufficient goal in their own right, so that increasingly, the generalisation of cognitive improvements to daily living skills was considered to be a key target for CR. This view has continued to prevail, and in 2009, Michael Green wrote in an editorial of *The American Journal of Psychiatry*, that 'Community functioning is the ultimate goal ... [for CRT] ... improving cognition in schizophrenia is *not* the end in itself'. This new goalpost has set a high threshold for acceptance of CRT, and in the last guidelines produced by the UK National Institute for Health and Clinical Excellence (NICE), CRT was not recommended, on the basis of there being insufficient evidence to demonstrate its benefits for functional outcome (NICE 2009).

The field has embraced this view, and consequently most studies of CR have included measures of functional outcome, and researchers have made explicit attempts to target general functioning, for example, by:

a   tying specific CRT programmes to other more traditional rehabilitation programmes such as vocational rehabilitation (Bell *et al.* 2014),

b   including additional 'bridging' components to CR, in which adjunctive sessions are offered which aim to help people generalise or transfer new cognitive skills to other settings (e.g. McGurk *et al.* 2005), or

c   basing the CRT itself on a model for the relationship between cognitive and functional change, and incorporating targeted processes to facilitate the transfer of new cognitive skills to everyday life into the CRT programme itself (Wykes and Reeder 2005).

The fruits of these developments were apparent in the most recent meta-analysis of CR, which form a pool of more than 2000 participants across 40 controlled studies, showed a mean effect size of 0.45 for global cognition – which was durable at follow-up (at least six months) – and a similar moderate-sized and durable effect size of CRT on general functioning (Wykes *et al.* 2011). Small, significant but non-durable effects of CRT were also apparent on symptoms.

The evidence to support the efficacy of CRT for schizophrenia is now substantial, and continues to grow. Consequently, the preoccupations of the research community are changing. On the one hand, there is a clear drive to understand the mechanisms of change in order to refine treatments. Studies of CRT now frequently focus on predictors of response, in terms of patient and therapy factors (a quick review of the literature revealed reports from six Randomized controlled trials investigating predictors of response to CR in schizophrenia since 2013: Scheu *et al.* 2013; Vita *et al.* 2013; Kontis *et al.* 2013; Mak *et al.* 2013; Panizzutti *et al.* 2013; Bell *et al.* 2014); and model-building studies – which investigate the link between cognition and functioning both cross-sectionally and longitudinally, and with putative mediating or moderating factors such as metacognition, social cognition or learning potential – are common (Reeder *et al.* 2014; Stratta *et al.* 2009; Miles *et al.* 2014; Wykes *et al.* 2012).

On the other hand, there is a focus on broadening the implementation of CR, both to target more diverse patients groups, particularly inpatients and first episode or at-risk samples (e.g. Urben *et al.* 2012), but more generally to consider which factors might be important if we are to facilitate the widespread dissemination of CR within health services across the world (Wykes and Spaulding 2011). This highlights procedural issues about the mode of delivery, particularly since a key feature of CR for schizophrenia has been massed practice, and there is a general consensus that sessions need to be offered intensively (several times a week) for a period of at least several months (Keefe *et al.* 2010). Consequently, questions arise regarding, a) how much therapist support is required and the extent to which patients can conduct sessions independently using a computer, b) whether CR can be effectively delivered in groups, and (c) the level of training of therapists that is required, and are in hot debate.

What is cognitive remediation?

The developmental process for CRT for schizophrenia that we have described is perhaps an unusual one as far as psychological therapies go, in being driven by the attempt to rehabilitate a specific symptom (i.e. cognitive functioning), rather than being focused on a particular model of change. Numerous different CRT programs have been developed, and whilst they usually adhere to core principles of massed practice, errorless learning, self-motivation and the promotion of the generalisation of new cognitive skills to everyday functional goals (Wykes and Spaulding 2011), their theoretical underpinnings and mode of delivery are notoriously diverse.

CRT delivery can be with pencil and paper versus computers; individually versus in groups; with or without a therapist; using software designed for the general population versus that designed specifically for people with a schizophrenia diagnosis; with or without adjunctive therapy. The list continues. Most crucially, there has traditionally between a discrepancy between programmes which lean primarily on drill-and-practice based approaches, relying on rehearsal and practice on highly repetitive basic cognitive tasks for improvements, as opposed to strategy-based CRT therapies, which also incorporate high levels of repetitive practice, but which have an additional focus on the development of new cognitive processing strategies to support or compensate for impairment in both basic and complex cognitive functions. The two approaches are underpinned by different conceptual camps.

The drill-and-practice approaches tend to draw heavily on the principles of neuroscience, particularly the notion of harnessing neuroplasticity to describe how well-rehearsed basic cognitive improvements can have a knock-on effect on more complex skills by providing secure cognitive building blocks upon which they are based (Vinogradov et al. 2012). This camp tends to de-emphasise the role of a therapist and focus on the improvement of brain functioning. This necessitates the use of adjunctive rehabilitation to provide the opportunity and generalisation training by which new cognitive skills may be transferred to functional outcomes.

By contrast, the strategy-based approach favours a more holistic cognitive conceptualisation, emphasising the development of more generic cognitive schemas to guide behaviour, and focusing on recovery-based goals – which are also likely to result in neuroplastic changes (Wykes and Reeder 2005). The therapist's role is considered to be key amongst a range of non-specific therapeutic effects, including providing positive reinforcement, a clear rationale for change, and encouraging a sense of self-efficacy.

In a recent sabbatical, one of us (TW) visited established CR services within the USA and noted that despite these divisions, in practice there is considerable overlap between programmes in terms of the delivery of CRT for schizophrenia. However, the debate regarding the nature of CR has had important implications for the development of the field.

Firstly, it was as recently as 2012 that a definition for CRT was agreed by the Cognitive Remediation Experts Workshop in an international schizophrenia conference in Florence:

> A behavioural training-based intervention that aims to improve cognitive processes [e.g. attention, memory, executive functioning, social cognition or meta-cognition] with the general aim of durable benefits on community functioning.

This definition remains very broad and says little about what the CRT programme should look like. Consequently, in terms of dissemination, for clinicians seeking to adopt a CRT within their services, there is little to guide them in selecting an appropriate programme or mode of delivery. It is not clear,

a   what techniques should be used in order to train cognitive processes,
b   which cognitive or functional processes should be targeted,
c   which, if any, non-specific therapy factors are intrinsic to any CRT programme,
d   whether or not it should be delivered by a therapist, and
e   which mental health professionals are best placed to deliver the therapy.

Similar uncertainties face advisory bodies in making clinical recommendations regarding the implementation of CRT in clinical services.

Whilst this situation is clearly complex and somewhat political, we feel that resolutions are in sight, and may be important drivers for future research. For example, the current focus on studies investigating the relationship between cognitive and functional change is likely to enable us to develop models to refine CRT treatments. This may be particularly important as evidence emerges that cognitive functions which are strongly predictive of functioning – and which consequently appear to be promising targets for intervention – are frequently not the ones which appear to be most beneficial for functioning when they are improved. Whilst a wide range of cognitive functions (e.g. working memory, long-term memory, speed of processing) may predict outcome at any one time in schizophrenia, it appears to be primarily executive function *improvements* that are beneficial for social functioning (Reeder *et al.* 2004; Wykes *et al.* 2012; Eack *et al.* 2009).

We may need to include within this model-building, studies of the role of non-specific factors in CRT, particularly the therapeutic relationship, and factors which improve motivation and self-efficacy. A clearer conceptualisation of the way in which case formulation and the use of collaboratively defined, recovery-based goals informs the delivery of CRT, may be particularly important in this regard.

Developing CRT in anorexia

The experience of developing CRT for schizophrenia has led to a number of lessons, which in hindsight it may have been helpful to address earlier on in the process. We leave you with a number of questions which relate to CRT in general which may be worth considering in relation to anorexia nervosa specifically, in order to smooth the developmental pathway of CRT. Some of these questions have already begun to be addressed in the chapters of this book.

1. What are the therapeutic targets for CRT for anorexia nervosa? One advantage that the field seems to have is the clear cognitive targets – identified and tested in a hypothesis-driven manner, particularly by Kate Tchanturia's group. But an added complexity may be the combination of cognitive deficits (e.g. impaired performance on set-shifting tasks) with cognitive styles (e.g. attention to detail at the expense of the bigger picture). On a separate note, in Chapter 7, Brockmeyer and Friedrich say that it will be important to discover whether CRT has any direct or indirect impact on eating disorder symptoms. We might state this more strongly, and suggest that it will be important to clarify whether cognitive targets are considered sufficiently meaningful in their own right or whether benefits to other outcomes are essential for the sustainability of CRT. If eating symptoms become a necessary target for CRT, then it will be important to investigate whether the current cognitive targets in CRT for anorexia nervosa, are the ones which drive symptom change if they can be improved.

2. Is there a testable model for the relationship between the cognitive targets and eating disorder symptoms or other outcomes, which may underpin the development of CRT? This may be crucial to guide the refinement of CRT to maximise effectiveness. In particular, there may be specific moderating and mediating effects that have still not been included or measured in current studies.

3. Which non-specific elements to the therapy are critical to its success and form part of the defining features of CRT for anorexia nervosa? The experience of developing CRT in schizophrenia, is that little is apparent to unify CRT programmes, and that in essence they can be perceived as a series of techniques to improve brain functioning, rather than a psychological therapy which targets cognitive functioning within a whole-person context.

References

Bell, M.D., Bryson, G., Fiszdon, J.M., Greig, T. and Wexler, B.E. (2004). Neurocognitive enhancement therapy and work therapy in schizophrenia: Work outcomes at 6 months and 12 month follow-up. *Biological Psychiatry, 55,* 335.

Bell, M.D., Choi, K.-H., Dyer, C. and Wexler, B. (2014). Benefits of cognitive remediation and supported employment for schizophrenia patients with poor community functioning. *Psychiatric Services, 65* (4), DOI: 10.1176/appi.ps. 201200505.

Bellack, A.S. (1992). Cognitive rehabilitation for schizophrenia – is it possible – is it necessary? *Schizophrenia Bulletin*, *18*, 43–50.

Eack, S.M., Greenwald, D.P., Hogarty, S.S., Cooley, S.J., DiBarry, A.L., Montrose, D.M. and Keshavan, M.S. (2009). Cognitive enhancement therapy for early-course schizophrenia: effects of a two-year randomized controlled trial. *Psychiatric Services (Washington, D.C.)*, *60*, 1468–1476.

Goldberg, T.E., Weinberger, D.R., Berman, K.F. *et al.* (1987). Further evidence for dementia of the prefrontal type in schizophrenia – a controlled study of teaching the Wisconsin Card Sorting Test. *Archives of General Psychiatry*, *44*, 1008–1014.

Keefe, R., Vinogradov, S., Medalia, A. *et al.* (2010). Feasibility of multi-site cognitive remediation in the schizophrenia trials network (CRSTN). *Schizophrenia Research*, *117*, SI, 394.

Kontis, D., Huddy, V., Reeder, C. *et al.* (2013). Effects of age and cognitive reserve on cognitive remediation therapy outcome in patients with schizophrenia. *American Journal of Geriatric Psychiatry*, *21*, 218–230.

Krabbendam, L. and Aleman, A. (2003) Cognitive rehabilitation in schizophrenia: a quantitative analysis of controlled studies. *Psychopharmacology*, *169*, 376–382.

Mak, M., Samochowiec, J., Tybura, P. *et al.* (2013). The efficacy of cognitive rehabilitation with RehaCom programme in schizophrenia patients. The role of selected genetic polymorphisms in successful cognitive rehabilitation. *Annals of Agricultural and Environmental Medicine*, *20*, 77–81.

McGurk, S.R., Mueser, K.T. and Pascaris, A. (2005). Cognitive training and supported employment for persons with severe mental illness: One-year results from a randomized controlled trial. *Schizophrenia Bulletin*, *31*, 898–909.

Meichenbaum, D.H. (1969). Effects of instructions and reinforcement on thinking and language behaviour of schizophrenics. *Behavior Research and Therapy*, *7*, 101–114.

Miles, A.A., Heinrichs, R.W., Ammari, N. *et al.* (2014). Stability and change in symptoms, cognition, and community outcome in schizophrenia. *Schizophrenia Research*, *152*, 435–439.

Panizzutti, R., Hamilton, S.P. and Vinogradov, S. (2013). Genetic correlate of cognitive training response in schizophrenia. *Neuropharmacology*, *64*, SI, 264–267.

Pilling, S., Bebbington, P., Kuipers, E., *et al.* (2002). Psychological treatments in schizophrenia: Meta-analysis of family intervention and cognitive behaviour therapy. *Psychological Medicine*, *32*, 763–782.

Reeder, C., Newton, E., Frangou, S. and Wykes, T. (2004). Which executive skills should we target to affect social functioning and symptom change? A study of a cognitive remediation therapy program. *Schizophrenia Bulletin*, *30*, 87–100.

Scheu, F., Aghotor, J., Pfueller, U. *et al.* (2013). Predictors of performance improvements within a cognitive remediation program for schizophrenia. *Psychiatry Research*, *209*, 375–380.

Stratta, P., Daneluzzo, E., Riccardi, I. *et al.* (2009). Metacognitive ability and social functioning are related in persons with schizophrenic disorder. *Schizophrenia Research*, *108*, 301–302.

Urben, S., Pihet, S., Jauget, L. *et al.* (2012). Computer-assisted cognitive remediation in adolescents with psychosis or at risk for psychosis: a 6-month follow-up. *Acta Neuropsychiatrica*, *24*, 328–335.

Velligan, D.I. and Miller, A.L. (1999). Cognitive dysfunction in schizophrenia and its importance to outcome: The place of atypical antipsychotics in treatment. *Journal of Clinical Psychiatry*, *60*, 25–28.

Vinogradov, S., Fisher, M. and Villiers-Sidani, E. (2012). Cognitive training for impaired neural systems in neuropsychiatric illness. *Psychopharmacology*, *37*, 43–76.

Vita, A., Deste, G., De Peri, L. *et al.* (2013). Predictors of cognitive and functional improvement and normalization after cognitive remediation in patients with schizophrenia. *Schizophrenia Research*, *150*, 51–57.

Wykes, T. (1994) Predicting symptomatic and behavioural outcomes of community care. *British Journal of Psychiatry, 165*, 486–492.

Wykes, T., Huddy, V., Cellard, C., et al. (2011). A meta-analysis of cognitive remediation for schizophrenia: Methodology and effect sizes. *The American Journal of Psychiatry, 168*, 472–485.

Wykes, T. and Reeder, C. (2005). *Cognitive Remediation Therapy for Schizophrenia: Theory and Practice.* London: Brunner Routledge.

Wykes, T., Reeder, C., Huddy, V., et al. (2012). Developing models of how cognitive improvements change functioning: Mediation, moderation and moderated mediation. *Schizophrenia Research, 38*, 88–93.

Wykes, T. and Spaulding, W.D. (2011). Thinking about the future cognitive remediation therapy – what works and could we do better? *Schizophrenia Bulletin, 37*, (2), S80–S90. DOI:10.1093/schbul/sbr064.

APPENDICES

Childhood Personality Traits in Eating Disorders

Appendix A: The Childhood Retrospective Perfectionism Questionnaire (CHIRP) – Proband Version

Permission is given for the questionnaire to be used but it should not be modified without written permission from the authors.

Name: _____   Date _____

Please think back to the time when you were a child, *up to the age of 12 years.* Then judge if the following behaviours described you at that time. However, only judge if a behaviour was present if you:

Either,

- took longer than others doing things because of attention to detail or high standards and if in your judgement this interfered with other activities (e.g. leisure time, school or hobbies)

Or,

- this behaviour was so extreme that other people (e.g. siblings, relatives, friends, teachers) commented on it.

		Yes	*No*
1a)	At school, did you put more effort into your schoolwork because of attention to detail or perfectionism, than your friends/ classmates?		
1b)	In your opinion did you spend more lime on homework than others?		
1c)	Was your work always exceptionally neat? For example, would you redo a piece of work if it had errors in it, even if there was just one mistake?		
1d)	Did you always strive for the best mark at school or get upset if you were not always top of the class?		
With regard to self-care and appearance, were you excessively concerned with . . .			
2a)	Making sure your appearance was just right, e.g. your hair parting was straight or symmetrical etc, without bumps etc?		
2b)	Making sure your clothes were coordinated (e.g. colour and style)?		
2c)	Order and symmetry with your appearance (e.g. hair/hems/ cuffs)?		
2d)	Spending excessive time and effort on matters of personal hygiene (e.g. cleaning your teeth, washing your hands etc)?		
3a)	Did you spend an excessive amount of time making your room tidy and organised?		
3b)	Did you like to make sure that everything was 'just so' and in its proper place?		
3c)	Were you excessively concerned about order and symmetry (e.g. lining things up)?		
4a)	If you had pets, did you take looking after them to extremes? (e.g. diligently taking a dog on long walks no matter what the weather or your family schedule)		
4b)	Did you have any other hobby, which was taken to extremes or where you put in supreme effort to the exclusion of other activities?		
5a)	Were you excessively careful to obey rules and not put a foot wrong?		
5b)	Were you excessively careful and cautious, e.g. with a tendency to hoard money, sweets, toys etc?		

6a)	Could you have been described as someone who was inflexible?		
6b)	Did you find periods of transition more difficult than your peers, e.g. difficult to adjust to changes in school, home or the family?		
6c)	Could you cope with changing plans at short notice?		
6d)	Would you like to have written plans or have intricate details about events or activities spelled out so you knew what was going to happen?		
6e)	Could you have been described as stubborn (determined)? For example, if you made up your mind to do something, would you have carried it through no matter what?		

I estimate that my account is _____% reliable (where 0% is not at all reliable and 100% is perfect).

Reference

Southgate L, Tchanturia K, Collier D, and Treasure J. (2008) The development of the childhood restrospective perfectionism questionnaire (CHIRP) in an eating disorder sample. *European Eating Disorder Review* 16(6): 451–462.

Appendix B: Detail and Flexibility Questionnaire (DFlex)

Below is a list of statements. Please circle the response that *best describes* to what extent you agree or disagree with each statement.

1. I get angry if people do not do things my way	1	2	3	4	5	6
2. I sometimes bore others as I go on to an excess about some things	1	2	3	4	5	6
3. I get upset if other people disturb my plans for the day by being late	1	2	3	4	5	6
4. I have difficulty making decisions	1	2	3	4	5	6
5. When others suggest a new way of doing things, I get upset or unsettled	1	2	3	4	5	6
6. I find it difficult to remember the story line in films, plays or books, but can remember specific scenes in great detail	1	2	3	4	5	6
7. Once I get into an emotional state, e.g. anger or sadness, it is very difficult to soothe myself	1	2	3	4	5	6
8. I spend as much time on more- or less important tasks	1	2	3	4	5	6
9. I like to make plans about complex arrangements, e.g. journeys and work projects	1	2	3	4	5	6
10. I can get hung up on details when reading, rather than understanding the gist	1	2	3	4	5	6
11. I have high levels of anxiety/ discomfort; I can see/feel/taste that things might not be quite right	1	2	3	4	5	6
12. I tend to focus on one thing at a time and get it out of proportion to the total situation	1	2	3	4	5	6
13. I like doing things in a particular order or routine	1	2	3	4	5	6

14. I can get lost in details and forget the real purpose of a task	1	2	3	4	5	6
15. I can be called stubborn or single-minded as it is difficult to shift from one point of view to another	1	2	3	4	5	6
16. I find it difficult to do several things at once (multi-tasking)	1	2	3	4	5	6
17. I need clarity and rules when facing a new situation. Without rules, I easily feel lost	1	2	3	4	5	6
18. I find it hard to see different perspectives of a situation	1	2	3	4	5	6
19. I get very distressed if plans get changed at the last minute	1	2	3	4	5	6
20. I can get overwhelmed by too many details	1	2	3	4	5	6
21. I dislike change	1	2	3	4	5	6
22. I depend on others to help me get things into perspective, as I tend to have a rather blinkered view on things in my life	1	2	3	4	5	6
23. I often feel vulnerable and unsafe as I am unable to see threats (or opportunities) that are out of my field of vision	1	2	3	4	5	6
24. I find it hard to write concisely; I often overrun word limits and find it difficult to decide which details can be left out	1	2	3	4	5	6

Notes: Cognitive rigidity subscale – odd numbered items. Attention to detail subscale – even numbered items.

Reference

Roberts M, Barthel S, Tchanturia K, Lopez C and Treasure J (2011) Development and validation of the detail and flexibility questionnaire (DFlex) in eating disorders. *Eating Behaviours* 12(3): 168–174. DOI. 10.1016/j.eatbeh.2011.04.001

USEFUL WEBLINKS

Cognitive Remediation Therapy for Anorexia Nervosa clinical manual:
www.national.slam.nhs.uk/wp-content/uploads/2014/04/Cognitive-remediation-therapy-for-Anorexia-Nervosa-Kate-Tchantura.pdf

Cognitive Remediation Therapy for Anorexia Nervosa clinical manual in Spanish and Italian:
www.katetchanturia.com/#!publications/c1y51

Dr. Kate Tchanturia's website also has presentations, protocols and links to relevant papers:
www.katetchanturia.com

For full papers, follow Dr. Kate Tchanturia on Research Gate:
www.researchgate.net

Professor Til Wykes speaking about CRT:
www.youtube.com/watch?v=VUtvoCgM57s

Professor James Lock speaking about CRT for eating disorders:
www.youtube.com/watch?v=r1zB_ekde-Q

A TO Z OF CRT FOR EATING DISORDERS

Kate Tchanturia and Samantha Lloyd

'**A**ll work and no play makes Jack a dull boy' – CRT for eating disorders is a light-hearted and playful form of therapy which creates opportunities for learning new skills and ways of thinking. Children learn and develop in play, and this way of learning may be particularly important for patients with eating disorders – significantly those with early onset of illness – who may have missed these opportunities to learn through play. In CRT, cognitive exercises are introduced in a playful manner with both patient and therapist participating.

Bigger picture thinking – is one of the target areas of CRT for eating disorders. Specific exercises to develop bigger picture thinking include summarising and generating 'headlines' or bullet points to summarise a story, film or holiday. This type of approach draws on some of the principles of Gestalt psychology ('the whole is greater than the sum of parts') and applies these to practical experiential exercises. It is also helpful to link CRT work to a 'bigger picture' of recovery.

Curiosity – CRT for eating disorders aims to encourage patients' curiosity and interest in their thinking style and approach. Developing a sense of curiosity is an important first step in engaging patients in CRT work.

Doing – is a key part of CRT: carrying out experiential exercises and beginning to make small achievable changes to everyday life. Small changes to promote flexibility may include changes in daily routines, changing the journey to work/hospital, wearing hair differently, reading a different newspaper at the weekend. These provide the opportunity to think about what may be difficult – or easy – about making changes, and for noticing and reflecting how this went and any thoughts which arose as a result. The active nature of CRT extends to the therapist who also engages in the tasks and activities.

Evaluation – as with any intervention, ongoing evaluation is essential. This should include a range of methods including quantitative self-report, qualitative and experimental. In this book we have outlined some of the assessment tools used by our team in order to evaluate changes and the effectiveness of CRT. Existing studies have shown improvements in neurocognitive performance, acceptability of CRT to both patients and therapists, and low drop-out rates. Further evaluation of adaptations of the CRT model to group formats is an area where further evaluation is needed.

Flexibility – is an important skill in life, as research shows that people who are flexible have a better quality of life and are more adaptable to change (when they need to change job, relocate, meet new people). CRT for eating disorders promotes this skill with cognitive exercises, thinking about alternatives and practising a variety of ways to solve a problem.

Global perspective – is what many of the CRT exercises encourage. This is also extended by encouraging the patient to foster a global image of their life and consider what they would like to achieve without an eating disorder, as well as thinking globally about recovery and what it means to them. After individual or group work, patients are encouraged to think more globally about the CRT principles they have learned and to place them in the context of their overall journey to recovery.

How to connect thinking style to eating disorders and a patient's journey to recovery is a big challenge. In the early stages of the development of CRT for eating disorders, our main focus was tailored to this approach in a way that was relevant to severe anorexia and also to facilitate 'thinking about thinking'. We then tried to use CRT as a means of improving engagement in therapy. As CRT has developed further, we are now trying to make the most of the reflective meta-cognitive aspects of CRT and to encourage patients to translate the knowledge and skills learned in sessions to real life behaviours. Increasingly, further adaptations of CRT for anorexia attempt early on to extend CRT practice outside of the sessions – for example to the dining table – and we have found surprisingly that this is often initiated by patients themselves. Involvement of families and support networks in finding creative ways to put into practice what is achieved in CRT sessions will also be extremely helpful.

Identifying strategies in tasks – an important part of CRT is identifying what strategies are employed in each task as a starting point to explore alternative or more effective ways of approaching them. The patient is then encouraged to think about when these strategies might be used in a real life context.

Joint goals and an action plan – are a key part of any therapy, but may be particularly challenging in the context of CRT in introducing a style of working which is different to other types of interventions the patient is more familiar with. It is therefore important to convey the aims and relevance of CRT and to work with the patient to plan what they might like to get out of it, as well as placing CRT work in the context of the patient's overall recovery. After that, we try with the patients to create mind maps and their own formulation of how this work on cognition will help them in the journey to recovery.

Key areas which CRT for anorexia nervosa targets are: flexibility, bigger picture thinking and perfectionism. We introduce specific and simple tasks to create the opportunity to target these areas and then reflect on the process of approaching the tasks and associated thinking styles.

Learning – is the basis of any talking therapy and each therapy is based on the principle of helping patients to unlearn unhelpful thinking and behaviour and to learn or relearn more adaptive and helpful behaviours. In non-directive therapeutic approaches, the process of therapy is based upon listening to the client, appraising motivationally, and summarising the content of their story in order to facilitate them to find their own solution. In a behavioural approach, the main focus is behavioural change and making changes by doing, learning about one's own thinking style and then unlearning unhelpful thinking and learning more helpful ways of thinking. CRT includes all of these aspects and is strongly focused upon learning.

Mistakes – are a very important part of learning and a motto which many of our patients have found useful is 'every mistake is a treasure'. In CRT we promote the benefits of trying without having to do something perfectly. Making mistakes in the session provokes uncomfortable feelings for patients with high standards and perfectionist tendencies. This is a good opportunity to discuss why mistakes are important in learning and to challenge thinking around mistakes and how we treat ourselves following mistakes. It also provides the opportunity to place the small mistakes made in the CRT session into a wider context.

Novelty and the unusual format – are two of the most important elements of CRT. From our clinical and research experience, patients who have been in treatment for a long time appreciate the novel format of CRT where food, weight and body-related cognitive content is replaced with 'thinking about thinking' – as our patients have difficulty discussing feelings and emotions when so acutely ill. In contrast to psychological treatments for eating disorders in general, CRT has been found to be associated with low drop-out rates, which is likely due to this novel focus. Our observations and evidence so far presented in this book show that both patients and therapists value this novel way of working. In real life our patients avoid novel situations and novel experiences – as demonstrated by research led by Professor Walter Kaye and colleagues into the biological mechanisms implicated in this area. Whilst CRT by no means addresses the area of 'novelty seeking', it does create an environment where patients can observe their tendency to avoid novel ways of thinking.

Opportunity to think about thinking – is not something which is widely available to us in our busy lives, and we act and think without having the space to think about the ways in which we think, approach tasks, which strategies we use and what might be alternatives. For people with eating disorders it can be helpful to think outside of eating disorders and to use CRT to reflect and develop skills. CRT sessions provide the time and space to do so.

Perfectionism – is a personality feature characteristic of AN, and is increasingly seen as an important target for treatment. In CRT we tap into this area through specific exercises such as those requiring estimation (e.g. line bisection) where patients are encouraged to practise estimating, and doing something to a standard that is 'good enough' rather than perfect. In line with these high levels of perfectionism, in the past some patients have suggested that more challenging and difficult tasks should be added to the manual. Our experience is that the tasks should be designed in such a way as to enable patients to reflect, rather than feeding competitive and perfectionistic tendencies.

Quality of CRT delivery – is likely become increasingly problematic as the model becomes more popular in the field of eating disorders. CRT can be delivered by any member of the multidisciplinary team: nurses, occupational therapists, psychologists. However, after nine years of supervision, our observation is that the quality and clinical use of the material generated in CRT sessions will vary greatly. For this reason regular supervision is essential. Observation of sessions is extremely useful (see work described in Chapter 9). In our own work we also assess session fidelity by recording sessions and through supervision notes. In the context of Randomized treatment trials of CRT, the use of ratings of recordings of sessions is hugely important in checking the fidelity of the intervention being delivered.

Reflection – is a central part of CRT for eating disorders. Psycho–education about how the brain works, research evidence, cognitive styles and doing cognitive exercises are only effective when we reflect on how these problems relate to real life. CRT guides patients through a process of self-reflection and self-discovery. The exercises are designed to be engaging and easy enough to allow both patient and therapist to reflect upon what they observed in the process of doing the task, and then to step back and reflect on the wider process of thinking.

Supervision – is a big part of the work we have promoted in this book. CRT is a low intensity treatment requiring a relatively minimal length of training compared to some other therapies. However, although training in CRT can be delivered in several days, ongoing regular supervision is essential. A really positive aspect of CRT is that it generates lots of enthusiasm, and ideas for games and tasks. However, clinicians with experience in clinical and neuropsychology are able to advise what might be CRT-specific or non-specific exercises, and this will form an important part of supervision. Supervision allows the tailoring of this approach for patients, and also allows therapists to make this piece of work meaningful – linking it to the patient's bigger picture and formulation. As CRT can be delivered by a range of people – from experienced clinicians to PhD students and trainees in our group – the types of issues which are raised in supervision will vary greatly, and a challenge for supervisors will be to address this and to ensure quality across delivery of CRT.

Thinking about thinking – CRT encourages a focus not on the content of thinking but the process or way of thinking itself. This enables us to notice and change our mental default settings. Engaging patients in this non–threatening way – with a focus on thinking style rather than content of thinking or symptoms – provides a safe and good working alliance and can be a good starting point for engaging patients.

Understanding – of our own patterns of thinking and our strengths and weaknesses is actively promoted in CRT in a very motivational way. Understanding of ways of thinking gradually gives patients and therapists the confidence to change maladaptive strategies. Our research shows that patients with eating disorders tend to have a higher than average IQ and if this is used effectively they will be able to start to make changes to their own lives. Understanding is the important first step before starting to make changes.

Variation and variety of tasks – is important, and it is a good idea to explore this with the patient collaboratively. CRT can also provide variation from other aspects of treatment for eating disorders which are more focused upon eating, shape and weight.

'Wood and trees' – CRT encourages patients to see 'both the wood and the trees' through acknowledging that both detail focus and bigger picture thinking are important in a range of tasks, and the advantages of learning to use a combination of strategies flexibly rather than being stuck on one strategy.

eXample – an important role of the therapist in CRT is to lead by example by actively engaging in the tasks and modelling a flexible and non-perfect approach, just as we are modelling a flexible approach here in dealing with the letter x.

'You are what you think' – the brain is shaped by how we use it. However, the brain is also very plastic and capable of reorganisation and the positive message of CRT is that it is possible to change our brain and our ways of thinking and behaving. This is supported by a wealth of very good research. We hope that the ideas offered in this book will help people who work with eating disorders or who have an eating disorder to make positive changes.

'Zoom in and zoom out' – is a great metaphor to use in CRT and captures a very important thinking strategy in everyday life. We need to 'zoom in' to focus on details such as the essay we write, the card we make, the novel we read or picture we look at, whilst at the same time 'zooming out' and thinking about the context of the literature, piece of art, person we write the card to, etc. Some patients we have worked with have found it helpful to stop and think, 'I find it difficult to solve the problem. Shall I zoom in or zoom out?'

INDEX